THE WINNING MINDSET

Professor Damian Hughes combines his
practical and academic background within sport,
organization and change psychology to work as
a trusted adviser to business, education and
sporting elite, specializing in the creation of
high-performance cultures. He has written
several successful business texts, including
Liquid Thinking and *How to Think Like
Sir Alex Ferguson*.

DAMIAN HUGHES

THE WINNING MINDSET

What Sport Can Teach Us About Great Leadership

PAN BOOKS

First published 2016 by Macmillan as *The Five STEPS to a Winning Mindset*

This paperback edition first published 2018 by Pan Books
an imprint of Pan Macmillan
20 New Wharf Road, London N1 9RR
Associated companies throughout the world
www.panmacmillan.com

ISBN 978-1-5098-0437-5

9 8 7 6 5 4 3 2 1

A CIP catalogue record for this book is available from the British Library.

Printed and bound by CPI Group (UK) Ltd, Croydon, CR0 4YY

Visit **www.panmacmillan.com** to read more about all our books
and to buy them. You will also find features, author interviews and
news of any author events, and you can sign up for e-newsletters
so that you're always first to hear about our new releases.

THE WINNING MINDSET

PROLOGUE

Ringside in San Remo, Milan, 1996.
WBC World Super-Middleweight title fight.

Crouched down in the challenger's red corner, I watched the action intently as the ever fiercer left hooks of Runcorn's Robin Reid continued to swing and connect with the Italian champion, the redoubtable Vincenzo Nardiello. Whenever Reid made an impression, I noted that he immediately skipped away from the champion's flailing retort and evaded the shot. I watched his trainer, Brian Hughes, who himself watched the proceedings with a silent intensity that enthralled me.

I'd read about the state of flow – defined by the wonderfully named psychologist Mihaly Csikszentmihalyi (pronounced *six-cent-mihaly*) as the place where mind and body work in harmony to produce their optimum performance – and I watched him completely in sync with the action, anticipating events seconds before they happened. His game plan, prepared after hour upon endless hour in front of video footage and then repeated in the dusty old gym where he had presided for my whole life, had now taken its physical form and he watched for any slight insights where he could tinker and adapt.

'Ten seconds,' I offered. This was the signal for the corner to become the boxing equivalent of a Formula One pit crew, busily applying fluids, respite, direction and advice in their minute-long intervention. My voice was loud enough to rise above the raucous Milanese crowd, urging their hometown hero to victory, but I was mindful of the mantra which had been drilled into me over the years: 'Keep your voice calm and your body language still during the fight. You need to present an image of complete control because it can panic the fighter.' Brian Hughes had been learning his craft as master coach since he was a boy and these insights always came packed with common sense hewn from years of experience. 'Listening to his wisdom, presented with a mix of gruffness and enthusiasm delivered in the kind of accent and phraseology that seems to have stepped straight from the pages of an Alan Bennett script, is one of life's pleasures,' was how the *Daily Telegraph* once described his instruction.

I played through the different instructions he could offer to Reid, who was coming back to the corner and gulping oxygen into his lungs. There were only sixty seconds to deliver the message, so it needed to be concise. Reid could be instructed to increase the pace of the fight, trusting his superior conditioning to take effect in the later rounds. He could receive a torrent of encouragement for executing the plan so diligently. How about a warning not to get complacent? The easiest option would be to remind him to keep on doing what he was doing. Why rock the boat? Why disrupt a winning plan? I moved closer to listen to the instructions, delivered in just five words.

'Sit down when you punch.'

'Sit down when you punch.' I knew exactly what he meant because of the simplicity and the clear image in my head which it evoked. The plan had been to throw punches whilst the legs identified their escape route. 'Sitting down' was a change of plan. It meant stillness as opposed to speed.

He had seen that the punches were hurting but that his fighter was preparing to move away as the punches landed, reducing the power each punch contained. The instruction to 'sit down' suggested that, rather than look to move, Reid should plant both feet, increasing the leverage and the associated power of a punch, as Hughes had seen that Vincenzo Nardiello's resistance was falling fast.

Most importantly, Reid understood it too. He nodded his understanding, stood up, adjusted his shorts, punched his gloves together to indicate his readiness to continue and stepped back into the centre of the ring's canvas for the seventh round of the WBC World Super-Middleweight title fight, the most prestigious of the alphabet titles which confusingly littered the sport.

Two minutes and fifty-nine seconds later, I scrambled into the ring to celebrate a victory for Reid and Brian Hughes, my dad, who had become the first Manchester man in fifty years to train a world champion.

INTRODUCING THE FIVE STEPS

Sport as an industry is unique – in the breadth of its appeal, the scale of its support and its ability to generate emotion. For generations, it has created extraordinary memories, offering us visions of sublime skill and moments of great passion. It has also generated pain and anguish. Across the world, it both divides and unites people of different races, nationalities and every conceivable status. It is sport which binds workers and rulers, children and the elderly.

Professional sport is, therefore, a crucible. The people working inside that crucible, charged with the task and privilege of leading sports teams, are generally known as the managers. In fact, their role has only a little to do with management, and much more to do with leadership. Those that do this in the upper reaches of sport are truly extraordinary. The work they perform is intensive, personal, technical and critical – critical to the success of their teams, the growth of their sport, and the happiness of many. It is also subject to intense personal scrutiny: their every move – whether witnessed, surmised or merely imagined – is subject to widespread analysis in almost every forum imaginable, from bar rooms through offices to Internet blogs and live television or radio broadcasts. They have their leadership publicly examined, challenged, lauded and ridiculed on a daily basis. Some of us feel we could do a better job if asked. Others stand back in admiration of the great achievers, and cast a sympathetic backward glance at the ones who look like they've failed. But we actually have very little appreciation of the full scope of their work.

The role of a sports team leader is fascinating, complex and tough. Fantasy football leagues may convince us that it's about buying players and selecting a team. In reality it is about creating winning environments, recruiting, developing and nurturing talent, effectively communicating a shared vision with a diverse collection of individuals, delivering on enormous expectations from a range of stakeholders, overcoming significant challenges, handling pressure and staying focused throughout – a set of challenges familiar to leaders in all sectors.

The aim of this book is to distil the lessons I have accumulated in my own work as an adviser to sporting and business leaders, enabling them to create winning cultures in sports as diverse as international and domestic rugby league, Premier League football, rugby union, athletics, water polo, swimming, diving, professional boxing, squash, golf and Australian Rules Football, where I have soaked up information about creating a winning mindset. This book is me wringing myself out. This is not to say that one leader has all the answers – or even that a full cohort has cracked it between them. But there is a set of circumstances from which emerges a compelling language, one of creating a winning mindset, that will be useful to leaders in any and every setting.

HOW TO APPLY IT?

The broad question, then, is how do you create a winning mindset?

During my visits, and in working with great – and equally illuminatingly, not-so-successful – coaches, I have begun to see the same themes, the same attributes, reflected in a wide range of successful environments. What I found was that their ideas shared certain key traits. There is no 'formula' for a winning culture – I don't want to overstate the case. But these cultures do draw on a common set of traits, which make them more likely to succeed.

It's like discussing the attributes of a great basketball player. You can be pretty sure that any great player possesses some subset of traits including height, speed, agility, power and court sense. But you don't need all of these traits in order to be great. Some great players are five feet ten and scrawny. And having some of these traits doesn't guarantee greatness: no doubt there are plenty of slow, clumsy seven-footers. It's clear, though, that if you are ever in the position of choosing a team from among strangers, you should probably take a gamble on the seven-foot player.

Winning cultures and mindsets work in much the same way. One skill we can learn is the ability to *spot* those ideas: those that have naturally occurring features, like the seven-foot basketball player. But here's where our basketball analogy breaks down: in the world of leading and shaping mindsets, we can genetically engineer our players. We can *create* them with an eye to maximizing their success.

As I have pored over the thousands of notes and observations from what I have seen and studied, I have recognized, over and over, the same principles at work.

These five principles to develop a winning mindset are: *Simplicity, Thinking, Emotional Intelligence, Practical, Storytelling.*

An astute observer will note that this sentence can be compacted into the acronym *STEPS*. This is sheer coincidence, of course.

No special expertise is needed to apply these principles. There are no licensed STEPSologists. Moreover, many of the principles have a common-sense ring to them: didn't most of us already have the intuition that we should 'be simple' and 'use stories'? It's not as though there is a powerful argument in favour of overcomplicated, lifeless prose.

'Common sense is not always so common,' is how one leading coach proudly responded to my observation that his approach to his work was profoundly simple. This book – and the exercises contained within it – show you how it can be the same for you.

It is a book to help you create a winning mindset both in yourself and others. Usually these topics are treated separately – there is 'change management' advice for businesses, 'self-help' advice for individuals and 'change the world' advice for activists. That is a shame, because all change has something in common: for anything to change, someone has to start acting differently. Ultimately, all leaders, in any field of endeavour or in any context where individuals lead other individuals in the pursuit of success, are charged with the same mission: can you get people to start living up to their potential?

Here's our STEPS checklist for creating a winning mindset:

1: Simplicity

How do we find the essential core of our culture?

Great sporting leaders strive for the ultimate model of simplicity: a one-sentence statement of their intentions, so profound that an individual could spend a lifetime learning to follow it. Sir Alex Ferguson summarized the culture he had shaped at Manchester United as an obdurate unwillingness to accept defeat. 'We never get beat,' he once said. 'We occasionally run out of time, but we never get beat.'[1]

Bill Walsh, coach of NFL giants the San Francisco 49ers, reversed years of underachievement to win three Super Bowl titles through a relentless focus on every individual doing their job to the highest possible standard. This commitment to the details of the job was articulated in the title of his bestselling coaching bible, *The Score Takes Care of Itself.*

Sir Graham Henry's mission as the New Zealand Rugby Union coach is to help his players 'enhance the All Blacks jersey and pass it on in a better state than what it was when you got it'.[2]

This simple understanding was underscored in the jubilant scenes after the team had retained the World Cup in 2015. When fourteen-year-old fan Charlie Lines attempted to join the team's lap of honour, he was forcibly ejected from the pitch by an overzealous security guard. Sonny Bill Williams, the team's high-impact substitute, broke away from the celebrations to intervene and present the young fan with his winner's medal. 'I tried to make the night more memorable for him. Better it to be hanging around his neck than mine,' he said.[3]

One former New Zealand player explained to me that the thing he feared most was to be an All Black with just one appearance. 'You had the talent but you lacked the attitude to leave the jersey in a better state than you found it.'

George Carman, the legendary defence lawyer, once said, 'If you argue ten points, even if each is a good point, when they get back to the jury room they won't remember any.'[4] To strip an environment down to its core, leaders must be masters of exclusion. They must relentlessly prioritize.

Two of the great boxing trainers, Cus d'Amato, the mysterious coach who played a seminal role in Mike Tyson's ascent to the status of youngest ever world heavyweight champion, and Emanuel Steward, the Detroit-based trainer of twenty world champions including Lennox Lewis and Thomas Hearns, both understood that they had just sixty seconds between rounds to affect a fight. 'We must communicate ideas that are both simple *and* profound,' said d'Amato.

To emphasize the need for leaders to be ever mindful about communicating one simple message at a time, I use an exercise of throwing and catching a tennis ball. If I throw one ball to you, it's quite likely that you will catch it. Now if I throw you two balls simultaneously, it will be quite difficult to catch both. Much more likely, in your confusion over which one to catch with which hand, which one to catch first and which one to catch second, you will succeed in catching neither. If I throw three, it's odds-on that all will hit the floor.

Saying something short is not the mission – sound bites are not the ideal. Barry Gibbons, the former head of Burger King, articulated his frustration with company mission statements: 'I arrived in the headquarters and found that the only piece of paper left in my office was the old mission statement hanging on my wall. It was so full of crap and humbug that there and then I invented a new word to describe the language normally used in mission statements: "crumbug".[5]

2: Thinking

How do we get our audience to pay attention to our ideas, and how do we maintain their interest when we need time to get the ideas across?

Like elite coaches, we will learn how to violate people's expectations. We need to be counter-intuitive. We can use surprise – an emotion whose function is to increase alertness and cause focus – to grab people's attention. But surprise doesn't last. For a culture of a winning mentality to endure, we must generate *interest* and *curiosity*. We can engage people's curiosity over a long period of time by systematically laying tripwires or 'opening gaps' in their knowledge – and then filling those gaps. I aim to show you not only how these tripwires can be laid, but what they require in order to fulfil their purpose: that is, first to open the gap, and then, most importantly, to lead people to fill it in themselves through their own thinking and discovery.

Psychologically, it's much more satisfying and validating to find the solution to a problem yourself than to have someone else solve it for you. José Mourinho understands this. He calls his tripwire approach 'guided discovery', a technique he learned under the tutelage of Louis van Gaal, who in turn was introduced to it by the Dutch master coach Rinus Michels, the father of Total Football. We will learn more about this soon.

'A great pianist doesn't run around the piano or do push-ups with the tips of his fingers,' Mourinho reasons. 'To be great, he plays the piano. He plays all his life, and being a footballer is not about running, push-ups or physical work generally. The best way to be a great footballer is to play.'[6]

Before his Inter Milan team played Barcelona in the 2010 Champions League second leg semi-final, Mourinho explained how he had prepared his players.

'I have had to train with ten men. How to play with ten men, because I go there [to Barcelona] with Chelsea, I finish with ten, I go there with Inter, I finish with ten and I have to train to play with ten men because it can happen again.'

Inevitably, when his midfielder Thiago Motta was sent off, the hours of rigorous training paid off. Mourinho organized his team into defensive lines to smother the incursions of Lionel Messi and the star-studded Barcelona team. Inter Milan offered a steely, white-shirted resistance and no amount of criticism about possession statistics, or killing the game, or ugliness smothering beauty could alter the fact that they emerged victorious.

'It's the greatest moment of my career,' declared Mourinho.

3: Emotions

How do we get people to care about our ideas? We make them *feel* something. Research shows that people are more likely to make a charitable donation to a single individual than to an entire impoverished region. We are wired to feel things for people, not for abstractions.

We will look at how this understanding has prompted many elite coaches to delve into the world of neuro-anatomy and learn how to harness emotions to create a winning mind-set.

The amygdala, the almond-shaped structure in the brain, forms part of what is known as the brain's limbic system – a set of primitive brain structures involved in many of our emotions and motivations. In particular, those emotions – such as fear, anger and pleasure – that are chiefly related to survival.

'If you think of your brain as your own personal "government", then the amygdala may be seen as the Ministerial Office of the Department of Emotion,' suggests Dr Kevin Dutton. It is the part of the brain which provides some of the main ingredients for success, most notably described by Smokin' Joe Frazier, the former world heavyweight boxing champion, as 'Inspiration, perspiration and dedication'.

'It is an ancient system, steeped in evolutionary tradition, and wields a heck of a lot of power,' says Dutton. 'It has the authority to veto ordinary, everyday decision-making processes – to order a Code Red – if it thinks it is in our interests to do so.'[7]

The amygdala is easily persuaded and reacts too readily. These are the times when we run instead of fight, dream instead of do, turn on the telly rather than do the work.

The prefrontal cortex, on the other hand, is the official headquarters of the Department of Rational Thought. This is the part of our brain that tells us that we should be working: that we should turn off the telly and start doing that work.

Compared with the amygdala and the limbic system, it is a relative new build and it is responsible for the heightened self-control that separates us from our ancient ancestors and the rest of the animal kingdom. It enables us to plan, weigh up different courses of action, and refrain from responding to immediate impulses and doing things we will probably later regret. It is the cornerstone of wisdom and willpower.

When we set out along the pathway of learning to create winning mindsets, we often experience crossroads or decision points where it can feel like there is an argument going on inside our heads. An argument between our 'good', rational side and our 'bad', emotional side. More specifically, this argument is between our logical, conscientious, forward-thinking PFC and our emotional, hedonistic, heat-of-the-moment amygdala. Great coaches know how to mediate between these two sides.

This was the internal argument taking place inside the South African golfer Louis Oosthuizen's head in the build-up to the 2010 British Open Championship.

'His pre-shot routine was all over the place. He told me that when he played in the US Open, he was making split-second decisions instead of thinking about what he should have been doing,' said his performance coach, Dr Karl Morris.[8]

However, when he entered the final round of the prestigious championship, most of the pundits fully expected his amygdala to take over and that he would surrender the four-shot lead he was carrying. He was expected to 'choke', a sporting term meaning that he would become overly emotional and lose.

But they were wrong, and the reason was very simple. A small red spot, just below the base of his thumb. On his glove.

The spot was the brainchild of his coach. A short time earlier, Oosthuizen had paid Morris a visit, seeking help in dealing with intrusive thoughts of failure that had begun to creep into his mind at exactly the wrong moment – such as when he was about to play a crucial shot.

And they identified a very simple solution.

Whenever Oosthuizen was about to play a shot, he was to deliberately distract himself. He was to zone in on the dot at the base of his thumb and concentrate on that. At the critical moment, it was the dot, not the shot, that mattered. The golfing part of his brain knew very well how to play the shot. The emotional part didn't need to get in the way and screw things up.

The red spot on Oosthuizen's glove was one way of focusing his mind on the process of playing a shot, rather than thinking of the consequences of victory or defeat.

He won by seven strokes.

4: Practical

How do we make our ideas clear? We must explain them in terms of human actions, in terms of sensory information. This is where so much business communication goes awry. Mission statements, synergies, strategies, visions – they are often ambiguous to the point of being meaningless. Naturally winning mindsets are full of concrete images because our brains are wired to remember concrete data. We will learn the science which validates the former US secretary of state Colin Powell's assertion that, 'If you can't explain what you are doing to your mother, maybe you don't really understand it,'[9] alongside methods to ensure your winning ideas are completely understood.

Peter Coe could have paraphrased Colin Powell's comment and suggested that the ability to explain what you're doing to your son is equally relevant.

When Sebastian Coe had set three world records – consecutively 800 metres, one mile, 1,500 metres – in the space of forty-one days in 1979, what intrigued the public about this twenty-three-year-old was the seemingly experienced head upon his young shoulders and the cadence of his limbs which imparted an aesthetic quality, provoking the *New Statesman* magazine to compare him to Rudolph Nureyev, the celebrated ballet dancer.

More than 20 million Britons tuned in to watch his attempt to add the 1980 Olympic gold medal to his haul. 'The Moscow

800 metres final had been mine to lose,' said Coe, 'and I lost it.' The balletic cadence, for which his father and coach Peter had been striving throughout the previous twelve years and thousands of hours of coaching, disappeared. He trailed in a distant second behind his great rival, fellow Briton Steve Ovett.

According to the younger Coe: 'My father said, "You're the fastest man on earth at eight hundred metres, and at the biggest moment of your career you run three seconds slower than if you were running back home in Sheffield. There is only one thing to do now," he reasoned. "You'll have to win the bloody fifteen hundred metres title instead."'

As the watching world dismissed Seb as a failure unable to win the biggest race of his life, his father would quietly, shrewdly advise his son just how to storm to victory in the 1,500 metres, universally regarded as a dead cert for Ovett, unbeaten in nearly fifty races over that distance.

'You *have* to maintain contact with the athletes at the front,' he told him, before adding an Anglo-Saxon twist. 'And I don't care if Steve Ovett runs off to the shitter, you are in there with him before you've even realized you've left the track. You sit so tight into that action you can smell his armpits.'[10]

True to his father's instructions, Sebastian Coe stayed on the shoulder of the leading athletes until he reached the final bend, where he kicked and swiftly overtook them to come home four yards clear.

Great leaders are able to explain themselves in clear, understandable language. Martin Luther King Jr didn't stand at the Lincoln Memorial in Washington D.C. in August 1963 and use complicated jargon such as, 'I have a critical path schedule . . .' to bring about the civil rights revolution. Equally, John F. Kennedy didn't challenge his people to 'strengthen the moon programme' or 'create strategic alliances to uncover possible synergies'. Their words were entrenched in the understanding that speaking in practical terms is the only way to ensure that our ideas will mean the same thing to everyone in our audience.

5: Stories

How do we get people to act on our ideas? We tell stories. Coaches naturally swap stories after every coaching session and by doing so they multiply their experience; after years of hearing stories, they have a richer, more complete mental catalogue of situations they might confront during a session and the appropriate responses to those situations.

We will understand why leaders who mentally rehearse a situation perform better when they encounter that situation in the physical environment. Similarly, learning how to tell stories can act as a kind of mental flight simulator, preparing others to effectively respond to the challenges that can potentially prevent success.

Nowhere was this approach better evidenced than The Boot Room; three legendary words infused with success and soaked in nostalgia for Liverpool Football Club. For this was the hub which provided the foundation for the club's domination of English and European club football in the 1970s and 1980s.

When Bill Shankly arrived in 1959, Liverpool were languishing in the Second Division, despite having been League Champions only ten years before. He was an outsider with a personality forceful enough to wake a sleeping giant and lay down a template of enduring success.

In an unglamorous part of Anfield, the team's home, Shankly told his staff, including Bob Paisley, Joe Fagan and Reuben Bennett, 'Fellows, your jobs are safe. Some managers bring their own people with them. Not me. I have my own system and it will work in cooperation with you. I will lay down the plans and gradually we will all be on the same wavelength. I demand only one thing: loyalty.'[11]

The four men – Paisley, Bennett, Fagan and Shankly – formed the nucleus of the little meetings that would take place every afternoon after training. Over the next two decades, their stories and insights helped shape a winning formula.

These stories were a mixture of searing insight into how to sustain success, and unashamed humour. When Liverpool progressed to the 1965 European Cup quarter-final, they played the champions of Germany: FC Cologne. They played in Cologne and they drew. In the replay in Liverpool, they still could not be separated. They played a deciding game in the neutral venue of Rotterdam, where they remained deadlocked, even after extra time. After 400 minutes of football, the game was decided on the toss of a coin, which Shankly's team won.

When they returned to England, three days later, they had to face Chelsea in the semi-final of the FA Cup. On the flight back, Shankly mentioned to his coaching staff that the players appeared spent. The fatigue hung over them even whilst they sat in the dressing room before the game.

Shankly stood and looked at the team. He said, 'Listen, lads, I've got something here I didn't want to show you in case it upsets you. But there's nothing to lose now, so I might as well.' He removed from his pocket a brightly coloured brochure and held it up. 'This,' he growled, 'is the leaflet that Chelsea have had printed for when they get to the final at Wembley.

'They think that tonight is a formality, because they think you're too knackered to win. They think you left everything on the field in Rotterdam. They think flying over there and playing the Germans took it out of you. That's why they've printed up their brochure for when they get to Wembley. After the formality of brushing Liverpool aside.'

He paused, allowing his words to hang in the air, suspended like a cartoon anvil, whilst he looked into the eyes of his players.

'What do you think, lads, is it a formality?

'Can they brush you lot aside?

'Are you too knackered to win?

'Are you finished?'

'Each question felt like a punch,' recalled star striker Ian St John. 'With each one, the players began to get irritated, then annoyed, then furious.'

Shankly's team went out and ran the legs off Chelsea, winning 2–0 and progressing to the FA Cup Final.

After the match, Bill Shankly walked over to Chelsea's manager, Tommy Docherty, to shake hands. Docherty described himself as 'shell-shocked. I said, "Bill, how did they manage a performance like that? They just come back from playing against the German champions in Rotterdam. How come they've got so much energy?"'

Shankly handed him the Chelsea Cup Final programme. He said, 'There you are, Tom, a little souvenir.'

Docherty looked at it and said, 'What the fuck's this?' He didn't recognize it.

He didn't recognize it because Chelsea hadn't printed it.

Bill Shankly had just the one copy printed to show his team before the match.

TRAPDOORS

'A journey of a thousand miles begins with a single step.' As clichés go, that's a pretty wise one. But you know what else starts with a single step? A walk in the wrong direction.

So, yes, whilst the journey to understanding how to create a winning mindset does start with a single step, a single step doesn't guarantee a long journey, or the right one.

Before we begin to look at how you can apply the STEPS to your own situation, it's important to identify the obstacles – or trapdoors – which are commonly found along the way and which can prevent you applying the lessons contained in this book to their fullest impact.

Even though the thinking that inspired this book is taken from the practices of those coaches operating within their chosen sport at an elite level, that doesn't mean you have to work in sport to apply it – far from it. The approach is both broader and simpler than that. It relies on an understanding of human beings and their ways of thinking and learning.

You don't need to be a coaching genius to use the STEPS process to create a winning mindset within your own field of endeavour. There is nothing magical about this way of think- ing. It usually traffics in the obvious and places a huge premium on common sense. We all have the ability to apply the STEPS and make a difference.

What's perplexing is that so few people actually do.

I have met many gifted coaches who haven't succeeded in creating a winning mindset. I have come away from my meetings with them and wondered why these smart, talented people can't quite help other people to understand their thinking and ideas.

Consequently, I've identified three common trapdoors that we need to beware of falling through.

Double-Loop Thinking

Listening is to hearing what seeing is to looking. Check this out:

I got a dig bick.
You that read wrong.
You read that wrong too.
Shocking, isn't it?

Not the message, which after all, makes no sense, but the fact that we can get it so wrong. The reason, as you have probably guessed, is all down to one simple thing: our brain's persistent and hard-wired tendency to take shortcuts.

When we look at a word, we tend to swallow it whole instead of taking each of its constituent components in turn. As a result, as long as the first and last letters remain the same, our refined cognitive palates are more than happy to swallow it down in one go as opposed to chewing it over.

It's the same when we hear someone talking. Most of the time, as long as we see the lips moving in sync and detect words coming out, we are perfectly happy to let our brains flick over to autopilot and let whatever someone happens to be saying go in one ear and out of the other.

Think about the last time you were genuinely surprised.

When I speak to any group of coaches or athletes, I often

start by putting a picture of Susan Boyle on the screen and asking how many recognize her. Even with an international contingent sitting in front of me, I can almost always guarantee that 80 per cent of my audience will know of the Scottish singer who sprang to prominence on the TV show *Britain's Got Talent* in 2009.

'Why,' I ask, 'do you know the person who came second on a show so many years ago, yet would struggle to recognize the numerous winners since?'

The most common answer to the question is that Susan Boyle wasn't what they expected. 'She wasn't as useless as I thought she'd be,' is the politest response.

Note the most important four words:

Wasn't what they expected.

Think of the great discoveries of our time – Columbus setting sail to the edge of a world considered to be flat; Edison discovering light without heat; Wilbur and Orville Wright achieving the very first powered flight; Neil Armstrong setting foot on the moon. These were all achieved by people who refused to let their own horizons represent the limits of what can be achieved. In sporting terms, think how Sir Dave Brailsford didn't merely look at the world of cycling to recruit members of his support team, or how Clive Woodward utilized the best minds in business and education to help him create an elite culture in rugby.

Breakthroughs in sport have come from innovators. Think of Kevin Pietersen introducing the switch hit to international cricket, or Sonja Henie winning the gold medal in figure skating at the 1928 Olympics by going outside the traditional skating 'box' and introducing ballet into her routine. Some have even given their name to an innovation: the Fosbury Flop in the high jump, the Cruyff Turn and the Panenka in football, and Federer's SABR (Sneak Attack By Roger) in tennis.

In other words, doing what wasn't expected – not so much pushing the envelope as ignoring it.

Most people possess a model of the world, a script for how things should be. What prevents innovation is the lack of willingness to double back and revisit our scripts and determine whether they are helpful or not. When I hear coaches respond to a defeat by declaring that they will 'work harder', I often wonder whether they are making a mistake similar to thinking that simply shouting louder at someone who speaks a foreign language will make them understand. It's not working harder but working smarter that double-loop thinking requires us to do.

Chris Evans recounts that he knew he was in professional trouble when his best friends were all on his payroll. 'They were paid to laugh at my jokes,' he recalls. The best coach resists the urge to run with the herd, recruiting people from outside his own area of expertise and allowing them to challenge him.

It is easy to run with the herd. Even on the most important issues of the day, we often adopt the views of our friends, families and colleagues. At some level, this makes sense: it is easier to fall into line with what your friends and family think than to find new family and friends. But running with the herd means we are quick to embrace the status quo, slow to change our minds and happy to delegate our thinking.

There is no obligation for you to agree with or do everything suggested in this book. While I want you to walk away having finished the book and be able to apply the ideas directly to your own life for immediate effect, I want to give you more than just a set of prescriptions. I want to make you think.

The Knowledge Trap

When asked by John Syer, the Tottenham Hotspur sports psychologist, what he felt like on a big match day, Glenn Hoddle replied: 'Lord of the Manor'. Syer told him to write the phrase down and put it in his wallet, which is precisely what Hoddle, regarded as the outstanding player of his generation, an artist of rare touch and vision, did throughout his glittering career for Spurs, Monaco, Chelsea and England.

It was expected that a player of his intelligence and ability would make a seamless transition to football management. After a promising start at Swindon Town and Chelsea, he was appointed the manager of the national team. His poor judgement and inability to engage with players were thought to be the root cause of his downfall.

Hoddle's pedigree and coaching nous are unimpeachable. His man-management, however, has left a bit to be desired. Tony Cascarino tells in his book *Full Time* of an early training session with Hoddle at Chelsea. One drill exposed numerous technical deficiencies which Hoddle then exacerbated with a flawless exhibition of how to do it. 'Grown men were made to feel as if they are being treated as children,' he wrote. The players returned to the changing rooms somewhat disgruntled. 'No player likes being belittled,' Cascarino says, 'and one grunted, "If he was an ice cream, he'd lick himself."'[1]

Hoddle appeared unable to transmit his own technical understanding of football to others. He became a victim of the trapdoor which many leaders fall through: the Knowledge Trap.

This is a worthy adversary, because in some sense it's inevitable.

Let's say that you are excellent at a given thing, a true master of your domain. Does this mean you are also more likely to excel in a different domain?

Creating a winning mindset has two stages: the answer stage and the 'telling others' stage. In the answer stage, you use your expertise to arrive at the idea that you want to share. Doctors study for a decade to be capable of giving the answer; business managers may deliberate for months to arrive at the answer; Glenn Hoddle accumulated twenty years of high-level playing experience.

The problem is that the same factors that worked to your advantage in the answer stage will backfire on you during the telling others stage. To get the answer, you need expertise, but you can't dissociate expertise from the Knowledge Trap. You know things that others don't know, and you can't remember what it was like not to know them. So when you get around to sharing the answer, you tend to communicate *as if the audience were you*. As a consequence, an insight shared is often an insight halved.

You'll stress the statistics that were pivotal in arriving at the answer and then find that no one remembers them afterwards. You'll share the punchline – the overarching truth which emerged from months of study and analysis – and no one will have a clue how your punchline relates to their day-to-day work.

I worked with the coaches of one rugby team that reached a Wembley Cup Final. The experienced coaches were meticulous in their preparations, ensuring that no stone was left unturned in the quest for the trophy. My role was redundant in the technical discussions about the tactics required to win.

We had several players who had never played in a big final and so I insisted that we step into their shoes and plan from their perspective. There's an old boxing maxim – a fight is never won on the walk to the ring, but it can be lost. Many fighters lose their nerve on the way to the ring – think of dry-mouthed Frank Bruno repeatedly making the sign of the cross on his second walk to face Mike Tyson in 1996. The months of preparation can be undone in these crucial few minutes.

The day before the final, we enjoyed the customary visit to the west London stadium, where we spent our time rehearsing how we would behave in the dressing rooms, stand in the tunnel, walk onto the field and the positions we would take on the field when we had scored the points that would clinch the trophy – which we comfortably managed the next day.

There is a curious disconnect between the amount of time we invest in training people how to arrive at the answer and the amount of time we invest in training them how to tell others. It's easy to graduate from medical school or an MBA programme without ever taking a class in communication. University professors take dozens of courses in their area of expertise but none on how to teach. A lot of engineers would laugh at the idea of a training programme about telling others.

Business managers believe that when they have clicked through a PowerPoint presentation showcasing their conclusions, they've successfully communicated their ideas. All they've really done is share data. If they're good speakers, they may have created an enhanced sense, amongst colleagues and peers, that they are decisive or motivational. But the surprise comes when they realize that nothing they've said has had a lasting impact. They've shared data but they haven't created ideas that are useful and lasting. Nothing stuck.

This book isn't about improving your technical know-how. This book shares ideas that are designed to stick.

Courage

Carpe diem! Stand up and be counted! Put your neck on the block! Take the bull by the horns! Grasp the nettle . . .

When a subject is as rich in metaphors as this, there must be lots to learn about it. Given the obvious importance of courage to successful coaches, it is amazing to note how little coverage it receives. There are loads of books about risk avoidance and management and very little about the positive nature of courage. It's like going into a bookshop to buy *The Joy of Sex* and being told that there is nothing on this subject but over twenty different books on reducing impotence. Whilst courage is no guarantee of success, it is obvious that to take action without displaying some sort of bravery is an effective way of preventing success.

So why don't we see more of it?

A clue is found in one long word: allodoxaphobia, which is the official name given to the fear of being ridiculed by other people. It is the second most common phobia in the UK (behind our fear of spiders).

Don't believe me? I've regularly tested it out with a simple experiment on a number of different groups and audiences, of all ages and experience, where I take £10 out of my pocket, hold it up and ask if anyone wants the money. You'd think it would be a no-brainer, wouldn't you? Who would say no to free money?

The outcome is always the same. Silence. Followed by a little more silence, followed by nervous laughter. I even hear people telling their friends to go up and get the money. Eventually someone runs up and grabs the money out of my hand, at which point everyone claps and the lucky winner immediately tries to give the money back! Even though it was offered to them with no strings attached.

There is one reason why I am never trampled by a rush of people coming to grab the money. It is that voice in your head (if you are wondering, 'which voice?', it's that one!) which is shouting, 'It's an evil trick! If I run up there to collect the money everyone will laugh at me. I don't understand the game. It can't be that simple. I will make a fool of myself.'

In short, this is allodoxaphobia in action.

What is courage? My favourite definition of the word is the original meaning of it, which is 'to speak your own mind with all your heart'.

The STEPS approach is intended to help you to achieve this with maximum impact.

THE FIRST STEP

SIMPLICITY

Everything should be made as simple as
possible, but not simpler.
Albert Einstein

1.i   THE HEART OF THE MATTER

Date: Sunday 9 July 2006
Time: 9.45 p.m. EST
Location: Olympiastadion, Berlin, Germany

Imagine that you are standing in the patent-leather shoes of Marcello Lippi, the coach of your national football team, a very fine one. You've led your nation to the brink of a World Cup victory, having orchestrated a tactical masterclass and guided your team to a penalty shoot-out. All you must do now is watch five of your players take a single penalty kick.

You can almost taste the champagne; you can imagine lighting the victory cigar, delivering the winner's acceptance speech, being feted as a national hero. You have one final task to complete before you can celebrate your success. You have to speak to the players charged with the responsibility of dispatching the penalty.

What words of wisdom will you share with them before they start the long walk from the centre circle, a journey described by Andrea Pirlo, your elegant Italian midfielder, who has been the conductor of your orchestra throughout the whole tournament, as 'a truly terrible journey, right through the heart of your fear'?[1]

As you approach the first player, the noise of the 77,000 people gathered in the arena reaches a deafening crescendo.

The end is now fast approaching of an epic contest, one which has witnessed both the drama of Zinedine Zidane, the great French captain, prematurely ending both his involvement in the game and his career with a vicious headbutt into the chest of one of your defenders, and the subtlety of a tactical game of cat and mouse played out against your French opponents.

You step forward and look into the player's eyes, seeking to determine the emotions of the man charged with making millions of dreams come true. You can see a mixture of fear and confusion. 'That moment really is a torment. A blizzard of agony.' Gary Lineker, the former England striker, once thus described his emotions. 'There's a storm raging inside and all around you.'[2]

'My thoughts are all over the place, drunken ideas at the wheel of fairground dodgems,' recounted Andrea Pirlo, one of the five Italian players charged with the responsibility of winning the coveted trophy. '*I was thinking, I'll go right; no, left, because that's the keeper's weaker side. No, I'll put it in the top corner, there's no way he's reaching that. But what if I get it wrong and the ball flies off into the stand?*' The noise both inside and outside his mind doesn't abate. '*I really don't know what to do,*' he admits to you, his coach.[3]

The responsibility lands squarely on the shoulders of your handmade suit.

Let's start with the basics. The goal is a mere twelve yards away; it is eight yards wide and eight feet high. Once the ball leaves your player's boot, it will travel towards the goal at eighty miles per hour. At such a speed, no goalkeeper can afford to wait and see where you kick the ball; he must take a guess and fling his body in that direction. The odds, therefore, are firmly in your favour: roughly 75 per cent of penalty kicks at this, the elite level, are successful. If the keeper guesses wrong, the odds rise to about 90 per cent.

This is pretty basic stuff. He knows this and doesn't need reminding. Come on, you can do better than that.

How about explaining that the best option is to aim towards the corner of the goal? Even if the keeper guesses correctly, he won't save it. This shot leaves little margin for error, though: a slight miskick and he may miss the goal completely. So you may want to advise him to ease up a bit, or aim slightly away from the corner.

Is this really the best you can offer?

What about suggesting that he chooses between the left corner and the right? If he is right-footed this will translate to more power and accuracy – but of course the keeper knows this too. That's why keepers jump towards the kicker's left corner 57 per cent of the time, and to the right only 41 per cent.

This is more specific. However, what would you suggest, strong side or weak?

Has your team taken penalty kicks against this keeper before? – and if so, where did they aim? And where did he jump? As you think all of this through, you also think about what the keeper is thinking, and you may even think about what the keeper is thinking about what you are thinking.

Come on. Time is ticking. What will you say?

You know the chance of becoming a hero is about 75 per cent, which isn't bad. But wouldn't it be nice to up that number a bit? Might there be a better way to think about this problem? What if you could outfox the keeper by thinking beyond the obvious?

You know that the keeper is guessing between jumping right or left. But what if . . . what if . . . what if you kick neither to right or left? What if you tell him to do the silliest thing imaginable and kick into the dead centre of the goal?

Yes, that is where the keeper is standing now, but you are

pretty sure he will vacate that spot as the kick is taken. Remember what the data says: keepers jump left 57 per cent of the time and right 41 per cent – which means they stay in the middle only two times out of a hundred. A leaping keeper may of course still stop a ball aimed at the centre, but how often can that happen?

Hold on, you know this answer.

Your team of analysts just happen to have that: a kick aimed towards the centre, as risky as it may appear, is 7 per cent more likely to succeed than a kick to the corner.

Are you really willing to tell your player to take the chance? Is going straight up the middle really the boldest move of all?

Now, let's start the action again and let's go back to you – the coach. What are you going to say?

How about just five words?

What is your clear intention?

Marcello Lippi, a serial winner in the challenging domain of managing football teams, was the first man to win both the Champions League and the World Cup. He was described by Sir Alex Ferguson as, 'somebody who is in command of himself and his professional domain'. He was, Ferguson asserted, a man whom 'nobody could make the mistake of taking lightly'.[4] Indeed, Fabio Grosso, the player who took the fifth – and final – penalty, later said that the look of confidence in Lippi's eyes 'helped transcend us'.

Before each penalty, he stepped forward, looked into the eyes of each player charged with the responsibility of taking the kick and simply asked, *Qual è la tua chiara intenzione?* What is your clear intention?

Pirlo described the effect of Lippi's intervention. 'I responded immediately and said, "I'll hit it straight down the middle, put a bit of height on it. Barthez will definitely dive and there's no way he's getting to it, even with his feet."'

Each of the five selected players successfully converted his penalty to beat France 5–3 and win the coveted golden trophy, the ultimate accolade. All because of five simple, well-chosen words.

In his book, *A Game of Ideas: Thoughts and Passions from the Sidelines*, Lippi explained, 'When we ask ourselves questions in real, simple terms we often receive a simple answer too.'[5]

Lippi understood the first lesson of great coaches.

Just like taking a penalty, the power of simplicity is fundamental.

1.ii THE KEY INFORMATION

The power of simplicity is particularly valuable in this age of data deluge when we struggle to differentiate between the important and the noise by which we are constantly surrounded.

This is an age in which advertisers, marketers and media outlets tweet us, text us and follow us online. An age of Facebook, newsfeeds and Amazon Recommends. An age in which we are overwhelmed with information, increasingly to breaking point.

The statistics which detail the volume of data we are subjected to are also numerous. A *New York Times* weekly edition contains more information than the average person in the seventeenth century was likely to come across in their entire lifetime. In 2012 we were consuming three times as much information as we were in 1960. By 2020 we'll be generating forty-four times more data than we are producing today.

Add to the barrage of data another twenty-first-century form of Chinese water torture – the drip, drip, drip of 'continuous disruption'. Time and time again we find ourselves giving people information they don't really need. In 2012, more than 204 million emails were sent every minute of every day. Harvard professor John Kotter estimates that 'the total amount of communication which an employee receives in a three-month working period is 2.3 million words or numbers'.[6]

And that is just email. Add to this the constant droning background noise of open-plan offices, the *rat-a-tat-tat* of mobile phones, texts, instant messages, Skype calls, Facebook groups, Twitter feeds, phone calls, the lure of websites demanding your attention, and you'll start to get the picture, usually in high-definition 3G. These days, we spend three-quarters of our waking lives receiving information. Most of us can't absent ourselves when we have decisions to make. Instead, we have to operate in a state of nothing less than continuous and relentless interruption.

On average, computer users change windows and check email or another program thirty-seven times an hour. Forty-three per cent of college students say they are interrupted by social media three or more times an hour whilst they are working. And when someone tries to reach us nowadays, not only will they email us – they'll text us, tweet us, phone and voicemail us too. Often, it can feel like there is no room in our heads to stop and think.

And often, there isn't. Studies reveal that we can't hold more than seven separate pieces of information in our minds at once. This is why telephone numbers were originally just seven digits long. Once we have stored those seven bits of information, we start forgetting things in order to house new ones. If you can recall the experience of hearing a clock chime the hour, you may find yourself asking yourself how many times it struck afterwards. Up to seven chimes and we can recall the sound; after that, we have no chance.

Try it yourself.

Read the following string of numbers quickly and only once, then look away and write them down on a sheet of paper in the same order they appear below.

7 2 0 9 6 3 1 4 8 5

How many did you get right?

The chances are you will have got at least one wrong. Remembering ten numbers in the correct order overloads your conscious mind. Even if you did write them down in the correct order, you would not have been able to think about anything else whilst you were doing it, because the space is so limited.

How can we find the space to think clearly, with all this data raining down on us? How can we discern intelligence from all this noise? How many emails do you receive every day? What are all these messages doing to your ability to concentrate, to think, to plan, to decide?

These are questions which are worth answering because the relentlessness of this bombardment has an impact.

A Microsoft Research study which tracked over two thousand hours of employee computer activity found that, once distracted by an email alert, computer users take an average of twenty-two minutes to return to the suspended task with the same level of focus. In 27 per cent of cases, it took them more than two hours to return to the task they were doing in the first place. Other studies have revealed that tasks take a third longer when interrupted by email.

The psychiatrist Edward Halliwell has identified a syndrome that he calls Attention Deficit Trait. This is not a neurological condition like the closely related and better known Attention Deficit Disorder; instead, it is created by the way we work. In a study of employees at the communications firm Porter-Novelli, he posited that the combined effect of incessant phone calls and emails can lead to a temporary drop in our IQ of an extraordinary and disturbing ten points.

'When you are confronted with the sixth decision after the fifth interruption in the midst of the search for the ninth missing piece of information on the day that the third deal has collapsed and the twelfth impossible request has blipped unbidden across your computer screen, your brain begins to panic,' explained Halliwell.[7]

In short, our Stone-Age bodies can't cope with this modern-day deluge. Evolution is slow; the avalanche of information generated by technology has come fast. Confronted with so much data, our hearts beat faster, our breath becomes more shallow, we sweat: our body shifts into crisis mode.

We'll explore this in more detail later; but when your frontal lobes become overburdened, the lower, more primitive parts of your brain shift into survival mode, dimming intelligence. When ADT kicks in, you lose your perspective, flexibility, and sense of humour. You are increasingly likely to make impulsive judgements or even avoid making any decisions at all.

The drip, drip, drip doesn't just make us less able to think, it's exhausting us too. We are spent. Unable to sleep, headaches ever looming, always tired; our bodies cope with these new demands by keeping us in a state of hormone-induced stress.

According to Barry Schwartz, the author of *The Paradox of Choice*, this abundance of information is overwhelming. 'We become overloaded. Choice no longer liberates, it debilitates. It might even be said to tyrannize.'[8]

In summary, it's hard to be heard in a noisy, unpredictable, chaotic environment.

To combat this increasingly frenetic atmosphere, the very first step we need to take to create a winning mindset is this: Be simple. In a world where we struggle to differentiate between the constant drone of background noise and the really important information, your audience needs as much help as possible. I don't use the term 'simple' in the sense of 'dumbing down' or offering 'sound bites'. You don't have to speak in monosyllables to be simple. What I mean by 'simple' is *finding the core of the idea you want to communicate.*

There is a famous story about Michelangelo which illustrates how to do this. One day Michelangelo welcomed a stranger into his studio. On the floor in the middle of the studio, he had a large lump of rock. The visitor asked Michelangelo what he intended to do with it. 'From that rock, I will sculpt a lion,' the great artist replied.

The visitor was taken aback. It was hard to imagine how anyone could create anything from such a rock. In obvious awe of Michelangelo, he asked the master nervously what, how, where one might start the process of creating a lion from such an unpromising block of stone.

'Oh, it's very simple,' Michelangelo replied. 'I just take my chisel and knock off all the bits that don't look like a lion.'

'Finding the core' is similar. It means stripping an idea down to its most critical essence. To get to the core, we need to weed out superfluous and tangential elements. But that's the easy part.

The hard part is weeding out ideas that may be really important but just aren't *the most important* idea.

You can't have five North Stars; you can't have five 'most important goals' and you can't catch five tennis balls. It's about discarding a lot of great insights in order to let the most important insight shine.

In fact, I'll follow my own advice and strip this book down to its core.

Here it is: there are two steps in creating a winning mindset – Step One is to find the core, and Step Two is to translate the core using the STEPS checklist. That's it. We'll spend the next half-chapter on Step One and the rest of the book on Step Two.

EXERCISE – THINK LIKE YOU TWEET

When I work with leaders, to help them understand the need for clarity I encourage them to communicate as they would tweet.

For the uninitiated, Twitter is a micro-messaging site where you can send messages (or tweets) of 140 or fewer characters. The mark of an effective tweet, like the mark of any effective communication, is that it engages the recipient and encourages them to take the conversation further – by responding, clicking a link, or sharing the tweet with others. The few scholars who have studied this new medium have found that only a small category of tweets actually accomplish those goals. It is similar for many leaders.

This approach worked really effectively when I once agreed to be the medium for a rugby coach when he wished to pass on instructions to his support staff – and, indirectly, to the players – during a game. He sat in the stands and would issue his radio instructions, and because I didn't possess the technical knowledge, he had to keep those instructions clear and concise.

How would you fare in your organization if you were obliged to think like you tweet?

1.iii   INFORMATION IS INSPIRATION

When I was growing up, the two best movies about coaching were *Dead Poets Society* and *Stand and Deliver*. More recently, Al Pacino's *Any Given Sunday* has assumed its place alongside them. The key moments in each of these films are when the coach delivers an eloquent and amazing speech that makes the hair stand up on the back of your neck; it is the moment when suddenly the students – and you – see the world in a new and wonderful way. These movies are totally great.

Also, they are totally wrong.

That's not how great coaches really operate. They don't make inspiring speeches to groups, like when Al Pacino delivers his impassioned plea to 'climb out of Hell, one inch at a time'. They don't try to deliver instinctive, creative, last-minute, improvised bursts of genius that will change everything.

Instead, they send short, simple and super-clear information.

Think about how many of your life's most important, most emotionally charged moments, were captured in the simplest of phrases:

'I love you.'

'I do.'

'It's a girl.'

'I'm leaving.'

'He's dead.'

Simple ideas have more impact than complicated ideas because our brains have a preference, a hardwired preference, for simplicity over complexity. They are more memorable in the short term, they are easier to pass on by word of mouth and in the longer term the message endures.

In 1970, two educational psychologists, Ron Gallimore and Roland Tharp, were given a dream opportunity: to set up, from scratch, an experimental programme at a school in a poor neighbourhood in Hawaii to help children learn to read.

One afternoon while playing basketball in his back yard, Gallimore had an idea: they would perform a detailed, up-close case study of the greatest teacher they could find and use the results to help them at their school. Both men instantly thought of the same teacher. This particular teacher was so brilliant and highly acclaimed that they doubted the likelihood of their chances. Still, with nothing to lose, they decided to write and ask anyway. They mailed their request to Mr John Wooden, the head basketball coach of University of California, Los Angeles.

To describe John Wooden as a good basketball coach is quite an understatement. 'The Wizard of Westwood', as Wooden was known, was a former English teacher from small-town Indiana who quoted the English poet William Wordsworth and lived by Christian values of discipline, morality and teamwork. He had also led UCLA to nine national championships.

In the previous ten years, his team had recorded an eighty-eight-game undefeated stretch that had lasted for nearly three years. This was just one of the many historic feats that would lead ESPN to name Wooden as 'the greatest coach of all time in any sport'.

Given his status within the sport, Wooden had no reason to submit himself to the prying of a couple of inquisitive scientists, so Gallimore and Tharp were more than a little surprised when Wooden's answer arrived: yes.

A few weeks later, the psychologists settled eagerly into courtside seats to watch Wooden open the coaching for the season's first practice. As fans of the team, as well as former athletes themselves, they thought they knew what to expect: lots of talks around a blackboard, inspiring speeches, punishment laps for slackers, praise for the hard workers. Then practice began.

'We thought we knew what coaching was,' Gallimore said. 'Our expectations were completely wrong. Completely. All the stuff I'd associated with coaching – there was none of it.'[9] Wooden didn't sound or act like any coach they'd ever encountered.

Wooden ran an intense session of drills which lasted between five and fifteen minutes, issuing a rapid-fire stream of words all the while. The interesting part, however, was the content of those words. As their subsequent article, 'Basketball's John Wooden: What a Coach Can Teach a Teacher' put it, Wooden's 'teaching utterances or comments were short, punctuated, and numerous. There were no lectures, no extended harangues . . . he rarely spoke longer than twenty seconds.'

Here are some of Wooden's more long-winded 'speeches':

'Take the ball softly; you're receiving a pass, not intercepting it.'

'Do some dribbling between shots.'

'Crisp passes, really snap them. Good, Richard – that's just what I want.'

'Hard, driving, quick steps.'

Gallimore and Tharp were confused. They'd expected to find a basketball equivalent of Moses intoning sermons from the mount, yet this man resembled a busy telegraph operator. They felt slightly deflated. This was great coaching?

Gallimore and Tharp kept attending practices. As the weeks and months went by, an ember of insight began to glow.

It came partly from watching the team improve, rising from third in the conference at the midpoint of the season to winning its tenth national championship. But it came mostly from the data they collected in their notebooks.

Gallimore and Tharp recorded and coded 2,326 discrete acts of teaching. Of them, a mere 6.9 per cent were compliments. Only 6.6 per cent were expressions of displeasure. But 75 per cent were pure information: what to do, how to do it, when to intensify an activity. One of Wooden's most frequent forms of teaching was a three-part instruction where he modelled the right way to do something, showed the incorrect way, and then remodelled the right way, a sequence that appeared in Gallimore and Tharp's notes as M+, M−, M+; it happened so often that they named it a 'Wooden'. As Gallimore and Tharp wrote, Wooden's 'demonstrations rarely take longer than three seconds, but are of such clarity that they leave an image in memory much like a textbook sketch'.

The information didn't slow down the practice; on the contrary, Wooden combined it with something he called 'mental and emotional conditioning', which basically amounted to everyone running harder than they did in games, all the time.

As former player Bill Walton said, 'Practices at UCLA were nonstop, electric, supercharged, intense, demanding.'[10] While Wooden's practices looked natural and unplanned, in fact they were anything but. The coach would spend two hours each morning with his assistants planning that day's practice, then write out the minute-by-minute schedule on three-by-five cards. He kept the cards from year to year, so he could compare and adjust. No detail was too small to be considered.'

What looked like a flowing, improvised series of drills was in fact as well structured as a libretto. What looked like Wooden shooting from the hip was in fact closer to planned talking points.

Gradually a picture came into focus: what made Wooden a great coach wasn't praise, wasn't denunciation, and certainly wasn't pep talks. His skill resided in the simplicity of the messages he fired at his players.

'Don't look for the big, quick improvement. Seek the small improvement one day at a time. That's the only way it happens – and when it happens, it lasts,' he wrote in *The Wisdom of Wooden*.[11] 'The importance of repetition cannot be overstated,' he said in *You Haven't Taught Until They Have Learned*, authored by Gallimore and former Wooden player Swen Nater. 'Repetition is the key to learning.'[12] The wizard's secret, it turned out, was: the simpler your message, the better your understanding.

Gallimore and Tharp began to apply what they'd learned in the classroom. They combined praise with 'Woodens'; they demonstrated and explained; they spoke in short, imperative bursts. 'We refocused our work,' Gallimore said. 'We started approaching the school with the idea of, what would John Wooden do?'

Slowly, steadily, things began to take off. Reading scores rose, comprehension improved, and the school, which had previously lagged far behind national averages, was soon exceeding them by a healthy margin. In 1993 Gallimore and Tharp's project received the Grawemeyer Award, one of education's highest honours; their success was chronicled in their book, *Rousing Minds to Life*.

'It's not so simple as to say John Wooden made the school work,' Gallimore said. 'But he does deserve a lot of the credit.'[13]

1.iv INVERTING THE PYRAMID

So how do you do this?

Let's begin with a lesson from General John Sedgwick, a highly decorated Union Army general in the American Civil War. He had forged a considerable reputation as a fighter, including the three separate occasions when he had been wounded by bullets yet continued to battle on. 'He was,' according to one report, 'seemingly immune to fear.'

Despite his military achievements, the soldier referred to as 'Uncle John' by his troops was destined to become a long-forgotten name but for the unfortunate assertion he made just before he drew his last breath. General Sedgwick's story inadvertently helped influence journalistic techniques and practices long after his death and can help you to master the art of simplicity.

In May 1864, a skirmish at Spotsylvania Court House, Virginia, had settled into its third day. Sedgwick was deploying his men to face the enemy, but Confederate snipers continued to hinder their preparations.

In an attempt to bolster the morale of his troops, the general wandered along the front line urging his men not to fear the enemy snipers. As he began directing the troop placement, General Sedgwick made a point of not responding to distant enemy gunfire, and he laughingly chided the soldiers who dodged when they heard the long shrill whistle of a bullet cutting through the air.

'What! What! Men, dodging this way for single bullets!' scolded Sedgwick. 'What will you do when they open fire along the whole line? I am ashamed of you.'

A second round of fire whistled by, and a young soldier reacted to the general's mocking laughter and told of the occasion when he dodged a shell that would otherwise have taken his head off. Sedgwick curtly told the man to take his position.

Before the third attempt to hit them, Sedgwick scoffed at the enemy's efforts and was heard to declare, 'They couldn't hit an elephant at this dist—'

A sniper's bullet prematurely ended his final words.

The story of John Sedgwick's demise is said to have influenced the news reporters who wanted to use military telegraphs to transmit their stories back home. They knew they could be cut off at any moment: they might be bumped by military personnel, the communication line might be lost completely – a common occurrence during battles – or a fate similar to that of General John Sedgwick might befall them. In short, the reporters never knew how much time they would get to send the story, so they had to learn to send the most important information first.

Today, journalism schools instruct their reporters to start their stories with the most important information. 'The importance of your first sentence must never be underestimated,' the writer Norman Mailer warned. This first sentence, called the lead, contains the most essential elements of the story. After the lead, information is presented in decreasing order of importance. Journalists call this the 'inverted pyramid' structure – the most important information (the widest part of the pyramid) is at the top.

Trevor Beattie, a leading figure within the advertising industry and the man responsible for modern-day classic campaigns such as the 'Hello Boys' slogan for Wonderbra, French Connection's FCUK and Peter Kay's John Smith's bitter commercials, suggests that this can be addressed by focusing on the core. 'Thirty seconds is too long to get your message across. Five seconds,' he asserts, 'is the right length.' Beattie continues, 'Boil your message to a succinct headline and you'll have people noticing your ideas.'[14]

The inverted pyramid is great for readers. No matter what the reader's attention span – whether they read only the lead or the entire story – the inverted pyramid maximizes the information they glean. Think of the alternative: if the news stories were written like mysteries, with a dramatic pay-off at the end, then readers who broke off in mid story would miss the point. Imagine waiting until the last sentence of a story to find out who won the election or the cup final.

The inverted pyramid also allows newspapers to get out of the door on time. Suppose a late-breaking story forces editors to steal space from other stories. Without the inverted pyramid, they'd be forced to do a slow, careful editing job on the other articles, trimming a word here or a phrase there. With the inverted pyramid structure, they simply lop off paragraphs from the bottom of the other articles, knowing that those paragraphs are – by construction – the least important. Ernest Hemingway, who trained as a journalist before achieving literary success, said, 'Writing is architecture, not interior decoration.'

'Journalism leads are like first impressions,' says former national newspaper editor Kelvin MacKenzie. 'You want to make sure they're good.'[15] The most traditional lead is meant to give a reader a quick summary of the story in as few words as possible. It contains the essence of the story. 'It should have the most important, but not necessarily all, of the five Ws and H – who, what, when, where, why and how,' says the sportswriter Derek Allsop.

Think about the greatest speeches in our history, the speeches that really changed the world. Those who wrote and delivered them never used words for words' sake; the central ideas were always stated in the simplest of language. Abraham Lincoln, who wrote the Gettysburg Address using just 272 words, once said, 'Give me six hours to chop down a tree and I will spend the first four sharpening the axe.'

This is the same approach that journalists take. Michael Buerk, the BBC journalist who highlighted the effects of famine in Africa in 1984, believes that the investment of time in finding the core is the key. 'Take time and space to sort out your thoughts and emotions,' he urges. 'Television news hardly ever gives you that luxury, but it can take a few hours to get the opening words right, working and reworking the sentences.'[16]

The opening lines of Buerk's famous report, which was the catalyst for the Live Aid famine campaign, are still cited by journalists as a great example of delivering the core of a message. He allowed the camera to pan across a scene of devastation and he said nothing for the first few seconds. When he spoke, his words were sparing but had a devastating impact: 'Dawn, and as the sun breaks through the piercing chill of night on the plain outside Korem it lights up a Biblical famine, now in the twentieth century. This place, say workers here, is the closest thing to hell on earth.'

When the report was aired in the USA, the power of its message was enough to displace the presidential election between Ronald Reagan and Walter Mondale from its usual leading slot. Tom Brokaw, the veteran NBC anchorman, recalls, 'The entire newsroom came to a stop. Not a breath was taken. All the side talk, the gossip, the scuttlebutt about the presidential election, just stopped. Tears came to your eyes and you felt you had just been hit in the stomach.'[17]

So if finding a good lead makes everything else easy, why would a journalist ever fail to come up with one?

You can get hamstrung by your own intelligence. You recognize the value of all the material. You can see different perspectives. But while detail and intellectual rigour are all very well when you're working out what to say, when you're working out how to say it, you need what the great advertising mogul Maurice Saatchi describes as 'brutal simplicity of thought'.

The process of writing a lead – and avoiding the temptation to bury it – is a helpful metaphor. Finding the core and writing the lead both involve forced prioritization. Suppose you're a wartime reporter and you can telegraph only one thing before the line gets cut. What would it be? There is only one lead and only one core. You must choose. Similarly, imagine you have to get a room of elite athletes to listen to your words. What is your most important message?

EXERCISE – READ ALL ABOUT IT!

When I started my career as a coach, the most effective lesson I ever received came from the tutor – an experienced Premier League coach – at the very start of the day's training, and which I referenced in the introduction.

'You are all excellent coaches,' he intoned, 'but you all have one great weakness.' He paused and glared around the room. He certainly had our full, undivided attention. 'I will highlight what it is,' he promised. 'Can I have a volunteer?'

Everyone in the room suddenly took a very real interest in the weave of the carpet at our feet, hoping to avoid meeting his glare. As I furtively looked up, it seemed as if he was waiting for me. 'Come here,' he beckoned.

He threw a tennis ball at me, with the simple request to catch and throw it back. 'Easy, huh?' he asked. I nodded. It was.

Then he threw two balls simultaneously and although I had to concentrate, I managed to catch both. 'Good,' he purred.

'Well done.' I felt my confidence growing. Then he threw three balls and despite my best efforts, I managed to catch just one. When four balls were introduced, I didn't know which one to focus on. Even less so, when five were thrown.

'That,' he declared, 'is your weakness.'

His point was that we often believe that including lots of lessons in our sessions – like throwing five balls simultaneously – was a sign of effective coaching. My coaching mentor dissuaded us from this notion. 'Great coaching is not about how many balls you can throw. It is understanding how many your team can catch.'

This is a point echoed in business by Seth Godin, the marketing guru, who argues that 'if you can't state your position – what you offer – in eight words or less, you don't actually have a position'.[18]

I have helped both individuals and teams create their own visions by acting as a news reporter: interviewing people involved in the task and then focusing on what they would see, hear, feel, touch, taste and sense when success has actually happened. This helps us then create our headline to summarize the intent.

Why not get someone to interview you about your own vision and then come up with an attention-grabbing headline?

This difficult quest – to wrestle priorities out of complexity – takes practice but in a world of noise, the impact can be profound. Equally, the consequences of failing to do so can be disastrous, as one of the world's biggest football clubs discovered.

1.v FERGUSON VERSUS MOYES: THE SORCERER AND THE APPRENTICE

In 1986, Sir Alex Ferguson left behind an as yet unsurpassed legacy of success in Scottish football with a previously unheralded Aberdeen team, to take over at Manchester United when the club was at perhaps its lowest point since the tragedy of the 1958 Munich air disaster. It had experienced a startling fall from grace since the European Cup triumph of 1968, and had not won an English league title in nearly twenty years. By prioritizing the development of young players, rebuilding the team, being shrewd in the transfer market, emphasizing attacking football, and bringing the best out of his players through his creation of a culture of constant innovation, Ferguson eventually turned United's fortunes around. He delivered football of rare beauty. He brought trophies, glory, prestige and the kind of happiness, over twenty-six years, that United supporters once only dreamed of. No other coach has performed at the highest level for so long, or with such competitive courage. Nobody has beaten the system the way he has and accumulated so many trophies. He outlasted thirteen different Manchester City managers. He saw off prime ministers Thatcher, Major, Blair and Brown. He has been knighted and immortalized in bronze, and he turned Manchester United into one of the most prolific trophy-grabbing machines in the modern game, with a list of honours encompassing thirteen league titles, two European Cups, five FA Cups, one European Cup Winners' Cup, two League Cups, plus enough individual awards to fill a museum – it amounts to an overall haul nearly double that of the next most successful English club manager.

Ferguson understood that great coaches don't amass such a record by spending their time talking. They spend most of their time watching and listening. 'He never misses anything,' his former captain Gary Neville recalled. 'He's always alert. There's nothing that his eyes and ears don't pick up.'[19] When such coaches do communicate, they don't just start talking, and risk burying the lead. Ferguson understood that in the world of high-pressure coaching, delivering concise, useful information, via the method of the inverted pyramid, tends to make that information stick.

He was once asked: 'If the average coach says a hundred words to his players, how many words should a great coach say?' Ferguson delivered a simple response.

'Ten words,' he said. 'Fewer, if possible.'[20]

Roy Keane, his most successful but now-estranged captain, described this ability to remain succinct as Ferguson's greatest strength. 'I was never once confused by one of his team talks or his tactics, or training sessions,' he said. 'I must have heard him talk before a match close to five hundred times. Never once, in all my years at United, did I think, "I don't know where you're going with that one." I always thought, "Yeah – that was good."'

Keane played under both Ferguson and the Scot's fellow double European Cup winner Brian Clough. When he considers the qualities that made them a part of the coaching elite, Keane's own observation also tends towards the brevity he admired in them. 'I played under good managers and bad managers,' he reflects. 'The top managers get a feel for the group, they know what you need.'

Keane, whose illustrious United career ended following a controversial interview with the club's in-house TV station, MUTV, continued, 'It could have been a European semi-final, it could have been Leeds away, it could have been a home League Cup tie – Alex Ferguson always had a feel of the group and could express it in clear terms. Whatever Alex Ferguson's strengths and weaknesses, that was by far his biggest strength.'

The Irish midfielder recalled one particular pre-match team talk which reflected Ferguson's ability to deliver the lead headline, and create a space to allow his players to complete the rest of the story.

'Before one game against Tottenham at home, I thought I knew what the group might need,' Keane said. 'We didn't need a big team talk.' Keane summarized the feelings of his teammates. 'I thought, please don't go on about Tottenham, we all know what Tottenham is about, they are nice and tidy but we'll fucking do them.'[21]

'Every time I went into a team talk, I bounded in, chest out, making sure I conveyed authority and control,' Ferguson told Alastair Campbell. 'I never slunk in without anyone noticing.'[22] On this occasion, he presented the core message in just three words.

'Lads,' he declared, 'it's Tottenham.' He paused, watching to ensure that the impact of his words was as he intended, and then walked back out.

'That was it,' Keane marvels, stopping to add the epithet, 'brilliant.'

Ferguson's team cantered to a 3–0 win.

In May 2013, Ferguson retired as British football's most decorated coach and anointed his successor, David Moyes. Ferguson recognized the Everton coach as someone who shared many of the same coaching and personal characteristics as himself, shaped in part by their Glaswegian upbringing.

Despite Ferguson's instructions to the club's fans when he delivered his emotion-drenched leaving speech, demanding they offer Moyes the same levels of patience and support he himself had enjoyed, the performances during the following ten months saw the team which Ferguson had led to the title slump to a disastrous seventh place, and the board chose to remove Moyes from his job.

Rio Ferdinand, the elegant England defender who enjoyed a hugely decorated career at the club, contrasted his experiences under the two managers. Like many of the 212 footballers who played for Ferguson during his twenty-six-year reign, he regarded Ferguson's ability to offer succinct advice as his greatest strength.

'I think perhaps the biggest thing was that Sir Alex Ferguson never confused us with too much detail – just a few key points and a mindset that there's no doubt we were going to beat the other team,' he said. 'If you go out with a clear, strong idea, you'll execute that in a more decisive manner. Clarity and energy: that's what he gave us.'

Ferdinand continues, 'The truth is that football is not as complicated as some people make out. People like to pretend there's a big mystique to winning football matches. But a lot of it is simple: don't make things too intricate and let people play off the cuff a little bit. Management is easy, but people often try to overcomplicate it.'

When trying to dissect what went wrong in the months following Ferguson's retirement, Ferdinand was unequivocal that his successor's apparent tendency to 'bury the lead' created confusion and misunderstanding. 'Moyes wanted us to change our style but we were never quite sure what he wanted us to change it to,' he observed.

'There were a lot of mixed messages. Sometimes he'd say, "I want you to pass the ball," other days it was, "I don't want you to pass the ball." What the fuck do you want us to do, man? You heard a lot of guys complaining, "I just don't know what he wants." He had me doubting everything,' Ferdinand said. 'We wanted clear and concise information,' he added, 'but everything was mixed.'

Ferdinand described one example of this confused communication. In the week after the team had been soundly beaten by cross-city rivals Manchester City, who had invested unprecedented amounts of money in new players, Moyes asked Ferdinand and his defensive partner, the Serbian Nemanja Vidić, to meet in his office and review the game.

'I want to show you a few things,' said the manager.

Ferdinand said, 'He had about fifteen separate clips to show us, but we never got past clip five.'

Following the heated forty-minute exchange, Ferdinand recalls how he and Vidić came out of the meeting, and his words should serve as a warning shot for anyone not convinced of the need to strive for simplicity.

'We looked at each other and said, "I don't know what the fuck he just asked us to do."'[23]

1.vi ONE THING AFTER ANOTHER: COGNITIVE FLUENCY

But the evidence for simplicity's hold over us isn't just anecdotal. There's science in the mix as well.

When asking why our brains love simplicity, we need to understand that whenever our prehistoric ancestors faced a difficult situation – let's say, a predator – those who came up with the correct solution to such a predicament, be it fight, flight or freeze, would have been most likely to survive and to pass on their genes to future generations. And among them, the most likely to survive and procreate would have been those who came up with the correct answer *most quickly*.

As we have seen, the data deluge happens way too fast for us to work in any other way. So, over the years, the millions of years of our evolutionary history, our brains have learned to take shortcuts; to use mental rules of thumb to make decisions; to employ learned associations; to assimilate millions upon millions of bytes of previously stored information to generate response outcomes.

Information travels around your brain like electricity around a circuit. It takes the path of least resistance. And the simpler you make your argument, the more clearly you present your case, the faster and more powerfully that information flows.

There lies great beauty in simplicity – and such essential, elemental elegance is a honeytrap for the brain.

Mathematicians constantly strive to find the shortest possible formula to describe a complex phenomenon. It's called, in their language, 'algorithmic irreducibility'. It is from Hollywood, however, that we can learn how to find simplicity within complexity and apply it to our situation. We must learn to BLUF – put your Bottom Line Up Front.

At the epicentre of the entertainment business is the pitch. Television and movie executives take meetings with writers and other creative types, who pitch them ideas for the next blockbuster film or hit TV series.

Motion pictures offer a glimpse of these sessions. 'It's *Out of Africa* meets *Pretty Woman*,' promises an eager writer in the Hollywood satire *The Player*. 'It's like *The Gods Must Be Crazy* except the Coke bottle is an actress!' But what really goes on behind those studio walls is often a mystery, which is why two business-school professors decided to helicopter behind the lines for a closer look.

Kimberly Elsbach of the University of California, Davis, and Roderick Kramer of Stanford University spent five years in the thick of the Hollywood pitch process. They sat in on dozens of pitch meetings, analysed transcripts of pitching sessions, and interviewed screenwriters, agents and producers. The award-winning study they wrote for the *Academy of Management Journal* offers excellent guidance even for humble movie watchers.

Now, whilst it may be hard to muster sympathy for the life of the studio execs who make these decisions, let's try for a moment.

Each Hollywood studio works on a ratio that for every movie it will produce, it will consider and reject hundreds of pitches or screenplays. Imagine the process of reaching a decision that they must go through. If they invest in a movie, they are, in effect, betting millions of dollars – and their own hard-earned reputations – on what is essentially an intangible idea that has come from the mind of a writer.

Contrast this decision with the kind you are more regularly faced with – for example, if you were buying a brand-new house. In the beginning, an architect creates a blueprint for your home, and someone else puts up the money for its construction. At each stage of this process, you can feel pretty confident that you'll have a home that realizes the architect's original vision.

A movie pitch, on the other hand, is destined to change. When a screenwriter is hired, the story will change. When a director is hired, the artistic feel of the movie will change. When stars are hired to play the parts, their personalities will change how we perceive the characters in the story. When producers are hired, the storytelling will become subject to financial and logistical constraints. And when the movie is completed, months or years later, the marketing team will need to find a way to explain the plot to the public in about thirty seconds – without giving away too much.

Imagine investing millions in an idea that will change as it is filtered through the consciousness of a succession of individuals with giant egos: directors, stars, producers, marketers. That idea had better be good.

In Hollywood, the official term for these core ideas is 'high-concept pitches'. You've probably seen some of them on the movie posters:

> **The general who became a slave. The slave who became a gladiator. The gladiator who defied an emperor.** (*Gladiator*)
>
> **Mischief. Mayhem. Soap.** (*Fight Club*)
>
> **An adventure 65 million years in the making.** (*Jurassic Park*)

The Oscar-winning movie star turned producer, Ben Affleck, understands the importance of achieving this. 'I had wanted to be a director for a long time, but I also felt insecure and not confident and not sure of myself about it. I thought, "Well, I'll learn. I'll use being an actor as a kind of apprenticeship,"' he said.

'Sidney Lumet wrote a great book called *Making Movies*, which is almost a "how-to" manual, very matter-of-fact, from one of the real masters. He distils film-making to its essence as he saw it and he really believed firmly that you had to have a sort of one-sentence encapsulation of what a movie was about before you could make it.'

Affleck was initially reluctant to accept the power of this simplicity. 'I thought, when I read the book – before I had ever directed anything, and before I really had any idea what I was talking about – that it was an oversimplification. I've changed my tune on that. I've noticed that when I haven't had a clear sense, at its root, of what a movie is about, I've tended to get more lost and do work that wasn't as good.'[24]

Affleck won an Oscar in 2012 for his film *Argo*, about Americans caught in Iran during the 1979 uprising. Affleck summarizes this as: *The Great Escape: How the CIA Used a Fake Sci-Fi Flick to Rescue Americans from Tehran*.

But let's look closely at the high-concept pitch that was used to start one of the highest-earning franchises of all time, the 1981 movie *Indiana Jones and the Raiders of the Lost Ark*.

After *Star Wars* opened in 1977, George Lucas had sought refuge in Hawaii, where he was joined by his friend Steven Spielberg. Whilst building sandcastles on the beach, Spielberg, who had already enjoyed huge success with *Jaws*, told Lucas of his desire to direct a James Bond film.

Lucas convinced his friend that he had conceived a character 'better than James Bond' and explained the concept of

Raiders of the Lost Ark, a film that would recapture the rollicking adventures of the matinee serials of Lucas's youth. Spielberg loved it, calling it 'a James Bond film without the hardware'.

Between the two of them, they crafted a compact, seven-word summary of the film, '*James Bond with a hat and a whip*', which poured a breathtaking amount of meaning into the previously non-existent concept of Indiana Jones.

Before it was pitched, it did not exist in the minds of the execs, but now think of all the important decisions you – and the people who work on the movie – can make, just on the strength of those seven words.

Do you hire an action director or an indie director? *Action.*

Do you budget $10 million for the movie or $100 million? *$100 million.*

Big star or ensemble cast? *Big star.*

Target a summer or a Christmas release? *Summer.*

If high-concept pitches can have this power in the movie world – an environment filled with a greater density of egos – we should feel confident that we can harness the same power in our own environments.

EXERCISE – THE T-SHIRT LAW

When working with any team or business, one of the first things I look for is whether they can pass the T-shirt law test.

The T-shirt law states that on the front of any T-shirt, you can only get one picture or message across – *Frankie Says Relax*, anyone? If you can't emblazon what you stand for across a T-shirt, it's probably too complicated.

This isn't particularly easy but it is absolutely necessary. Winston Churchill understood this rule and once wrote a long letter to his wife, Clementine, which ended with the apology, 'I am sorry I wrote such a long letter, I did not have time to write a short one.'

As we have seen, Hollywood demands that the essence of a film should be boiled down to fit the T-shirt law, through stating your BLUF. There are a number of companies who can also successfully condense their mission down to its core message:

Bayern Munich FC: *more than 1–0*

Bayern Munich revised their mission and came up with this simple message which is applicable to everybody associated with the club, from the players through to the fans. They wanted to be a club which was about more than just results; they wanted to stand for something in the community and amongst their followers; they also wanted to be a club that looked to entertain as opposed to just winning by the bare minimum.

Harley Davidson: *to sell the ability to a forty-three-year-old accountant to dress in black leather, ride through small towns and have people be afraid of him.*

When Rich Teerlink was running the Harley-Davidson motorbike company, he spent a long time trying to convince Wall Street investors that the company was not a motorbike manufacturer but was instead a company selling experiences. They make more money selling associated products such as hats and clothing than though their motorcycles. When he was able to articulate his T-shirt law, he finally managed to convince them.

Waldorf Astoria Hotel: *creating customers for life.*

The origins of this world-famous hotel have their roots in a stormy night, many years ago, when an elderly man and his wife entered the lobby of a small hotel in Philadelphia. Keen to get out of the rain, the couple approached the desk and hoped to get a room. The clerk, a friendly young man, explained that there were three conventions in town and all the rooms were taken. He refused, however, to allow the guests to head back out into the night and offered them his own room instead.

Two years later, the young clerk received a letter from the old man with a return ticket to New York. He was invited to come to the city, where the old man led him to the corner of Fifth Avenue and 34th Street and pointed to a great new building, a palace of reddish stone with turrets rising into the sky. 'That,' he said, 'is the hotel I have built for you to manage.'

The old man was William Waldorf Astor and the hotel was named after him, the original Waldorf Astoria Hotel. The young clerk, George C. Bokit, then became the first manager and he insisted that all his staff understood the purpose of the hotel, which was to 'create customers for life'.

South West Airlines: *to democratize the skies*.

There are lots of ways in which airlines can compete: in-flight service, loyalty schemes, convenient schedules, route network, legroom, on-board entertainment, quality of food and wine, airport lounges, sleeper beds, punctuality, choice of airport and quality of connections.

Herb Kelleher, the founder of Southwest Airlines, has a simple response to all these competitive challenges: low cost, low cost, low cost, low cost, low cost, low cost, low cost, low cost, low cost, low cost and low cost.

This is very simple, very focused and very effective. Everyone, including the customer, understands what this means for them. They keep it low to ensure that anyone, whatever their budget, can afford to fly with them and, therefore, they truly democratize the skies.

What is your T-shirt law?

This same approach was employed by an East German coach to ignite the culture of British rowing.

1.vii WILL IT MAKE THE BOAT GO FASTER?

Henley is a picturesque malting town and former port that straddles the Thames about thirty-five miles from London. Here, the rowers are as much a part of the riverside furniture as the 1786 town bridge and the Angel pub. The modern sport of rowing was born on the mile-and-a-half straight of Henley Reach when the first Oxford vs Cambridge Boat Race took place in 1829.

The river, its idyllic setting and the drop-dead gorgeous views have remained essentially unchanged in nearly two hundred years. The only eyesore in this seductively picturesque backdrop is the Leander Club itself. A clumsy, rambling structure, it is a shrine to rowing, but its bulk lacks the grace and practicality of the sport's finest practitioners. Here, crews work under the hawk eye of the watch-tapping Jürgen Gröbler.

Ever since 1972, Gröbler has groomed medal-winning crews at every World Championships and Olympic Games, except Los Angeles in 1984, which was boycotted by the Soviet bloc, including his own East German team. When he arrived in England in 1991, Gröbler, who spoke schoolboy English and had little knowledge of the eccentrically amateur British way of sport, found the move from Germany a considerable culture shock. But the pull of a broader education for his son, Björn, who was eleven, and the need to prove himself as a coach outside the megalithic GDR system, brought him and his wife Angela to the banks of the Thames and into the intricate social fabric of the Leander Club.

He was the most professional person the majority of people in British rowing had ever met. The sport was coached by enthusiastic amateurs who were, in the main, school teachers. Gröbler was surprised by how primitive and amateurish British rowing was. 'Conditions were a lot worse than in the GDR,' he said. 'When I came over, I couldn't really understand that we had to go out and find the money to go to the World Championships. They carry the British flag for the country, people have to pay for it! A big shock for me.'[25]

Gröbler's approach to coaching technique seemed to be: if it ain't broke, don't fix it. He would say very little during outings. Out on the river, he might utter one prized word, such as, 'Acceleration'. Quite often, the crews might not notice him at all, until he would suddenly pop out from behind a bush with a stopwatch. Trainee coaches would turn up at Leander and follow him along the towpath to learn from him, and then complain that he didn't say anything.

'Bad coaches are forever asking how the boat feels and if the crew agree with what they are saying,' four-times Olympic champion Sir Matthew Pinsent said. 'Jürgen did so little of this it was scary. He would bring the boat in towards the towpath and give you a few pointers, nothing outlandish but definitely taxing. Most often he wouldn't open any negotiation with the crew at all; it was a swift monologue and then off you go again. It didn't take very long doing this to find out if the guy was a faker or the real thing.'[26]

When Gröbler arrived, he came with valuable data and new methods, but above all, with a commitment to be the best. Gröbler declared that, in order to win Olympic gold, every crew must up the intensity of their training by 10 per cent compared to the previous Olympiad.

Treading water wouldn't do. 'Redgrave's winning time in the coxed four in 1984 wouldn't have qualified him for the final of the coxed fours in Seoul in 1988,' Gröbler recalled. 'His gold-medal winning time in Seoul in the coxless pair wouldn't have even won him a medal in Barcelona in 1992, and so on and on.' At every four-year turn of the Olympic wheel, the bar was set higher. 'You have to find more every time,' Gröbler said.[27]

Without hard data, you could never be sure what made a boat go faster, or even if it were going faster at all. A numbers man, and a master of arcane calculations about wind speed against the performance of a crew, Gröbler focused on improving 'measurables': physiology, boat speed, ergometer times and physical strength. Boat speed over two hundred metres was the most important measurable, but that should be improved as other measurables improved. New ideas were introduced one at a time, and their effect measured if possible. When Gröbler spoke, in his sparing, heavily accented English, he tended not to waste words. He simply said, 'It was now possible to summarize your every move against the question: "Will it make the boat go faster?"'

The genuine hunger to try and become the best in the world, both as a team and as individuals, had a huge impact on the culture of the club and by default the sport as a whole. As Pinsent describes it, 'every event, every training session, even every meal you ate had meaning, and there was nowhere to hide. We were able to turn up to events knowing exactly where we stood against the best crews in the world.'[28]

Early on in his illustrious career, Steve Redgrave was openly dismissive of the idea that he needed to incorporate weight training into his regime. 'If I wanted to lift weights, I would have chosen to be a weightlifter,' he scoffed.

When Gröbler wanted to persuade him to adopt these new sessions into his training, Gröbler posed his golden – *will it make the boat go faster?* – question along with some statistics to help guide Redgrave's response.

'I sometimes compared his [Redgrave's] weights with my strongest German women,' Gröbler recalled. 'It was probably not the right thing to say, but I did it in a gentle way. I was always working with his competitive instincts.'[29] Soon after, Redgrave began to see the difference increased power developed in the weight room could make to his speed in the boat. He became one of the most committed trainers in the gym.

Perhaps the most celebrated crew with which Gröbler worked was the coxless four that won the gold medal at the 2000 Olympic Games in Sydney, not least because it propelled Redgrave to his fifth gold medal and sporting immortality and a knighthood.

In his book *Four Men in a Boat*, Tim Foster described how, twelve months before the Olympic finals, he put his hand through a window at a drunken party, severing tendons, lacerating an artery and losing two pints of blood in the process. Despite his obvious pain, Foster failed to appreciate the seriousness of his injury and the impact on his teammates.

In the consultant's room, he asked, 'How long will it be until I can play the piano?'

'Six weeks,' was the reply.

'That's brilliant. I couldn't play it before,' he deadpanned.

Despite his light-hearted view of the situation, the eight weeks during which he was eventually incapacitated and unable to row was not treated as humorous within the squad. Redgrave simply applied the golden question and announced that they would carry on with the next best bow-side oarsman.

Foster remembers his surprise at how quickly the crew shunned him. He would cycle the twenty-six miles from Oxford to Leander, train alone and then cycle home, having been ignored by his crewmates. Gröbler assured Foster that, once healed, he would be back in. He spun a different story to the four, telling them that if they were fast enough with the replacement (Luka Grubor), they'd stay as they were.

They weren't, finishing fourth in a World Cup regatta in Munich.

Gröbler convened a meeting back at Leander based around the question of Foster's return and whether it would help 'make the boat go faster'. The crew aired their views and Foster, healed, restored, scarred and forgiven, meekly apologized and was back on board. Thereafter, his attitude shifted. He took a serious look at his non-rowing life.

'Previously, I'd asked myself, "Will such-and-such activity harm my rowing?"' he said. 'Now, I began to ask myself, "Will this activity help my rowing?" It was a defining moment.'

1.viii   STRENGTH IN DEPTH

Anyone can come up with a compact phrase. Plenty of people can come up with a profound phrase. But very few can come up with a phrase that is both profound *and* compact. What I have tried to show is that the effort is worth it – that 'finding the core message', and expressing it in the form of a compact idea, can be enduringly powerful.

THE SECOND STEP

THINKING

I cannot teach anybody anything.
I can only make them think.
Socrates

2.i   IN THE MIDDLE OF THE MUDDLE

The revered former England and Newcastle United coach, Sir Bobby Robson, was signing copies of his autobiography in his home town of Newcastle.

When a little boy reached the front, the affable Robson engaged him in conversation. 'Thanks for coming,' he smiled. 'I hope you've not had to wait too long.'

'We've waited a while,' the young man replied. 'How about you, Sir Bobby? Have you signed a lot of books today?'

'Oh, hundreds, son. Absolutely hundreds,' the wizened coach replied in his usual avuncular manner.

That evening, when he returned home, the young boy opened the book and glanced down at the inscription: 'Best wishes, Bobby Hundreds.'

It is estimated that we have to make up to 10,000 trivial decisions every single day. 227 of them are just about food. Think about a visit to a coffee shop. Do you want: caffeinated or decaf? Small, medium, large or extra large? Colombian, Ecuadorian, Ethiopian? Hazelnut, vanilla or unflavoured? Cream or milk? Brown sugar or sweetener? You even have the dilemma of deciding whether to give the barista your real name or not. (I like to give the name 'Bueller' and then watch them inadvertently recreate the classroom register scene from the film *Ferris Bueller's Day Off*. 'Bueller . . . Bueller . . . Anyone? Bueller.')

To cope with this, we all have developed our routines, our ways of doing things. It is suggested that up to 95 per cent of behaviour is habitual, which means that our brain is operating on autopilot for much of the day.

In fact, it's very easy to demonstrate how detached our conscious mind is from our unconscious autopilot. If I gave you a £10 note, how confident would you be that what you had in your hand was a £10 note and not an illegal counterfeit which I had conjured up in my shed? My guess is that you would feel very confident you could accurately identify a £10 note when you are handed one as change in a shop. A cursory glance would inform you that you have a legitimate note in your hand.

However, if I asked you to describe a £10 note to someone who had never seen one so that they could create it from scratch, I'm guessing that you wouldn't get very close to reality. Are the '£' and '10' in the same colour? Does the word 'ten' appear on the note anywhere? If so, how many times? How many digits does the serial number have? Is it printed vertically or horizontally? What pictures are there? How big is the note exactly? Your unconscious mind has the answers but your conscious mind is evidently preoccupied with other things.

When you are learning something new, like walking, the process starts in the conscious mind. That is, you consciously took your first steps, showing great bravery and persistence, until you could walk without falling over. Over time, it was stored within your subconscious and became an automatic process. You can now perform the actions of walking without thinking.

Imagine that you're walking down the street, and you see someone on the other side who you do not want to meet, for whatever reason. You say to yourself, or if you are with someone else you say out loud to them, 'Just walk normally.'

On that instruction, you will immediately start to walk like a robot, walking anything but 'normally' and being acutely aware of each step you are taking and the strange movements of your arms.

Why is this? Conscious decisions are the territory of your thinking brain and because they require careful supervision, they tax the strength of it. The more decisions it has to make – remember, 10,000 a day – the more exhausted it gets, and the more exhausted it gets, the more likely it will go onto autopilot. We call it *decision paralysis*.

President Barack Obama tries to avoid this trap by 'paring down' the decisions he has to make, so he can spend the necessary amount of time thinking about the important ones. Whilst the fashion-conscious among us may feel his approach is a step too far, Obama explains: 'You'll see I wear only grey or blue suits . . . I don't want to make decisions about what I'm eating or wearing . . . you can't be going through the day distracted by trivia.'[1]

His approach has been proven to help. Consider these real examples of decision paralysis:

Scene one: When Procter and Gamble, who offer a wide range of products, from laundry detergents to prescription drugs, reduced the number of versions of Head and Shoulders, one of its very popular shampoos, from a staggering twenty-six to 'only' fifteen, they experienced a 10 per cent increase in sales.

Scene two: A local bar. It's speed-dating night. Singles meet a series of other singles, spending perhaps five minutes with each person, in the hope of making a romantic connection. But decision paralysis thwarts even Cupid. Those who meet seven other singles make more matches than those who meet twenty.

Bottom line: Decision paralysis disrupts our leisure, our shopping and our dating decisions, which suggests that it might affect decisions when creating a winning mindset, too.

Great coaches anticipate this and remove distractions so you can think about what matters most. This chapter focuses on two essential questions: *How do coaches get people to think for themselves?* And, just as crucially, *How do they keep them thinking?* We will look at each of them in turn.

Let's start this chapter by getting you to think about the important things. I'd like you to think about a specific context, let's say work, and compare your performance when operating at your very best against the occasions when you're at your very worst.

Now, honestly answer this question:

What percentage of the difference was mental?

When I do this exercise with elite performers, I get everyone in the room to stand up. I ask those who think the mental part was less than 10 per cent of the difference to sit down. Those who think that it was less than 20 per cent are then asked to take a seat. I repeat this process for those who believe that it is less than 30 per cent and then 40 per cent. When I finally get to 50 per cent at least half the room still remains standing. What about you? Would you still be on your feet?

If the answer to this question is yes, then answer my next question: if you believe that the difference between your very best and your worst day was at least 50 per cent mental, then how much time do you actually spend developing your thinking skills?

When was the last time you sat for an hour of pure, unadulterated thinking? If you're like most people, it's been a while. Is this simply a function of our high-speed era? Perhaps not. The absurdly talented George Bernard Shaw – a world-class writer and a founder of the London School of Economics – noted this thought deficit many years ago. 'Few people think more than two or three times a year,' Shaw reportedly said. 'I have made an international reputation for myself by thinking once or twice a week.'

When David Cameron took office as prime minister, President Obama reportedly advised him that, 'The most important thing you need to do is to have big chunks of time during the day when all you're doing is thinking. Without that, you lose the big picture.'

As one psychologist put it to me: 'Despite spending more time with themselves than with any other person, people often have surprisingly poor insights into their skills and abilities.' A classic example: when asked to rate their driving skills, roughly 80 per cent of respondents rated themselves better than the average driver.

David Dunning, professor of psychology at Cornell University, argues that in order to know how good you are at something, it requires exactly the same skills as it does to be good at that thing in the first place. Take the driving example. The best drivers will know exactly why they rate themselves so highly; what they do that distinguishes them from the rest. Alternatively, it also means that if you're absolutely no good at driving then you lack exactly the skills you need to know that you are absolutely no good at it. Tom Hanks' Forrest Gump described it best: 'Stupid is as stupid does.'

2.ii   THE WILDEBEESTS OF ELITE SPORT

Many environments appear to place little emphasis on thinking skills. Rio Ferdinand describes the experience of living as an elite footballer as like being a wildebeest. 'It must be weird looking at it from the outside, but what people have to understand is that as football players we are treated like children a lot of the time. We are ushered and ferried around from "A" to "B". When we go to airports, for example, we don't have to look for anything or think about anything – we just follow security and follow people telling us what to do. We're like a herd of wildebeest. None of us knows where we're going or what we're doing; we just follow each other. That's it – everything's on the board. We're told what to do at every stage.'[2]

There are numerous sportsmen, now working as after-dinner speakers, who specialize in regaling audiences with stories of such wildebeest-like behaviour, and there are some stand-out examples. Step forward Jason McAteer, the former Liverpool and Republic of Ireland midfielder, who was dubbed 'Trigger' during his career for his similarity to the numbskull character in *Only Fools and Horses*.

McAteer was once asked at a takeaway if he wanted his pizza cut into eight slices or four. 'Four,' he answered. 'I'm not that hungry.' On another occasion, McAteer applied for a credit card and on the application form was the question: 'What is your position at the company?' McAteer's answer was: 'Right full-back'.

Gary Neville, the former footballer now developing a career as coach, articulates the dangerous consequences of a culture which places too little emphasis on thinking. 'It is like being on the waltzer at a fairground. You're spinning around, it's exciting, but you come off dizzy, and it's hard to know whether what you just saw meant anything. As a result, player thinking tends to be really poor,' he said. 'Problem-solving too.'[3]

It is no coincidence that the best environments, where winning mindsets dominate, tend to invest time thinking about thinking.

Rinus Michels, the founding father of Dutch football's 'Total Football' movement – which heralded an era of success in the 1970s the ripples of which are still in evidence today – articulated its importance. 'My role is to train the players' brains, not their legs,' the former schoolteacher declared.[4]

His star pupil, Johan Cruyff, built upon this philosophy during his time as Barcelona coach. 'Intelligent guys are what it is all about,' he explained, 'because you play football with your head, and your legs are there to help you. If you don't use your head, using your feet won't be sufficient. Why does a player have to chase a ball? Because he started running too late. You have to pay attention, use your brain and find the right position. If you get to the ball late, it means you chose the wrong position. Intelligent players are never late.'[5]

So how do they do it?

2.iii COMMANDER'S INTENT

You can't prepare for every scenario. It's impossible. That would be like trying to predict the twenty-third move in a chess game. What great coaches seem to understand is that it's just the critical moves that count.

In the army, the same principle is true.

Every move a soldier makes is preceded by a staggering amount of planning. The plans are quite thorough, detailing what each unit will do, which equipment it will use, how it will replace munitions, and so on. These orders snowball until they are specific enough to guide an individual soldier at any one particular moment in time.

The army invests enormous energy in its planning, and its processes have been refined over many years. The system is a marvel of communication. There's just one tiny drawback: the plans often turn out to be useless.

The expression, 'No plan survives contact with the enemy' is true. You may start off trying to follow your plan but what if the enemy doesn't respond accordingly? What if the weather changes or a key weapon is destroyed?

The army's challenge is akin to writing instructions for a friend to play chess on your behalf. You know a lot about the rules of the game, and you may know a lot about your friend and the opponent. But if you try to write move-by-move instructions, you will fail. You can't possibly anticipate more than a few moves. The first time the opponent makes a surprise move, your friend will have to throw out your carefully designed plans and rely on their own instinct.

This is the reason why the US Army, led by Colin Powell, invented a concept called Commander's Intent (CI).

CI is a crisp, plain-talking statement that appears at the top of every order, specifying the plan's goal, the desired end-state of an operation. At the high levels of the army the CI may be relatively abstract, but as it goes down the ranks it becomes increasingly concrete. The CI never specifies so much detail that it risks being rendered obsolete by unpredictable events but it does align the behaviours of soldiers at all levels without requiring play-by-play instructions from their leaders.

The US Army recommends that all officers arrive at the Commander's Intent by asking themselves to complete two sentences:

If we do nothing else during tomorrow's mission, we must

_____

The single most important thing we must do tomorrow is

_____

Colonel Tim Collins gave a great example of how CI can be used. On Wednesday, 19 March 2003, he gathered around 800 of his men from the 1st Battalion of the Royal Irish Regiment, part of the 16 Air Assault Brigade, at their camp in the Kuwaiti desert, about twenty miles from the Iraqi border.

Colonel Collins delivered a rousing speech, packed with emotive oratory: 'We go to liberate, not to conquer.' 'The enemy should be in no doubt that we are his nemesis and that we are bringing about his rightful destruction.' 'It is a big step to take another human life, it is not to be done lightly.' 'Let's bring everyone home and leave Iraq a better place for us having been there.'

A journalist, Sarah Oliver of the *Mail on Sunday*, was standing nearby and made a note of his speech. She explained, 'It was just after a sandstorm and all the men were standing around him in a U-shape in the middle of a very dusty courtyard. A lot of them were very young and he wanted to explain something of the history and culture of Iraq to them whilst being very clear about the behaviours they should show in the heat of battle. They knew that the public at home had doubts about the war, and he wanted to reassure them and tell them why they were there. By the end, everyone felt they were ready for whatever unpredictable events lay ahead.'

In summary, his message was:

If we do nothing else during tomorrow's mission, we must liberate Iraq.

The single, most important thing we must do tomorrow is act with dignity.

EXERCISE – COMMANDER'S INTENT

I find these questions are especially useful when you are facing an urgent task. One Premier League team I worked with found themselves in a relegation dogfight and these questions helped to focus their efforts.

If we do nothing else during tomorrow's mission, we must **STAY IN THE PREMIER LEAGUE** was the obvious answer to the first question. Players knew that their contracts would be affected; others understood that their resale value would be, as well; some of them had proud records they wanted to maintain of only ever playing in the top division.

When we answered the second question, I asked them to identify the best performance they had delivered in the last six months. There was a universal agreement about one particular victory against a leading team.

I asked them to describe the performance and from this, we identified three 'trademark behaviours' – traits that they felt had distinguished them.

The three most important behaviours we must do tomorrow are:

1. *Sensible hard work*

2. *Resilience*

3. *Remaining united*

We agreed that by investing our time in demonstrating these behaviours we would achieve our mission of staying up.

In our next game, one player publicly remonstrated with a teammate who had spurned an opportunity to pass, elected to shoot and missed. The coaches were able to use the Commander's Intent questions to ask whether the behaviour was representative of 'remaining united' as opposed to letting the rest of the stadium know that his teammate had made a mistake.

In the next eight games, the team won four, drew two and escaped relegation.

If you adapted the Commander's Intent for your own situation, how would you answer these questions:

If you do nothing else during tomorrow's mission, you must:

The three most important behaviours you must do tomorrow are:

So, how do coaches script behaviours in less precarious situations?

2.iv THE PRIVILEGES AND DUTIES OF THE KING

It's common knowledge that British Cycling is a successful team, but there is a fascinating story that precedes its current dominance of track and the Tour de France.

The reasons for British Cycling's success could (and do) fill books but perhaps the single greatest factor in the organization's success is the dogged focus on getting their athletes to think. Every team would love to win, but British Cycling has been doing it for nearly two decades. For this effort to succeed, they must rely on hundreds of employees, ranging from chefs to cyclists, to work together.

British Cycling uses a version of the Commander's Intent – referred to as the King/Queen Strategy – to help guide this coordination.

Let's look at how the adoption of such a clear set of commands has been central to one of the greatest success stories in the history of British sport.

When Chris Hoy made his international debut at the European Under-23 Championships in 1996, the future track legend had to sign his team tracksuit out and then return it to the kit manager afterwards as somebody else would be needing it the following year.

Back then British Cycling was so cash-strapped it could not

afford to send officials to the Moscow event, so Hoy and his two teammates went on their own, with their own bikes and one set of race wheels each.

The entire operation had low expectations and even lower self-esteem. British Cycling looked, felt and acted unloved, so when the new performance director, Peter Keen, stood up at the sport's annual conference a year later and announced that he wanted to make Britain the world's top Olympic cycling nation, many in the room wondered where they had found this guy. Such ambition and enthusiasm. It was all so, well, un-British.

Fast-forward two decades, and the sport is the jewel in the British Olympic crown and the team the envy of the cycling world. The structure at the top of the sport is very, very good and it knows it. Such confidence and success is all so, well, un-British.

The British team that now arrives at major championships is more than a little different from the team that went to those 1996 European games. They now have more kit than Halfords and twenty-four teammates; they are surrounded by even more support staff, regarded as the best in sports science; they are cocooned in a feel-good bubble where no detail is left to chance; and they are ready to live up to some serious expectations.

So where did it all go right?

The answer to that question is both straightforward and complicated, and it is fitting that Peter Keen's current job as elite performance director for UK Sport, the body which effectively runs Olympic sport in Britain, is to help replicate what happened in cycling across all the sports.

Keen, however, is eager to point out that cycling's success story is not one man's tale.

The Moscow episode mentioned above comes from Richard Moore's excellent book, *Heroes, Villains and Velodromes: Inside*

Track Cycling with Chris Hoy, and it is clear from Moore's account that both Hoy and Keen join others in the 'Heroes' column; not that either would admit it.

In 1980, aged sixteen, Keen won the national junior ten-mile race. It would be the peak of his accomplishments on the bike but only the foothills of his impact on the sport.

Six years later, and the ambitious, slightly bookish sports studies graduate from High Wycombe had started working with an equally ambitious young cyclist from the Wirral. Six years after that, in 1992, Chris Boardman won Britain's first Olympic cycling gold since 1920.

But Keen knew that nothing had really changed within the sport's culture.

'What Chris and I were doing in the early '90s was classic British Alpinism,' remembers Keen. 'He was just another one-off success. Leave no ropes, leave no trail. There was no system so there was no legacy. I saw then the challenge was to convert those highly motivated, highly talented individuals into a system.'

Keen was given a chance to put his ideas into practice soon after Britain's Olympic Waterloo in 1996. The cycling squad contributed two bronzes to the Atlanta pot (not bad considering GB did not win a cycling medal during the 1980s), but Steve Redgrave and Matthew Pinsent's rowing gold was Team GB's only win. Keen's challenge was made easier by the almost simultaneous arrival of National Lottery funding. Not that the money was an immediate panacea.

'Actually, one of my biggest hurdles at first was dealing with this inflow of cash,' says Keen. 'First-generation performance directors like me were suddenly expected to write business plans. It was all very new.'[6]

Keen's first plan included a list of about a hundred athletes he wanted to fund. It was a large group but there seemed to be enough cash to go round. The performance at the Sydney Olympics, his first as performance director, seemed to vindicate this approach. Jason Queally stormed to gold in the 'kilo', added a silver in the sprint, and Keen watched Yvonne McGregor and the team pursuit boys chip in with bronzes. Despite this success, he was not convinced of its sustainability.

'We had some good results but we couldn't really argue there was a system in place or that we had developed a culture,' he explains. 'I needed to clear out riders and coaches who weren't obsessed with winning.' Keen developed his own Commander's Intent. The mission was gold medals; the behaviour which everyone had to demonstrate was personal responsibility to deliver their best.

Keen also recognized that in this new culture of accountability, he had taken British Cycling as far as he could go – the next part of the journey would have to be led by others, the irrepressible Dave Brailsford, for one. 'Dave is better at people than me,' admits Keen. 'His man-management skills are incredible. He gets people.'

Brailsford was a relative unknown in cycling circles. He was born in Derby and was a keen amateur cyclist, whose passion for the sport was ignited on family holidays to France. He had studied sports science and psychology at university before later completing an MBA.

His early career included working as a business consultant within the perfume industry before he got a foot in the door of the sport in 1993 as a *soigneur* – a masseur, handler and all-round dogsbody – for a small cycling club and later the British national team.

Richard Moore, a former cyclist and author of *Sky's the Limit: British Cycling's Quest to Conquer the Tour de France*, has spent considerable time with Brailsford and knows him better than most. 'Dave is a curious mixture of appearing laid back, but actually being fairly obsessive,' he says. 'Attention to detail is his big thing. He conveys this sense of calm, but that doesn't always give a true indication of what's going on inside his head. It's like the classic metaphor of the swan gliding effortlessly across the surface of the water, but paddling furiously underneath.'

'He is a people person.' Moore echoes Keen's assessment. 'He always talks about having an athlete-centred approach where, in his own words, the athletes are "kings and queens" with everyone else there to support them. That philosophy runs through British Cycling and Team Sky.'[7]

If Keen identified the mission of British Cycling as an obsession with winning gold medals, Brailsford created a culture where the behaviours – defined under the acronym CORE, standing for Commitment, Ownership, Responsibility and Excellence – were clear. 'It's actually "Personal Excellence",' explained Steve Peters, who helped define it, 'but then it would spell CORPE, which is too close to "corpse".'[8]

Brailsford used the metaphor of each athlete being a king or queen of their discipline, with the performance support staff being there as 'aides and advisers' to help and guide them.

Elite cycling is about engineering, aerodynamics, fitness, endurance, teamwork, tactics, planning, diet, a mass of interlinking technical, logistical and human issues and characteristics. But to Brailsford, the mindset of his athletes is more important than any of those. 'Most teams will get to the same place in time, in terms of logistics and engineering, so it will be the performance of the athletes that makes the difference, and getting them in the best mental and physical shape is what coaching and leadership is all about.'

'I built a team, a hand-picked team of world experts, who can really support the athlete to be the best they can be,' Brailsford explained. 'The support team can help them create a culture, an environment, in which they can excel, in which they can embrace the expertise offered and where they can deliver.' Brailsford added, 'If that really doesn't get you excited and get you out of bed in the morning, then this was the wrong place for you.'[9]

'We function as a whole,' says Peters. 'We are not *The Waltons*. I believe it is more like *The Waltons* with a touch of *EastEnders*. We have our moments; we have differences of opinion and sometimes we have clashes – like any team does. We do have a respect for everybody's opinion.'[10]

Brailsford explains, 'We put the riders in the middle; they have the ownership and responsibility for what they're doing whilst we're just the minions around them giving them expert advice. It seems to work,' he adds with some understatement.

This approach took some time to become understood by the athletes. 'I remember going to a race in Scotland with two young riders in the car with me,' recounts Rod Ellingworth, the head coach of Team Sky. 'They both had their headphones on and wouldn't talk. I was thinking, "For the next few hours they've got a chance to get a whole load of information about bike racing out of me . . ." but they weren't interested.

'I asked them, "What have you got planned for next week?"' Ellingworth says. 'They said, "Nothing."

'"How do you mean, nothing? What races are you doing?"

'"We're not racing. You guys – the coaches – haven't entered us for anything."

'"But don't you want to race?"

'"We don't race unless you make us race."

'This was something I simply couldn't get my head around. I wanted them to be responsible for their own success.'

The king and queen strategy was an important step in obliging each athlete to start taking responsibility for their own individual levels of support and allowing them to make their own smart choices.

'If you want extra physiotherapy treatment, you have to ask for it,' Ellingworth explains. 'The consequences of poor performance are also clear to the athletes. You can't complain that you didn't get the treatment you wanted after you miss your targets. It forces you to be accountable.'[11]

Doug Dailey, the former national coach who became the British Cycling logistics manager, said, 'The beauty of this model is that it empowers athletes and treats them with autonomy and respect, but has the safety check of performance goals the athletes are aiming to hit, with clear consequences if they don't perform.'[12]

Under this new approach, there was no place for excuses. 'The rider eventually assumes control over their own programme,' Dave Brailsford explains. 'I then say, it is your responsibility. I will give you all the tools: an elite environment, a high-performance focus; we give you the best people: medical, mental, technical, tactical, and I will manage that.

'You know – Bradley Wiggins is in control of Bradley Wiggins, Victoria Pendleton is in control of Victoria Pendleton, Chris Hoy is the boss of Chris Hoy. They have to move to this position; they don't become kings and queens overnight. You've got to have proved your worth. It doesn't happen in all sports. In some, you do exactly as you are told.'[13] That is, act like a wildebeest.

'There is some magic in the approach,' Keen enthuses. 'We managed to go beyond the individual and generate a critical mass of people pulling in the same direction but using their own initiative. That's what you need.'[14]

Think about the ideas driving British Cycling as circles. The central circle, the core, is 'gold medals'. But the very next circle might be the behaviour 'responsibility'. British Cycling employees know that it is OK to make a decision as long as it doesn't jeopardize their quest to deliver gold medals. The British Cycling team and Team Sky have excelled at this, right down to finding out what size and type of pillow the riders sleep on best at home, and taking the exact same pillows on the road, from hotel to hotel. For Team Sky, their favourite mattresses have followed. Anything that could legitimately assist performance has led to people taking responsibility to explore the possibilities.

A new member of the team can easily put these ideas together to realize how to act in an unscripted situation. For instance, is it OK to risk a time penalty in order to help a teammate in trouble?

This was the situation which Chris Froome experienced during his 2013 Tour de France victory. During the gruelling climb of Alpe d'Huez, Froome became hypoglycaemic – extremely low on sugar. The support car wasn't in position at the permitted time to hand the energy gels to his teammate, Richie Porte, and so it was too late, legally, to give Froome the sugar-rich food he needed. Porte ignored the rules that stated when cyclists could receive supplies and helped Froome avoid what academic nutritionists describe as 'bonking'.

There were no recriminations. 'If Richie hadn't broken the rule, the time loss might have been a lot more than the twenty-second penalty,' Brailsford explained.

EXERCISE – HOW TO THINK LIKE A KINGMAKER

The British Cycling model of appointing kings and queens, with the performance support staff being there as 'aides' to help and guide them, is a simple one with much crossover into your own world.

The kings or queens are able to pick and choose where they get their help from – but ultimately (and to carry on the comparison to monarchy), if they do not perform they can be overthrown. This allows individual levels of support and empowers the individual to make smart, intelligent choices. The consequences of poor performance are also clear.

The beauty of this model is that it treats individuals with autonomy and respect, but has the safety check of the performance goals the person is aiming to hit. This is vital. In fact, Professors Edwin Locke and Gary Latham's research estimates that allowing people control of how they meet targets can improve performance by up to 16 per cent (the equivalent of saving yourself an hour in an average eight-hour day). It is one worth considering.

The technique has started to be developed within education recently. The concept is called 'flipping the classroom'.

Here's how it works: in regular classrooms the teacher stands at the front of the room and explains an idea while the kids listen and absorb. Then they go home and do homework.

In a flipped classroom, the situation is reversed. First, the learners absorb the lecture at home, often via a video. Classroom time is devoted to doing the homework – grappling with the material, solving problems. Instead of being a sage on the stage, the teacher is a guide on the side, roving like a personal coach, spotting problems, giving individualized attention and guidance. Class time is about active construction, productive struggle and exploration.

The concept is flexible enough to be applied to other situations. Such as:

In the workplace – why not flip training sessions? Instead of listening to lectures, time could be spent practising real-life on-the-job skills.

In sports – why not flip the review session? Coaches could deliver theories, strategies, game plans, and fundamentals via video, and spend practice time actually working on the skills.

I like flipping because it's a nice way to highlight a home truth: sitting still and listening to someone talk is a demanding and inefficient way to learn. Learning is ultimately about doing – about struggling and reaching, often with the guidance of a good coach or a support network of experts – and the highest goal of a leader is to design a space that makes that happen.

In other words, leaders aren't really leaders – they are kingmakers. As Einstein put it, 'I never teach my students; I only attempt to provide the conditions in which they learn.'

If you want to think like a kingmaker, ask: what can you flip in your world?

2.v TRIPWIRES AND OTHER HAZARDS

We began this chapter with two questions: How do we get people thinking? And how do we keep them thinking?

We've looked at how you create an environment which encourages independent thinking. Let's look at how to keep people thinking by examining some tripwires of our own.

There's a children's game which can be used to prove how quickly humans adapt to consistent routines and patterns. It goes like this:

Spell out *silk* – S, I, L, K.

And again, S, I, L, K. And again, S, I, L, K. And again, S, I, L, K. Now answer this question: *What do cows drink?*

Most people say 'milk'. Cows, of course, drink water.

To understand the answer to the second of these questions, and keep people thinking and alert, we have to stimulate two essential emotions – surprise and interest.

Consistent sensory stimulation makes us tune out: think of the hum of an air conditioner, or traffic noise, or the smell of a candle, or the sight of a bookshelf. We may become consciously aware of these things only when something changes. The air conditioner shuts off. Your spouse rearranges the books. So, the most basic way to get someone's attention is this: break a pattern.

Our brain is designed to be keenly aware of changes. Smart product designers are well aware of this tendency. They make sure that, when products require users to pay attention, something *changes*. Warning lights blink on and off, because we would tune out a light that was constantly on. Old emergency sirens wailed in a two-note pattern, but modern sirens wail in a more complex pattern that is even more attention-grabbing. Car alarms make diabolical use of our change sensitivity.

Breaking a pattern evokes surprise, which is associated with a facial expression that is consistent across almost all cultures. In a book called *Unmasking the Face*, Paul Eckman and Wallace Friesen coined a term, 'the surprise brow', to describe this distinctive expression: 'The eyebrows appear curved and high . . . the skin below the brow has been stretched by the lifting of the brow, and is more visible than usual.'[15]

When our brows go up, it widens our eyes and gives us a broader field of vision – the surprise brow is our body's way of forcing us to see more. We may also do a double take to make sure that we saw what we thought we saw. By way of contrast, when we're angry, our eyes narrow so that we can focus on a known problem. In addition to making our eyebrows rise, surprise causes our jaws to drop and our mouths to gape. We're struck momentarily speechless. Our bodies temporarily stop moving and our muscles go slack. It's as though our bodies want to ensure that we're not talking or moving when we ought to be taking in new information.

So surprise acts as a kind of emergency override when we confront something unexpected and our autopilot fails. Things come to a halt, ongoing activities are interrupted, our attention focuses involuntarily on the event that surprised us.

Researchers who study conspiracy theories have noted that many of them arise when people are grappling with unexpected events, such as when the young and attractive die suddenly. There are conspiracy theories about the sudden deaths of JFK, Marilyn Monroe, Elvis Presley, Kurt Cobain and

Princess Diana. There tends to be less conspiratorial interest in the sudden deaths of ninety-year-olds.

In 1994, George Loewenstein, a behavioural economist at Carnegie Mellon University, provided the most comprehensive account of how to take advantage of surprise and generate interest. It is surprisingly simple. Curiosity, he says, happens when we feel a gap in our knowledge.

Try it yourself. Take a few seconds to look at the following lists; spend the same amount of time on each one.

A	B
Ocean/breeze	bread/b_tter
Leaf/tree	music/l_rics
Sweet/sour	s_oe/sock
Movie/actress	phone/b_ok
Petrol/engine	chi_s/salsa
School/college	pen_il/paper
Turkey/stuffing	river/b_at
Fruit/vegetable	b_er/wine
Computer/chip	television/rad_o
Chair/couch	l_nch/dinner

Now turn the page. Without looking, try to remember as many of the word pairs as you can. From which column do you recall more words?

If you're like most people, it won't even be close. You will remember more of the words in column B, the ones that had fragments missing. Studies show you'll remember three times as many. It's as if, in those few seconds, your memory skills suddenly sharpened. If this had been a test, your column B score would have been three times higher.

However, your IQ did not increase while you looked at column B. You didn't feel different. You weren't touched by genius. But when you encountered the words with blank spaces, something both imperceptible and profound happened. You stopped. You stumbled ever so briefly, then figured it out. You experienced a microsecond of struggle, and that microsecond made all the difference. You didn't practise harder when you looked at column B.

Loewenstein argues that gaps cause pain. When we want to know something but don't, it's like having an itch that we need to scratch. To take away the pain, we need to fill the knowledge gap. We sit patiently through bad movies, even though they may be painful to watch, because it's too painful not to know how they end.

In a recent study, volunteers were asked to answer five quiz questions and were told that after they had taken their best guesses, they would receive one of two rewards:

– *Either* they would learn the correct answers to the questions and whether they had got them right or wrong.

– *Or* they would receive a chocolate bar but never get to learn the correct answers.

Some volunteers chose their reward *before* they took the quiz and some chose *after* they took it. As you might expect, people preferred the chocolate bar before taking the quiz but would rather have the answers afterwards.

In other words, taking the quiz had made people so curious that they valued the answers more than a scrumptious bar of chocolate. Beforehand, volunteers who had not actually experienced the intense curiosity that taking the quiz produced simply couldn't imagine refusing the offer of chocolate for a few dull facts.

One important implication of the gap theory is that we need to *open* gaps before we *close* them. Our tendency is to tell people the facts. First, though, they must realize that they need these facts.

'I have the information inside of here,' said Goody Petronelli, pointing to the side of his head, 'that can make you millions and give you the chance to move your family to the best neighbourhood in the city. Do you want to have it?'

It was a well-rehearsed line which the boxing trainer would use with all the kids who entered the Brockton, Massachusetts gym he called home. The fifteen-year-old Marvin Hagler sat in front of him and silently nodded his agreement, 'but the eagerness in his eyes told me he'd be back,' Petronelli laughed.

Hagler continued to return every day for the next fifteen years, as the fighter sought to gain every last morsel of information available to help him continue his journey to the top of his chosen profession. 'I never stopped learning,' Hagler said, 'and Goody never stopped giving.'[16]

The trick to convincing people that they need our message, according to Loewenstein, is first to highlight some specific knowledge that they're missing. We can pose a puzzle or question that confronts people with a gap in their knowledge. We can point out that someone else knows something they don't. We can present them with situations that have unknown resolutions, such as elections, sports events or mysteries. We can challenge them to predict an outcome (which creates two knowledge gaps – *What will happen?* and *Was I right?*).

Commercial radio stations know that people switch off during the adverts. I do. What they use to combat this is a device that engages our natural curiosity, referred to in radio circles as 'throwing forward'. So you will hear things like, 'Coming up after the break, the funniest joke in the world', or 'the best advert ever', or 'the crudest thing anyone has ever said to anyone else ever!' They work because they tease you with something you don't know – in fact, something that you didn't care about at all, until you found out that you didn't know it.

The 'throw it forward' approach can be used with all sorts of ideas in all sorts of contexts. To generate interest, we need to shift our thinking from 'What information do I need to convey?' to 'What questions do I want my audience to ask?'

Rosser Reeves, an American advertising executive who was at his peak in the middle of the twentieth century, is the protagonist of one of the most famous stories in advertising, one that exemplified the need to think about your challenge from the audience's perspective.

The precise details of the story are somewhat in doubt. As it's been retold over the past fifty years, the particulars often change but the broad contours of the tale remain.

One afternoon, Reeves and a colleague were having lunch in Central Park. On the way back to their Madison Avenue office, they encountered a man sitting in the park, begging for money. He had a cup of donations and beside it was a sign, handwritten on cardboard, that read: I AM BLIND.

Unfortunately for the man, the cup contained only a few coins. His attempts to move others to donate money were coming up short. Reeves thought he knew why. He told his colleague something to the effect of, 'I bet I can dramatically increase the amount of money that guy is getting simply by adding four words to his sign.' Reeves's sceptical friend took him up on his bet.

Reeves then introduced himself to the beleaguered man, explained that he knew something about advertising, and offered to change the sign ever so slightly to increase donations. The man agreed. Reeves took a thick pen and added his four words and then stepped back to watch the effect.

Almost immediately, a few people dropped coins into the man's cup. Others soon stopped, talked to the man, and plucked dollar bills from their wallets. Before long, the cup was running over with cash and the once sad-looking blind man, feeling his newly earned wealth, beamed.

What four words did Reeves add? *'It is springtime and'*.

The sign now read: **It is springtime and I am blind.**

Reeves won his bet. And we learned a lesson. Getting people to act depends on the effectiveness of your tripwires in making them think.

To do this requires some planning. Great coaches will set up tripwires in their activities, moments that create knowledge gaps and therefore force people to think about the answer.

2.vi   BROWN SWEETS AND RED FLAGS

Dave Lee Roth was the lead singer for Van Halen from the mid 1970s to the mid 1980s, an era when the band cranked out one smash hit after another: 'Runnin' with the Devil', 'Dance the Night Away', 'Jump' and more. Van Halen toured tirelessly, with over a hundred concerts in 1984 alone, and behind the band's headbanging appeal was some serious operational expertise. It was one of the first rock bands to bring major stage productions to smaller markets. As Roth recalled in his autobiography, *Crazy from the Heat*, 'We'd pull up with nine eighteen-wheeler trucks, full of gear, where the standard was three trucks, max.'

The band's production design was astonishingly complex. The contract specifying the set-up was, according to Roth, 'like a version of the Chinese Yellow Pages' because it was so technical and complex it was like reading a foreign language. A typical article in the contract might say, 'There will be fifteen amperage voltage sockets at twenty-foot spaces, evenly, providing nineteen amperes . . .'

The band decided that they needed to know this contract was being taken seriously, so they introduced their very own safeguard or tripwire, which in turn became enshrined in rock folklore.

The 'M&M clause', perhaps the most infamous of all rock-star riders, was written into the band's contract to serve a very specific purpose. It was called Article 126, and it read as follows: 'There will be no brown M&M's in the backstage area, upon pain of forfeiture of the show, with full compensation.' The article was buried in the middle of countless technical specifications.

When Roth arrived at a new venue, he would immediately walk backstage and glance at the M&M bowl. If he saw a brown M&M, he'd demand a line check of the entire production. 'Guaranteed you're going to arrive at a technical error,' he said. 'They didn't read the contract . . . Sometimes it would threaten to just destroy the whole show.'

In other words, David Lee Roth was no diva; he was an operational master. He needed a way to assess quickly whether the stagehands at each venue were paying attention – whether they'd read every single word of the contract and taken it seriously. He needed a way, in other words, to snap out of the 'mental autopilot' and realize that a decision had to be made. In Van Halen's world, a brown M&M was a tripwire.

EXERCISE – MIRROR, MIRROR ON THE WALL . . .

Analysing your daily routine and identifying three potential tripwire opportunities where you can break out of autopilot mode and think about your own behaviours is a good trigger to help you refocus on the things that matter.

One senior manager I work with had a difficult relationship with an important customer. Their telephone conversations would often become heated and fractious.

Can you spot the tripwire opportunity here?

We simply changed the name of this customer on his phone. We identified how the manager wanted to behave in this relationship – remaining calm, speaking confidently and listening patiently – so now, whenever his problem customer rang, my client would receive an instant reminder of his desired response.

One business leader had an issue getting his staff to be honest with him. He combated this by positioning pertinent questions – *have you received enough training this year?* – behind two wastepaper bins marked *YES* and *NO* throughout the offices. He soon began to receive valuable feedback.

One retail business I worked with had a dress code that required all employees to wear a tie as part of their uniform. A mirror, with the perfect employee behaviours on it, was also distributed to all stores.

Can you spot the tripwire?

Staff had to use the mirror to put the tie on correctly and so when they checked their appearance, they were subconsciously reminded of the required behaviours.

Within the first twelve months, they had recorded a 5 per cent improvement in their execution, and customer feedback improved by 3 per cent. Significantly, the profits rose by 2 per cent.

Where could you build tripwires to help bring about the desired change in your life?

2.vii GUIDED DISCOVERY

This is a technique honed by one of the world's leading coaches.

FIFA have named him the World Coach of the Year on two occasions. In thirteen full seasons as a manager with Porto, Chelsea, Inter Milan and Real Madrid, he has won nineteen major trophies, including two Champions League titles, a unique Italian treble and nine domestic league championships. He didn't lose a league game at home in nine years. José Mourinho may be the best coach in any sport, anywhere.

'He's at the top, there's no doubt about that,' says the legendary former Manchester United coach Sir Alex Ferguson. 'You have certain criteria in terms of top management, and that is longevity of success – which is very difficult today – and what you win. You have to regard his achievements as really first-class.'[17]

'A football coach who only understands football is not a great coach,' says Mourinho. 'I never forget: my players are men. Men with different personalities, different cultures. To deal with this is very important. I think I have a gift.'[18]

It could be added that his gift is to make his players think.

José Mourinho grew up in the Portuguese city of Setúbal. His mother, Maria Júlia, worked as a schoolteacher and his father, Félix, played professional football (a goalkeeper, Mourinho senior won a single cap for Portugal). As a boy, José was at his happiest travelling with his dad (or by himself if he could) to Porto and Lisbon, at first to watch Félix play, and later, when his father became a coach, to help him scout the opposition teams. As a player himself, José wasn't very good. Enthusiastic, yes. Talented, not so much. After struggling through spells at Belenenses, Rio Ave and Sesimbra, he found his level: the Portuguese second division. 'I'm an intelligent person,' he admitted later. 'I knew I was not going to go any higher.' Compare the self-awareness of his response to the 80 per cent of us who declare ourselves better than the average driver.

Refusing to allow his limitations as a player to restrict his ambition, José decided to become a coach instead. He studied physical education and sports science at university in Lisbon, earned his coaching badges, took courses run by the Scottish FA and the Football Association, and ran youth teams and assisted with any small teams he could. Wherever there was an opportunity to learn, Mourinho took it. Then in 1992 he got his break. Sir Bobby Robson took the manager's job at Sporting Lisbon and José was hired as his interpreter.

Quickly establishing a working relationship that extended far beyond mere translation, Mourinho began to provide Robson with sophisticated dossiers on Sporting's opponents while learning as much as he could from the former England manager. Robson lasted barely a year at Sporting, but when he was sacked in December 1993 he was offered the coaching job at Porto and took Mourinho with him. The success they had together over the next few seasons attracted the attention of Barcelona and when they hired Robson the Catalans took Mourinho as well.

With Robson's attacking instincts and man-management skills, complemented by Mourinho's defensive abilities and committed organization, Barcelona went on to win the European Cup Winners' Cup. But when Robson was replaced – by Louis van Gaal – Mourinho stayed behind in Spain as the Dutchman's assistant.

'I owe him for so much,' Mourinho says of Robson. 'I was a nobody in football when he came to Portugal. He helped me to work in two clubs [in Portugal] and he took me to one of the biggest clubs in the world [Barcelona]. We are very different, but I got from him the idea of what it is to be a top coach.'[19]

Having learned all he could from Robson and van Gaal, Mourinho was ready for a head coach role and returned to Portugal. It was around this time – 2001 – Mourinho drew up his 'bible', a document that no one has access to and which steers his professional life. 'It's my training file, where I keep all my directives for my work. It contains all the objectives and methodologies for my practice and how to achieve these. If I had to give it a title, it would be the evolution of my training concepts. In 1990, I didn't think about training the way I did in 2000. After I had drawn it up, I was definitely ready to be a coach.'[20]

He had brief spells as the head coach of Benfica (just nine league games), then União de Leiria, and in January 2002 he took over at Porto. Putting into practice all the knowledge he had acquired, Mourinho combined scientific analysis with tactical theory, sports science and player psychology to turn his team, Porto, into one of the best in Europe, winning back-to-back national league and cup titles, as well as the Champions League in 2004, a significant achievement as Porto became the only team from outside the Europe's richest four leagues to win the tournament since 1995. His reward was the offer of a contract from Russian owner Roman Abramovich to become the new coach of Chelsea.

He knew it would be a challenge, but as he said when meeting the British press for the first time, 'If I wanted to have an easy job I would have stayed at Porto. Beautiful blue chair, the UEFA Champions League trophy, God, and after God, me.'[21]

Three successful seasons at Chelsea (two league titles, two League Cups and one FA Cup) were followed by two at Inter Milan (he won the Serie A title in his first season and completed the treble in his second, including a second career Champions League title) and another three at Real Madrid (winning La Liga title and the Spanish Cup) before Mourinho announced he was returning to Chelsea, where he picked up the title once again in his second season.

Mourinho has a few simple rules, which read like a Commander's Intent. 'People only have a general idea of what I do,' Mourinho told four university students who visited him when he was working in Italy for a thesis about his methods, 'and it's insufficient.'[22]

When he addresses his teams, he does so in the language of the team's country, the better to integrate the players into the club and the culture. (At Inter he spoke Italian, even though only four of his twenty-four first-team players were Italian.) When he starts with a new team, his first task is to emphasize his two behaviours that will help the team to win.

Rule one: 'I guarantee "quality work", with which they will improve, both on an individual and collective level.' If you work with and listen to him, he will improve you.

There are two individual players who highlight Mourinho's strict adherence to this rule and his FIFO – fit in or fuck off – application of it: 'If people support the team culture, there will be a role. If they are cynical about what we are trying to do, there won't.'[23]

EXERCISE – MY KIND OF PEOPLE?

The psychologist David Kantor once led what many people have described as the first incarnation of reality TV. In an effort to study how schizophrenia manifests in family systems, Kantor set up cameras in various rooms of people's houses, then pored over hours of footage of their lives. Kantor soon detected a pattern that emerged again and again within every group dynamic, regardless of whether schizophrenia was a factor.

After analysing the tapes, Kantor established that each individual within a family unit will fall into one of four distinct roles.

The first role is that of the initiator: the person who always has ideas, likes to start projects and advocates new ways of moving forward.

The second group are the initiator's opposites: blockers. Whatever new idea the initiator comes up with, the blocker finds fault with it. 'Let's go to Disneyland!' says the initiator. 'No. It's too expensive,' replies the blocker. 'Let's start a new company.' 'Most fail within the first year.'

If hanging out with initiators makes us want to go out and do something fun, spending a minute with blockers makes us reluctant to do anything. Of course, it is easy to think of blockers as pure curmudgeons, but we will see that they do play a vital role in maintaining balance within a group.

Initiators and blockers are bound to lock horns, which is where the third group – adapters – steps in, taking one side or the other. If there is a decision to be made, you can bet on the supporter siding with either the initiator or the blocker. The fourth role is that of the detached observer, who stays disengaged and neutral, tending merely to comment on what is going on.

So, when creating a winning mindset, answer three questions:

1. Make a list of the fifteen people you need to influence.

2. Now put these in the boxes below, according to how helpful and supportive they are. *Note:* There are no right or wrong answers here and it doesn't mean that a person is good or bad. It is about how supportive they are of you in terms of your change challenge.

3. Look at your list and decide if the balance is helpful. Is there any action you want to take to move someone from one box to another? For example, ask an 'adapter' for help and support to become an 'initiator'.

Initiator – really active; supportive, helpful; encouraging; interested

---

Adapter – doesn't really understand; not aware

```
┌─────────────────────────────────────────────────────────┐
│ Blocker – highlights the problems/difficulties            │
│                                                           │
│                                                           │
│                                                           │
│                                                           │
│                                                           │
│                                                           │
└─────────────────────────────────────────────────────────┘

┌─────────────────────────────────────────────────────────┐
│ Observer – not bothered in the slightest                  │
│                                                           │
│                                                           │
│                                                           │
│                                                           │
│                                                           │
│                                                           │
│                                                           │
└─────────────────────────────────────────────────────────┘
```

When Mourinho took over at Benfica, he organized a reserve team match and within two minutes, midfielder Maniche was sent off. Mourinho instructed the player to run around the pitch until the end of the first half. Maniche made a point of sulkily ambling round and so Mourinho stopped him and told him to head for the showers.

When Maniche arrived for training the next day, Mourinho was waiting for him. 'It took you eight minutes to run 800 metres yesterday. That means one of two things: you either have a problem on your mind that needs to be solved, or you have a physical problem, and you still need to find a solution for it. So you're going to train with the B team, and when you feel you no longer have a mental or physical problem, come and see me.'

At the end of the fourth day training with the B team, Maniche spoke to Mourinho, apologized for his unprofessional attitude and assured him he had no problems at all.

A few weeks later, Maniche was made Benfica's captain and eventually moved with Mourinho to Porto, where he was a central figure of the club's most successful team – endearingly nicknamed 'Mourinho's godson' – before briefly joining him at Chelsea.

In contrast, the Portuguese coach recounts a story about Mario Balotelli, the enigmatic Italian centre forward he deemed 'uncoachable' while both were at Inter Milan.

'I could write a book of 200 pages of my two years at Inter with Mario, but the book would not be a drama – it would be a comedy,' Mourinho noted.

'I remember one time when we went to play in the Champions League. In that match I had all my strikers injured. I was really in trouble and Mario was the only one.

'Mario got a yellow card in the forty-second minute, so when I got to the dressing room at half-time I spent about fourteen minutes of the fifteen available speaking only to Mario.

'I said to him: "Mario, I cannot change you, I have no strikers on the bench, so don't touch anybody and play only with the ball. If we lose the ball, no reaction. If someone provokes you, no reaction; if the referee makes a mistake, no reaction."

'The forty-sixth minute – red card!'[24]

Mourinho imposed his own suspension on Balotelli before he was eventually sold to Manchester City.

Rule two: you hear everything from him. 'Many clubs are influenced by information, counter-information, rumour and gossip,' he explains. 'No matter what decisions I take in relation to my players, they will always be the first to know, and they'll know it from me.'[25]

To achieve the second rule, in private meetings with individual players Mourinho communicates whenever possible in their native tongues. 'By speaking five languages I can have a special relation with them,' he says. 'A player feels more comfortable explaining emotions in the language where he has no doubts. So he has no problem to open his heart, to criticize, to be criticized.' We will see, in the next chapter – Emotions – quite why this is such a powerful lesson.

It is the first rule – his guarantee of 'quality work' – that fascinates. 'Every exercise is done with the ball. Most if not all sessions last 90 minutes, the duration of a game, or a maximum of 120 minutes, like one that goes into extra time.'[26]

Each one is devised with the aim of reproducing moments of a match, specific situations so that once they come into a competitive context the players know exactly what to do and where to be on the pitch, how to defend and how to attack in whatever formation they're in or up against and according to the circumstances they find themselves in too, be they a goal up or a goal down, a man up or down to ten men.

This is in contrast to how many teams choose to practise, preferring exercises which Mourinho describes as 'repetitive stimuli, such as shooting and passing drills, which the game has none of'.

Indeed, when Mourinho began coaching Benfica, Eusebio, the club's legendary goalscorer from the 1960s, was in charge of training the goalkeepers. 'Eusebio would place the ball near the penalty area and shoot nearly a hundred shots at goal,' Mourinho recalled. He recognized the futility of such an approach. 'A player will never stand in isolation and shoot one hundred times. This situation is out of context with reality and the complexity of the game,' he said.

Mourinho enjoys telling a story he read in *Fortune* magazine. It involves an episode usually attributed to Alfred Sloan, GM's legendary president, who served in the role for a quarter of a century. At a meeting with his general staff, Sloan raised the question: 'Gentlemen, it appears we fully agree with this decision, am I right?' As he saw everybody nodding in approval, he said: 'Therefore, I propose we suspend the definitive analysis of this matter until the next meeting, so we can have time to discover any contradiction and perhaps be able to better understand what this decision means.'

This story encapsulates a lesson Mourinho learnt at Barcelona. 'You can't help but learn when you coach some of the best professionals in the world – such as Ronaldo, Rivaldo, Figo, Guardiola, Stoichkov and Kluivert,' he said. 'Players at this level don't accept what they're told simply because of the authority of the person who's saying it. We have to show them that we're right. Here, the old story of "the Mister is always right" does not apply. In fact, it generally isn't applicable, and even less so with highly developed players, which is the case with any Barcelona player.'

Mourinho explained how this has become one of his core philosophies. 'The relationship I had with them taught me one of my main virtues as a coach. The tactical work I encourage isn't about there being a "transmitter" on the one hand and a "receptor" on the other. I call it the "guided discovery"; that is, they discover according to my clues.'[27]

Let's look at how Mourinho's guided discovery works. To demonstrate, I'm going to try a little magic trick. Magic doesn't really work very well on paper, but anyway. Here goes.

In front of you are five coins – a 50p coin, a 20p coin, a 10p coin, a 5p coin and a penny.

I am going to predict, in advance, which one you are going to hand me in a minute or so. In fact, I have already written my prediction down at the bottom of the page.*

Step One: What I want you to do first is pick THREE coins and push them towards me. Let's say, for the sake of argument, that you choose the 50p, 20p and penny coins – discarding the 5p and 10p.

Happy with that? Good.

Step Two: Next what I want you to do is choose ONE of the three coins and discard it. Let's say, again for the sake of argument, that this time you choose the 20p.

So now we are left with just two coins on the table.

Step Three: For your next move I want you to choose ONE of those coins and push it towards me. Let's say it is the 50p.

This means that you should be left with just ONE coin in front of you – the penny.

Step Four: Pick the penny up and hand it to me – and now look at the footnote to see if my prediction was correct.

Actually, it isn't magic at all. But then you knew that, didn't you? Instead, like Mourinho's guided discovery, it uses a clever piece of psychology called the Principle of Forced Choice.

I once worked with a French rugby team which adopted this principle of forced choice by asking players to complete an application form if they wished to be selected for the team. The form contained questions such as what kind of teammate they would be, how they responded to a crisis, how they preferred to receive feedback.

The process served two purposes. It allowed the coaches to adapt their approach to meet the players' needs. The second – and most powerful – purpose, however, was in obliging players to take responsibility, especially when things didn't go to plan.

* One penny.

On one occasion, a logistical issue meant that training was disrupted. One particular player seemed to relish the opportunity to loudly share his moans and complaints about the situation. After a short while, he was presented with a copy of his application form. It became difficult for him to sustain his grumbling when he saw that he had identified himself as a 'hard-working professional who gets on with the job'.

There is a simplicity to Mourinho's guided discovery approach which demands that all of his players have to 'buy in' to his methods. Vítor Baía, a goalkeeper who played for Mourinho, has described the effect. 'You're more in control. You're more lucid. You're more able to anticipate things, read the play and not only make better decisions but vary them too.'[28]

Mourinho has taken the old proverb 'You can take a horse to water but you can't make it drink,' and applied it to his training sessions. His aim is to make sure that whenever he introduces new formations or approaches his teams are consulted – he wants them to have their say.

'The objective,' he says, 'is that the players understand the playing system and trust it, that they take some initiative because they're convinced that it's the best thing to do and not because someone else says: "Do it that way."

'I know where it is I want us to get to, but instead of telling them: "Go that way," I want them to find their own way there.'

Crucially, Mourinho says: 'I don't want to create robots or automatons. They're predictable and I don't want my teams to be that way.'

Robert Bjork, the chair of psychology at UCLA, has spent most of his life delving into questions of memory and learning. 'We think of effortless performance as desirable, but it's really a terrible way to learn,' he says. 'Things that appear to be obstacles turn out to be desirable in the long haul. One real encounter, even for a few seconds, is far more useful than several hundred observations.

'The reason,' Bjork explains, 'resides in the way our brains are built. We tend to think of our memory as a tape recorder, but that's wrong. It's a living structure, a scaffold of nearly infinite size. The more we generate impulses, encountering and overcoming difficulties, the more scaffolding we build. The more scaffolding we build, the faster we learn.

'It's all about finding the sweet spot,' Bjorn suggests. 'There's an optimal gap between what you know and what you're trying to do. When you find that sweet spot, learning takes off.'[29]

And that sweet spot is the holy grail for any winning mindset.

EXERCISE: THE MISTAKE CLUB

Much of the research about how the brain learns could be distilled into a few simple words:

Mistakes are good. Struggle makes you smarter.

When it comes to applying this lesson to our lives, the problem is not with the science, but with our powerful natural aversion to mistakes and to struggling.

Try as we might to convince ourselves otherwise, mistakes feel horrible and struggling feels like a judgement. Also, mistakes often carry a social price – they can cost us our job, our money, our reputation. So we instinctively hide them.

The question is, how to fix that? How do you overcome your mistake allergy?

One good answer: do it as a group.

I once heard of a nice strategy from the headmaster of a

school I visited. It's called the Mistake Club, and it started, as most of these things do, by accident.

Backstory: a new assistant head teacher (let's call him Tom) had been asked to speak to one of the school's governors about a forthcoming project. For various reasons, the conversation didn't go well; by the time it ended the governors were disappointed. Tom's first instinct, naturally, was to hide the mistake; to tell no one.

But for some strange reason Tom did the opposite. He told the headmaster and the staff the whole fiasco, describing each detail of the disastrous conversation. Someone made a joke that they should start awarding points for each cock-up.

The Mistake Club was born. Meetings were weekly; points were awarded on a 1–10 scale — the bigger the mistake, the more you 'earned'. At the end of the year, a 'prize' was awarded to the person who had accumulated the most points.

The benefits, of course, reach far beyond the pleasure of the joke. The Mistake Club established a culture of trust and communication. When someone shares the details of their mistake, the whole group learns vicariously. Social ties are strengthened. The meetings turn into coaching sessions; the organizational brain becomes smarter.

Here are a few other ways to do that:

Control expectations: I've seen sports teams and businesses sign contracts at the beginning of a season affirming that people will make mistakes, struggle will happen.

Deliver praise during the struggle: instead of praising someone at the moment of their achievement, praise them during their effort — since this is the behaviour that really matters, and that you want to help to recreate.

Encourage fallibility in leaders: it's far easier for everyone to be transparent when leaders set the tone. For example, I recently heard of a hospital CEO who wanted to encourage handwashing. She offered a reward of £20 to any worker who noticed her entering a sterile area without washing her hands first. Showing her own fallibility makes it easy for others to show theirs.

Legislate risk: Some companies build risk-taking requirements into their culture. For instance, one company I work with encourages its people to take a business risk that scares them once a week.

The point is to find some way to create a safe social place where mistakes can be made and then used to guide discovery and accelerate learning – an inoculation for our natural mistake allergy. As with any inoculation, a small dose can have a big effect.

THE THIRD STEP

EMOTIONS

Follow your heart but take your
head along with you.
Nelson Mandela

3.i   FEELING ON TOP OF THE WORLD

You had to pass a small grocery store to get to the door of the police gym on Catskill's Shell Avenue. The door was heavy, with painted zinc nailed across its face and a sign reading, 'Catskill Boxing Gym', and when you opened the door, you saw a long badly lit stairway climbing into darkness. There was another door on the landing. 'This was the moment when a lot of tough New York kids would reach that landing and find themselves unable to open the second door,' recalls the author, Pete Hamill. 'They'd go back down the stairs, try to look cool as they bought a soda, then hurry home.'[1] Many others opened the second door. And when they did, they entered the tough, hard, disciplined school of a man named Cus D'Amato.

'First thing I want to know about a kid,' Cus said, 'is whether he can open that door. Then when he walks in, I look at him, try to see what he's seeing. Most of them stand at the door. They see guys skipping rope, shadow-boxing, hitting the bags. Most of all, they see guys in the ring. Fighting. And then they have to decide. Do they want this, or not?'

D'Amato viewed this moment as his own personal tripwire, the mental signal to start paying attention we discussed in the previous chapter. 'If they want it, they stay, they ask someone what they should do. Most of them are shy, for some reason. Almost all fighters. They whisper. You tell them to come back, and you'll see what can be done. They have to spend at least one night dealing with fear. If they come back the second time, then maybe you have a fighter.'

D'Amato's passion was boxing, but he himself never fought. At twelve years old, he had a street fight with a man – 'one of those men who push kids around because they know they can't push men around,' he described. It left him virtually blind in one eye.

This injury forced him towards the path of becoming one of the sport's greatest ever coaches. He took over the Gramercy Gym on New York's East 14th Street, where he lived alone in an office above the gym with his dog, Champ, and plotted the development of Floyd Patterson from a troubled thirteen-year-old to an Olympic gold medallist, and on to the world heavyweight championship through a combination of tough, intelligent coaching and a deep interest in what he described as 'the workings of the inner man'. D'Amato was a self-created psychologist, described by Norman Mailer, the great novelist and sports writer, as 'a student of Zen'.

D'Amato's success with Patterson and then with José Torres, a Puerto Rican boxer he guided to the world light-heavyweight championship, put him at odds with the people who ran the sport. This was an era when the Mob was all over boxing. The gangsters 'owned' fighters, arranged fixed fights and bribed judges. The notorious gang boss Frankie Carbo was often called the underworld's commissioner of boxing.

Tired of the corruption and refusing to compromise his principles, D'Amato left his New York gym in the late 1960s and relocated – locked in a deep sleep, as far as much of the boxing world was concerned – in Catskill, surrounded by the mountains of upstate New York.

He lived with Camille Ewald, whose sister had been married to his older brother, in a fourteen-room Victorian house, overlooking the Hudson. Thanks to the largesse of an entrepreneur friend, Jimmy Jacobs, he turned the house into a sort of year-round training camp. At any given moment there might be half a dozen fighters in residence, working under D'Amato's tutelage in a gym carved into the loft above the Catskill police station. D'Amato trained the local boxing talent, but many professional boxers sought him out for fine-tuning to their technique, including Muhammad Ali, who asked the boxing sage to manage him.

One evening in 1981, Bob Stewart, a former fighter who worked at the Tryon School – an austere and imposing New York prison for young offenders – brought over a fourteen-year-old kid for D'Amato's opinion on his prospects in the boxing game. 'I was used to dealing with losers in the school,' Stewart explained. 'But Mike Tyson had something.'[2]

'Cus looked exactly like what you'd envision a hard-boiled boxing trainer to look like,' recalled Tyson. 'He was short and stout with a bald head and you could see that he was strong. He even talked tough and he was dead serious; there wasn't a happy muscle in his face.'[3] D'Amato was often compared – outside his hearing range – to Colonel Kurtz, the character portrayed by Marlon Brando in the film *Apocalypse Now.*

Stewart said, 'I came because in the back of my mind was the knowledge that Cus took in fighters, and I thought that maybe if I brought Mike down six or seven times, he'd take a liking to him.' Stewart stepped into the ring to box three rounds. 'I had to fight my head off because Mike was charging me. He was keen to impress,' he recounts. 'Boom! I hit him early in the second round and his nose was blown all over the place and Cus says, "We better stop it at two." But Mike says, "No, I want to go three." He was eager to impress this potential saviour,' Stewart remembers.[4]

Tyson recounts that immediately after this first sparring session, 'We went to Cus's house for lunch. We sat down and

Cus told me what my future would be.' Tyson's eyes still express the amazement he felt as he heard the prophecy. 'He had only seen me spar for not even six minutes but he said it in a way that was like law. "You looked splendid," he said. "You're a great fighter." It was compliment after compliment after compliment.' He then stopped talking, allowing the impact of his words to register. Finally, he announced, 'If you listen to me, I can make you the youngest heavyweight champion of all time.'

Stewart shakes his head at the memory of D'Amato's declaration. 'Here I am hoping that maybe after two or three months, Cus will say something positive. But, no, this very first night what does Cus say? "That's the heavyweight champion of the world. If he wants it, it's his."'

'I didn't know what to say,' Tyson recounts. 'I had never heard anyone say nice things about me before. I just knew that I wanted to stay around this old guy because I liked the way he made me feel. I'd later realize that this was at the heart of Cus's psychology. You give a weak man some strength and he becomes addicted. My whole world had changed. In that one moment, I knew I was going to be somebody.'[5]

Within months of this meeting, fourteen-year-old Tyson was released from the Tryon School and moved into the Catskill home where he remained in D'Amato's care throughout his entire adolescence. Tyson, as with José Torres and Patterson before him, found D'Amato was no mere trainer. He spent two hours a day working with him in the gym but much of the waking portion of the remaining twenty-two teaching him about the psychology of the sport, and it is these teachings which provide us with important lessons about how to develop a winning mindset.

'What really separated Cus from most other trainers was his focus on the mental aspect of boxing,' said Teddy Atlas, a former charge who became an elite coach himself. 'Every night, we would sit around at dinner and Cus would expound on his life philosophy as it applied to boxing and his boxing philosophy as it applied to life.'[6]

D'Amato's favourite subject was the mastery of emotional control. 'Fear is the greatest obstacle to learning in any area of life,' D'Amato explained, 'but particularly in boxing. The thing a kid in the street fears most is to be called a coward. Sometimes a kid will do the most crazy, wild things just to show he's not scared . . .' His preferred description of his chosen sport – the noble art – was 'chess played with gloves on'. 'Whoever controls their emotions best, wins,' he would announce.

'At first,' Tyson recounts, 'Cus wouldn't let me box. He would sit down with me and we'd talk. He'd talk about my feelings and emotions and about the psychology of boxing. He wanted to reach me at the root. He knew how to talk my language and get through to me. The first thing Cus talked about was fear and how to overcome it.'

D'Amato learned that Tyson had grown up fatherless in the Brownsville section of Brooklyn, New York, stealing cars and robbing stores, sometimes sleeping in abandoned buildings. He discovered that the kid extended unqualified love only to his pigeons, the 'street rats' he caught in the park and cooped on the roof of a burned-out tenement. He learned that the boy was mortified by not being able to read, that this was the source of his truancy. 'My feeling is this,' he told him. 'There are no stupid people. There are only uninterested people.'

D'Amato got Mike private tutoring and gave him reading that would appeal to him – books about fight legends such as Joe Louis and Jack Dempsey and historical leaders like Napoleon and Alexander the Great.

D'Amato discovered that Tyson was not merely suspicious of white people, he was distrustful of everyone. 'See,' explained the grizzled veteran, 'people, especially if they come up in a rough area, have to go through a number of experiences in life that are intimidating and embarrassing. These experiences form layer upon layer over their capabilities and talents. So your job as a teacher is to peel off these layers.'

The raw potential which D'Amato had seen on his first meeting was refined, buffed and polished in his boxing workshop, and Tyson's impact on the sport soon began to tell. 'He was like a one-man hurricane, sweeping all before him,' announced one report in the boxing press. Within a year, he won the National Junior Olympics belt with an awesome exhibition of punching power.

His progress wasn't linear, however. Teddy Atlas recounts an occasion when he had to risk disqualification and lean into the ring to whisper in Tyson's ear, 'Don't you dare quit,' when one opponent proved surprisingly durable and wouldn't buckle beneath the furious onslaught of Tyson's wrecking-ball fists. 'The longer the guy stayed standing, the faster I could see his resolve disappearing,' Atlas said. 'After the fight, we were stood alone in a corridor. He looked at me and said, in a quiet voice, "Thank you." His studies at Cus's university were far from finished.'[7]

These lessons were accelerated following an emotional collapse an hour before a tournament final in the blue Colorado Mountains. Tyson began to sob, claiming that he couldn't fight any more. He was too scared to enter the ring. Once again, Teddy Atlas was on hand to wrap an arm around his shoulders, telling him how well he had done to reach that point. 'Come a long way,' Tyson snivelled, 'it's all right now . . . I'm Mike Tyson . . . everyone likes me, yes, everyone likes me . . . I've come a long way, I'm a fighter now, I'm Mike Tyson . . .'

His words were swallowed up by the tears. Tyson was consumed by the fear of losing, believing that a loss would expose his whole being as a loser. 'He managed to suppress the fear to win the tournament on a technical knockout,' Atlas said, 'but D'Amato's teachings moved on to another level, specifically addressing the topic of fear.'

'Fear,' he would say, 'is like a fire. If you control it, as we do when we heat our houses, it is a friend. When you don't, it consumes you and everything around you.' He would ask Tyson to 'Imagine a deer crossing an open field. He's approaching the forest when his instinct tells him, "Think! There may be a mountain lion in the tree." The moment that happens, nature starts the survival process. Normally a deer can jump five or ten feet. With adrenaline he can jump fifteen or twenty feet. Fear, you see, is nature's way of preparing us for struggle. Without it, we'd die.'

He would show Tyson archive footage of former heavyweight champions and dissect their approach. 'Any fighter who fought Muhammad Ali was intimidated by him,' he would explain. 'You see, Ali's secret weapon was a tremendous will to win, an ability to take his own fear and project it as an irresistible force, which immediately tended to inhibit the ability of his opponent to execute what he knew.'[8]

The psychological training paid off in spectacular fashion. Tyson left the amateur ranks and made his professional debut at eighteen. In the next nine months, he annihilated fifteen opponents, many in the first round. The boxing world began to sit up and pay attention once again to what D'Amato was doing. *People* magazine ran a story, beneath a headline stating: 'D'Amato is back.' Cus objected. 'I haven't been away.'

D'Amato, however, was engaged in his own private battle – with pneumonia. With his health beginning to fail, his lessons took on an increased urgency. Tyson could see that his mentor was fading and would listen whilst choking back tears. He confided, 'I don't want to do this shit without you, Cus. I'm not going to do it.'

'Well,' D'Amato would reply, 'if you don't fight, you'll realize that people can come back from the grave, because I'm going to haunt you for the rest of your life.'

Despite his outward optimism, the illness took its toll and finally, on a grey November morning in 1985, at the age of seventy-seven, D'Amato finally succumbed and passed peacefully away at his home.

One of D'Amato's dying commands to Tyson's managers, Jim Jacobs and Bill Cayton, was to help Tyson fight through the grief that would envelop him, by increasing the volume of his fights. Within just over a year, the nineteen-year-old manchild had amassed a winning streak of thirty-seven consecutive undefeated fights before finally fulfilling D'Amato's dinnertable prediction from six years earlier by becoming the youngest ever world heavyweight champion when he beat Trevor Berbick in November 1986. His final punch knocked his opponent down three times. 'Berbick must have felt he was back home in his native Jamaica, trying to find shelter from a hurricane,' suggested the boxing writer George Kimball.

Amidst the scenes of wild jubilation in the ring, Tyson's first words were to dedicate the win – and the title – to 'my great guardian Cus D'Amato. I'm sure he's up there in heaven,' Tyson said, choking back the tears, 'talking to all the great fighters, and saying his boy did it.'

The epitaph engraved on D'Amato's tombstone read: 'A boy comes to me with a spark of interest, I feed the spark and it becomes a flame, I feed the flame and it becomes a fire, I fuel the fire and it becomes a roaring blaze . . .'

Let's look at the tools used by Cus D'Amato to ignite his young heavyweight and understand how we can apply them for ourselves.

3.ii THE ELEPHANT AND THE RIDER

In his brilliant account of obsessive-compulsive disorder, *The Man Who Couldn't Stop*, Dr David Adam says: 'Only a fool or a liar will tell you how the brain works.'[9] It may weigh only a little over a kilo, but it is a kilo of such labyrinthine complexity, containing a whole lifetime of memories, that mere facts don't do it justice.

The brain is an extraordinary organ. Some basic facts about it will start to make your brain hurt. It consists of some 100 billion cells, each of which connects and communicates with up to 10,000 others. Together they forge an elaborate network of some one quadrillion (1,000,000,000,000,000) connections that control everything including how we talk, eat, breathe and move. James Watson, who won the Nobel Prize for helping to discover DNA, described the human brain as 'the most complex thing we have yet discovered in our universe'.[10] Woody Allen called it 'my second favourite organ'.

However, for all of the brain's complexity, we know that it isn't of one mind.

There is a model for understanding the brain that has been around since the 1940s and, like many neurological models, it works better as a metaphor than as an accurate description of brain functioning. Known as the Triune model, the theory, devised by Dr Paul MacLean in 1949, divides the brain into three core parts – three brains in one, if you like – that mirror our evolution.

To take you through it, let's create your own little model of the three-part brain. Wrap one hand round a clenched fist made with the other hand and hold it in front of you. The arm going up into the fist, think of as a spinal cord. The bottom wrist now is the part of your brain known as the reptilian brain, or brainstem, where you will find the five 'F's of basic human responses – fight, flight, flock, freeze and fu— . . . sex. Let's look at them in more detail.

There is a hierarchy of needs that this part of the brain needs to address. The first of these is a need to procreate and continue the evolutionary journey. The second is the desire for survival. When we feel this is threatened, our reptilian brain provides us with three options – hide, confront that danger or run. You'll know this better as the fight, flight or freeze response. The final need is our desire to belong – to fit in. This is where other basic responses such as territorial and ritualistic behaviour come in. Think of this brain as possessing the intelligence of a newt – not feeling, not hypothesizing, just getting by. What does a newt have to be able to do to live a fulfilled and productive life? Stay alive and try to have sex – there's not much to it, really.

The second part of the brain to evolve, so the theory went, was your bottom fist. Or to give it its full title, the limbic system. It is also known variously as the emotional brain or even the mammalian brain. Here we are working with emotions and here, too, are vital elements of our brain that help us lay down long-term memories. Long-term memory and emotion go together. You remember your first kiss (although perhaps not your last, but then that's marriage for you!). Think of the intelligence of a dog. It does all that the newt's brain can do, but, in addition, experiences emotion. Yet it cannot do the crossword.

This was the area Cus D'Amato spent much of his time attempting to understand and to help his boxers control; the part that he argued 'can consume you'. Many boxing observers maintain that had D'Amato been given more time, the impact of these teachings could have helped Tyson. Instead, his absence 'opened the door to some of the world's most able conmen', as Teddy Atlas described it.[11] Tyson's focus on maintaining emotional control waned and his subsequent spiral towards prison and bankruptcy began.

From your emotional brain, more of which later, we arrive at your top hand – the neocortex. This is the part that is proportionately so huge in humans, the bit with the squiggly lines – folds caused by the evolutionary squashing-up of a large surface area into a small space. Here are the centres that deal with speech, processing new information, abstract thought and reasoning, the faculties that move us to the top of the evolutionary ladder. This is the part that goes beyond newts and dogs.

The hierarchy of needs which this part of your brain addresses is what we may call a 'society agenda' – a desire to work with and help other humans plus a desire for logic. Remember what we learnt about conspiracy theories in the *Thinking* chapter. Researchers have noted that many of them arise when people are grappling with unexpected events, such as when the young and attractive die suddenly. Gossip is popular for the same reasons. We know a lot about some people, but there's some information that we lack. Celebrity gossip is particularly tantalizing. We have a sense of who David Beckham and George Clooney are, but we crave the missing pieces – their quirks, their romantic struggles, their secret vices.

In the past few decades, psychologists have learned a lot

about these systems, but of course mankind has always been aware of the tension that exists between them. The Greek philosopher Plato said that in our heads we have a rational charioteer who has to rein in an unruly horse that 'barely yields to horsewhip and goad combined'. Freud wrote about the selfish id and the conscientious superego (and also about the ego, which mediates between them). Behavioural economists dubbed the two systems the Planner and the Doer and more recently Daniel Kahnemann labelled them System 1 and System 2 in his groundbreaking book *Thinking Fast and Slow*.

The tension is captured best by an analogy used by University of Virginia psychologist Jonathan Haidt in his wonderful book *The Happiness Hypothesis* and popularized by the esteemed sibling authors Dan and Chip Heath. Haidt says that our emotional side is an elephant and our rational side is its rider. Perched atop the Elephant, the Rider holds the reins and tries to read the map (our memory bank) in order to appear to be the leader.

EXERCISE – UNDERSTANDING YOUR ELEPHANT

In one study, researchers telephoned people in different parts of the country and asked how satisfied they were with their lives. Where the weather was nice, people reported that their lives were relatively happy. But when people lived in cities that happened to have bad weather that day, they reported that they were relatively unhappy.

These people had tried to answer the question – directed at the Rider – but the Elephant enforced a kind of 'reality first' policy and insisted on reacting to the immediate situation instead of the bigger picture. They mistook their reality-induced feelings for fact.

When creating a winning mindset, understanding this distinction between the Elephant and the Rider is crucial.

You've probably been in a similar situation yourself. You've had an awful night's sleep and you wake up feeling out of sorts. You look out of the window and it's raining heavily. If at that moment you try to imagine how much you are looking forward to the working day ahead, you may attribute feelings to your imaginary day that are to do with your bad night's sleep ('it is going to be terrible').

In your own world, one effective solution is to create a transition zone. Supermarkets have been doing for this for many years. Few attempts are made to sell to you immediately inside the entrance. There may be a photo booth, some charity collection boxes and perhaps a ride-on car or horse for toddlers. Extending some twenty feet into the store, this is what retailers term the 'decompression zone'. Its purpose is to ensure that shoppers adjust, physically and psychologically, to their new surroundings. The pace at which we walk down a street or across a car park is a good deal faster than the 'grazing' speed at which supermarket managers want us to move through their stores. The 'decompression zone' not only slows us down but also helps us adapt to changes in light levels, temperature and humidity. Once this adaptation has been achieved we will be in an optimum frame of mind to impulse buy.

Your transition zone could be the time you spend in your car driving to work or even the time before this when you are getting ready for the day ahead. When you get dressed, open your mental wardrobe. With each article of clothing you put on – shirt, belt, shoes – let go of a problem you are worried about. By the time you are changed, you'll have shed all your unhelpful distractions and personal concerns and be able to focus on dealing with the present.

Think of your own triggers, which will stimulate you to ask the question, 'Is this my Elephant or my Rider answering?'

The Rider's control is precarious because the Rider is so small relative to the Elephant: five times smaller, in fact. Any time the six-tonne Elephant and the Rider disagree about which direction on the map to go, the Rider is going to lose. He's completely overmatched.

Most of us are all too familiar with real-life situations in which our Elephant overpowers our Rider. For example, have you ever entered an auction on eBay? Suppose you made your first bid on a Monday morning, for a watch, and at this point you are the highest bidder. That night you log on, and you're still the top dog. Same again the next night. You start thinking about that elegant watch. You imagine it on your wrist; you imagine the compliments you will get. But then you go online again one hour before the end of the auction. Someone has topped your bid! Someone else will take that watch! Your watch! So you increase your bid beyond what you had originally planned.

The feeling of partial ownership causes the spiral we often see in online auctions. The longer an auction continues, the greater the grip that virtual ownership will have on the various bidders and the more money they will spend.

Communicating with your Elephant first is the mainspring of the advertising industry. We see a happy couple driving down a beautiful coastline in a convertible car and we imagine ourselves there. We see a new dress in a catalogue and – *poof!* – we start thinking of it as ours. The trap is set, and your Elephant willingly walks in. We become partial owners even before becoming rightful owners.

You've also experienced this if you have ever slept in, overeaten, dialled up your ex at midnight, procrastinated, tried to quit smoking and failed, skipped the gym, got angry and said something you've regretted, abandoned your Spanish lessons, gone food shopping when hungry, refused to speak up in a meeting because you were scared, and so on.

The weakness of the Elephant, our emotional and instinctive side, is clear: it's lazy and unpredictable, often looking for a quick pay-off over the long-term pay-off. As D'Amato understood, when our efforts fail, it's usually the Elephant's fault, since the kinds of success which elite performers achieve typically involve short-term sacrifices for long-term pay-offs. All coaches have their stories of the talented athlete who never quite achieved their potential. This failure is often because the Rider simply couldn't keep the Elephant on the road long enough to reach the destination.

The Elephant's hunger for instant gratification is the opposite of the Rider's strength, which is the ability to think long-term, to plan, to think beyond the moment (all of those things your pet can't do). But what may also surprise you is that the Elephant also has enormous strengths and that the Rider has crippling weaknesses. The Elephant isn't always the bad guy. Emotion is the Elephant's turf – love and compassion, sympathy, loyalty and motivation. That willingness to get out of bed and run despite the early hour/cold/comfort of your bed – that's the Elephant. That spine-stiffening you feel when you need to stand up for yourself – that's the Elephant. That willingness to put your hand up and demand the ball when you are getting beat with a minute to go – that's the Elephant.

And even more important if you're contemplating getting things done: to make progress towards a goal, whether it is the world heavyweight championship or something less ambitious, requires the energy and drive of the Elephant. This strength is the mirror image of the Rider's great weakness: deliberation and procrastination. Because it deals with logic and an ability to see things from several angles, the Rider tends to overanalyse and overthink things.

One athlete I worked with asked the coaches to ignore his immediate responses when asked how he was feeling. He was frustrated because he would often be substituted soon afterwards. He understood that his Elephant would often answer first – 'I'm exhausted, get me out of here!' – but he needed them to check in again one minute later. If his answer was consistent, he was telling the truth. This is a tactic which is easily adopted in everyday life: when a decision must be made, but you don't want to make it hastily and overemotionally, give yourself a deadline to reconsider, then stick to what you have decided by then. It's reminiscent of the old trick whereby you toss a coin. While it's in the air, you may suddenly realize which side you want it to land on. That will tell you what you really want to do.

Chances are, you know people with the Rider problems: your friend who can agonize for twenty minutes about what to eat for dinner, your colleague who can brainstorm about new ideas for hours but can't ever seem to make a decision. The neurologist Donald Calne echoes this: 'The essential difference between emotion and reason is that emotion leads to action while reason leads to conclusions.'[12]

Neurological researcher Michael Gazzaniga confirms that, 'All we are doing in life is catching up with what our brain already knows.'[13] In understanding the interplay between the emotional Elephant brain and the neocortex Rider brain, neuroscientists and coaches are finally coming to agree with Plato when he wrote: *All learning has an emotional base.*

Cus D'Amato knew this, which is why once he had spotted Mike Tyson's undoubted potential he invested so much of himself in his young charge.

Unless we emotionally believe something to be true, we do

not fully believe it. Unless the emotional brain registers what the neocortex learns then it is not really believed. Otherwise, we would all be driving round in Skodas. Intellectually you know them to be fantastic cars these days, but emotionally . . . many just can't do it. Rita Carter, in her book *Mapping the Mind*, says, 'Where thought conflicts with emotion, the latter is designed by the neural circuitry in our brains to win.'

So what goes on in the subtle electrical and chemical interplay between these three areas of our brain when things start to hot up and we find ourselves feeling overwhelmed and unable and/or unwilling to cope with what life is throwing at us?

Essentially we go 'reptilian' and the Elephant is called into action. The blood, the energy, the oxygen – everything that fires the brain gets focused on our reptilian fight-flight-or-freeze instinct. The brain 'downshifts'. It goes into 'survival' mode. And while it is there, don't expect it to give two hoots about the tactics for your next match or learning the important free-kick routine you want to practise. It's as if I were to ask you to read this book while crossing a busy road. You would have to be heavily committed to the laws of motion to resist moving into survival mode.

As in Cus D'Amato's boxing laboratory, great coaches understand that great cultures have got to appeal to both. The Rider provides the planning and direction we discussed in the *Thinking* chapter, and the Elephant provides the energy. So if you reach the Riders of your team but not the Elephants, team members will have understanding without motivation. If you reach the Elephants but not their Riders, they'll have passion without direction. In both cases, the flaws can be paralysing. 'Passivity or a wild recklessness are dangerous responses in a boxing ring,' said D'Amato. However, when Elephants and Riders work and move together, success can come easily.

3.iii THE STORM AND THE T-CUP

Boxing's very nature has compelled its finest coaching practitioners to get to grips with this understanding, and many leading coaches in other sporting disciplines have recognized a need to spend time educating themselves and their players about this distinction. There may be different terms employed in the metaphors used but there is a consistency of messages used to achieve what the former England Rugby Union head coach Sir Clive Woodward claims is, 'The greatest critical component of success in sport – or life – in either a team or an individual context . . . the ability to perform and *think* correctly under pressure.'[14]

Woodward put the phrase 'Thinking Correctly Under Pressure' into the acronym T-CUP, which he spent time teaching to his England team during his seven-year reign. He had noticed that his team tended to cede control to the Elephant when losing games with less than ten minutes on the clock. 'We would become desperate and lacking control,' Woodward recounts. The focus on T-CUP allowed the players to access the Rider in the last minute of the 2003 World Cup Final. 'I don't think this team ever panicked,' recalls Mike Catt, the versatile centre. 'We just had to do our own thing and we knew we would win it.'

As legendary BBC radio commentator Ian Robertson described it, 'Martin Johnson has it. He drives. There's thirty-five seconds to go. This is the one . . . It's coming back for Jonny Wilkinson . . .' Woodward knew that they were executing a move they had rehearsed hundreds of time; they were, as Catt said, 'doing their own thing'. Robertson continued, '. . . he drops for World Cup glory . . . It's up . . . It's over! England have just won the World Cup . . .'

During this golden period for English rugby, New Zealand's All Blacks had cemented their reputations as one of sport's greatest 'chokers'. Accusing someone of 'choking' – being unable to cope with pressure – is one of the biggest insults in the sports world. It is what many performers believe sets the elite apart from those of us who left our composure behind on school sports day. The All Blacks, however, seemed to do little to dispel this notion, having acquired a reputation as the most talented players who could perform whenever the pressure wasn't so extreme. They were often heralded as the best rugby team in the world in between World Cup tournaments.

Graham Henry, the head coach, had noted that some of his players 'were having trouble controlling their emotions in key moments of matches'. This resulted in typical Elephant-type behaviours like trying too hard, being overly aggressive, and experiencing the tunnel-vision syndrome which navy pilots drily refer to as OBE: Overcome By Events.

'Just having knowledge of how the brain reacts to stress was a pretty important first step,' says Henry. 'What the players do, why they felt the way they felt.'[15]

With the help of Ceri Evans, a former Rhodes Scholar and psychiatrist, the players and coaches formed the 'Mental Analysis and Development Group' – they called it MAD for short – to confront the issue of pressure: what it is, what it does and what they could do about it.

They devised a tool that describes the mental state you want to avoid, and the one you want to be in. They called it Red

Head/Blue Head. Red Head is the negative state, when you are heated, overwhelmed, and tense (HOT, in the parlance). Your emotional engine is smoking, your perceptions are slow, the game feels too fast, and your decision-making is rushed.

Blue Head, on the other hand, is the precise opposite: the cool, controlled, pattern-seeing state, when you retain your awareness and your decision-making power, when you stay flexible and deliver your best performance.

'If you want to build up strength, you go to the gym and you work three times a week on your core strength,' says Gilbert Enoka, a member of the coaching staff. 'It just seems that if you want to develop your ability to concentrate and focus and be flexible in what you do from a mental perspective, wouldn't you apply the same approach?'[16]

Henry agrees. 'If you think of physical conditioning, technical understanding and tactical appreciation as forming three legs, the stool isn't balanced unless you have psychological strength as well.' All four aspects were on display when they were crowned World Cup winners in 2011 for only the second time in their illustrious history, and once again when they became the first team to retain the trophy in 2015.

EXERCISE – TIME MANAGEMENT

'Things that matter most must never be at the mercy of things that matter least.' – *Goethe*

1. **Think about Sir Graham Henry's four most important aspects of a winning mindset which enable you to deliver consistently high performance in your role. These are: physical conditioning (are you physically able to do it?), technical skills (are you capable of doing it?), tactical understanding (do you know both**

why you are doing it and how to go about it?) and psychological strength (have you the will to do it?)

2. **Grade them 1–10 on how happy you are with the amount of time you spend on developing them.
    (1 = not happy; 10 = very happy.)**

3. **Now think about what you would like the ratings to be. Work out what time you wish was spent on each, to deliver the rating you would prefer.**

This should give you a good indication of where you are spending most of your time. Is it in the areas where you want to be?

The epitome of this measured approach was the unlikely figure of Stephen Donald. A year earlier, Donald had delivered an unfortunate performance against Australia, when he had missed an important kick to offer his team a comfortable cushion and then gave the ball away in the last minute to allow their rivals to score the winning try. One national newspaper wrote that his performance was a 'nightmare', and his international career was generally considered to be over. As the World Cup unfolded, Donald went fishing with friends in Waikato.

But then a series of disasters hit the All Blacks.

First of all, Dan Carter, the fly half and arguably the best player in the world – not to mention the highest points scorer in the sport's Test match history – tore a tendon. The man considered essential for an All Blacks victory was ruled out of the tournament.

In the gruelling quarter-final victory against the rugged Argentinians, his understudy, Colin Slade, aggravated a groin injury and was ruled out. With just one fit fly half, head coach Henry tracked down Donald. 'I was out on the river whitebaiting. I'd had a good day, hauling in around eleven kilos,' he said. 'When the call came, my day got a lot better.'[17]

In the forty-third minute of the final against France, the third-choice playmaker, Aaron Cruden, fell to the ground with a knee injury and Donald, wearing a borrowed jersey that was two sizes too small, and having not played a game for six weeks, ran on to replace him.

In the tightest and most gruelling of finals, the French made a slight error which was duly punished with the award of a penalty. The player dubbed 'The Beaver' after a character from the US children's show *Leave it to Beaver* lived up to his nickname and took sole command. He stepped up, nodded at the goalposts and landed the kick. They proved to be the winning points.

'The key was to focus on just getting the job done,' Donald calmly explained afterwards. 'I didn't focus on just how big the job was.'[18]

Four years later, these exact words were echoed by Dan Carter just moments after his flawless kicking, including a penalty – kicked with his weaker right foot – had given his team the points to beat Australia in the 2015 Final.

The All Blacks had opened a commanding 21–3 lead over their Australian rivals before full back Ben Smith was sent to the sin bin, allowing Australia to regain some momentum and claw back the score line to 21–17. Enter Carter, who dropped a goal from 42 metres and then landed a penalty from near halfway, his longest of the tournament, to give the holders a cushion. 'He would probably emerge from half an hour in a sauna without any evidence of sweat' was how one newspaper report described his calm and measured response to the situation.

'It was an important part of the game,' Carter reasoned, 'and we needed some breathing space.' When explaining why he had kicked the final penalty with his weaker right foot, his blue-headed response was simple. 'It's always been a dream of mine to kick a conversion right-footed,' he said. 'The opportunity came. I've practised it in training many times and I just thought I'd give it a little go.'[19]

EXERCISE – WIN

Michael Phelps first met his coach, Bob Bowman, at the age of eight. Over the years, Bowman, who had originally worked as a child psychologist, would deliberately make Phelps uncomfortable at practices, including altering practice times at late notice, cancelling taxis to take him home and banning him from drinking water in his breaks. He once purposely stepped on Phelps' swimming goggles just moments before a race, forcing him to make do without them.

Bowman was effectively training Phelps to contain his Elephant. He was taught to defuse the emotional reaction by asking himself an important question, which he dubbed WIN: What's Important Now?

Is it allowing the Elephant an opportunity to complain or moan about the hand which fate has dealt you, or instead controlling your reaction?

You can change your thinking, your language and your behaviour. That is all you really have any control over anyway. Unfortunately, most of us never change our behaviour because we get stuck into conditioned responses.

Take a really close look at whatever it is that you want to change and figure out how the WIN formula applies.

For example, you may want to gain support from others for a new idea you want to implement. Now have a look at your behaviour towards achieving this outcome, so far.

Event: You need to gain support from your colleagues for a new idea you want to implement.

Elephant: You became short-tempered and angry with colleagues for their lack of support.

Outcome: You have upset colleagues and have no buy-in to your idea.

Event: You want to lose some weight for your eagerly anticipated summer holiday.

Elephant: You continue to snack on crisps and chocolate between meals.

Outcome: You are the same weight or heavier but unhappy with your shape.

Event: You want to enjoy getting close to your kids and putting them to bed.

Elephant: You refuse to say 'no' to your colleagues' requests and end up working late.

Outcome: You arrive home late and too tired to enjoy the experience.

Twelve-step programmes such as Alcoholics Anonymous define insanity as 'continuing the same behaviour and expecting a different result'. If you continue to adopt the same Elephant response your outcome will not change either.

Now apply the WIN question and look at how you could have changed your response to the facts in order to get a different outcome.

Event: You need to gain support from your colleagues for a new idea you want to implement.

WIN: You make time to speak to key people in private and explain your idea in detail.

Outcome: You have improved their understanding and support for the change.

Event: You want to lose some weight for your eagerly anticipated summer holiday.

WIN: You prepare healthy snacks to nibble on during the day.

Outcome: You start to lose weight and feel happier with your shape.

Event: You want to enjoy getting close to your kids and putting them to bed.

WIN: You meet with your boss and agree a plan to arrive early and leave early on certain days.

Outcome: You arrive home in plenty of time to enjoy the experience.

When Dave Brailsford was recruiting the members of his support staff, he describes his best decision as the appointment of Steve Peters, a professor of psychiatry at Sheffield University. Peters used to be a doctor at Rampton Hospital, one of England's three maximum-security psychiatric facilities, before embarking on a second, high-profile career working with elite athletes to improve their mental performance.

In the 1990s, Peters came up with what he calls the 'chimp paradox' to explain to first-year medical students how the mind functions. According to his analogy, there is a contest within the brain between its more rational 'human' parts and its anciently evolved 'chimp' regions.

The 'chimp' is essentially an emotional machine that behaves independently of us. It is neither good nor bad. It fulfils essential functions, but it is also powerful and prone to panic. 'A chimpanzee is five times stronger than us,' Peters explains. It competes with the 'computer' and 'human' brain, the logical and calculating sides of our character, and if it is left to dominate can result in bad decision-making. We are not responsible for the nature of our chimp but we are responsible for managing it. 'If you have this animal sharing your life with you, you have to treat it with respect,' he says.[20] Peters does not call himself a doctor when he is dealing with athletes. He thinks of himself as a coach, teaching them how to manage their chimps. Dave Brailsford concurs. 'If you understand that part of your brain, the part that reacts emotionally rather than logically, you'll be more effective.'[21]

Perhaps the most effective example of this emotional control was displayed by Chris Hoy. At the 2003 Stuttgart World Championships, Hoy had watched his German rival, Stefan Nimke, break the 1-kilometre time trial world record and it panicked him into abandoning his strategy and his form. 'I changed my plans and set off way too fast, which caused me to mess up towards the end,' he explained.

For many, the kilo is considered to be the most painful event in cycling: like the 400 metres in athletics, it requires acceleration and speed but there is also an endurance element. Hoy himself describes the event as 'gladiatorial. You have one chance. Your body is on the line and it's cruel because everyone cracks. You just have to try and remain smooth for as long as possible.'[22]

A year after his chastening experience in Germany, Hoy put himself on the line once again for a much bigger prize: Olympic gold. He was afforded the honour – and added pressure – of being the last man to race. It put him in the hottest of hot seats. In the final twenty minutes, he watched three of the final five riders break the world record. 'I'm going to have to do a personal best just to get a medal here,' Hoy remembers thinking.

'It's like the gallows. That's what it feels like – an execution,' Hoy said. 'In those last few minutes it's the last place in the world you ever want to be. There's no getting out of it.

You've put yourself in this position; you've committed four years to it; it seems ridiculous . . .'

He remembered the drills and mental rehearsals he had gone through: negative thoughts are natural, don't panic when you have one; displace it with positive thoughts. And always, always turn your focus to the start, and the routine: *bang!* You're in the start gate, breathing deeply, tightening your toe straps, sitting up, leaning forward, gripping the bars, pulling back, lunging forward.

1 minute 0.711 seconds – and an even newer Olympic record – later, Hoy crossed the line to win the coveted gold medal. 'I forgot to celebrate,' Hoy laughs. 'I was so focused on the ride itself, I hadn't considered the aftermath.'

EXERCISE – KNOW YOUR ELEPHANT / CHIMP / RED HEAD

When I work with leaders, one activity I encourage them to invest time in is preparing for their 'oh shit!' moments.

What's an 'oh shit!' moment, you ask?

One rather formal definition is: 'The reaction people have to excessive pressures or other types of demands placed on them. It arises when they worry they can't cope.' I prefer the more graphic description, 'The moments that cause you to wake up screaming before you realize that you haven't actually fallen asleep yet'.

Hans Seyle, a pioneer of modern stress research, says that these moments have three components:

- stimulus

- perception

- response

For example, if we are hiking in the woods and encounter a bear, this is a stimulus, we then perceive a life-threatening situation and a response is activated in our bodies, so we can run for our lives. This important response mechanism – in other words, our 'red head', chimp, or elephant's reaction – has been hardwired into our genes since the caveman days and is a key survival tool.

Our response to the stimulus of an 'oh shit!' moment can manifest itself in three ways:

– fight

– flight

– freeze

In this state we will do (or say) whatever it takes to get out of the situation. You cannot reason with people in this state, you cannot build true consensus, you won't hear the truth. You only have access to about 10 per cent of your own – and other people's – true abilities. In other words, you can't build a winning mindset unless this fight, flight or freeze mechanism is disarmed.

This is why you need to prepare for these moments.

The first step is to understand the role which your natural personality will play in determining the type of behaviour you will exhibit when feeling stress about making change happen. Depending on their personalities, some people display aggressive behaviour (fight), some people distance themselves from the situation (flight) and some give up and acquiesce to the pressure (freeze).

Consider in which of these potentially stressful situations you can recognize your own likely response. Knowing how you are likely to react is the best way to prepare yourself for such moments:

A. At a meeting for which you have thoroughly prepared, the chair criticizes you and accuses you of failing to attend to tasks that were, in reality, someone else's responsibility. As all eyes turn on you, you feel your face getting hot, your jaw tightening, and your fist clenching. You would not shout or hit anyone – doing so would only make things worse. But you *feel like* shouting or striking out.

B. Now consider another stress-filled scenario. You walk into your weekly night class a few moments late, only to find everyone putting books and notes away – apparently preparing for a test you did not realize had been scheduled for today. Your heart seems to stop, your mouth is dry, your knees feel weak and you momentarily consider hurrying back out of the door. Your life is not really in danger, and running away will not solve your problem – so why should you feel a physical urge to escape?

C. Finally, imagine walking alone down a dark street. You hear a startling noise. Without thinking, you stop dead in your tracks. Your senses become razor sharp. Your eyes widen and scan the scene, taking in as much visual information as possible. You may even hold your breath in an effort to be completely silent and still, and to hear better. You become 'an alarmed-looking human statue'.

These three scenarios illustrate the fight, flight or freeze response, a sequence of internal processes that prepares you for struggle or escape. It is triggered when we interpret a situation as threatening. The resulting response depends on how you have learned to deal with threat, as well as on an innate fight, flight or freeze 'programme' built into the brain.

3.iv CONTAIN, ENTERTAIN, EXPLAIN

As with all neat theories about the brain, it is obviously far more complicated than these models would suggest, yet as metaphors they are still very useful in our own scenario of creating a winning mindset. Once we understand what is happening inside our heads, we can then know what to do to manage our emotions to the best effect.

Emanuel Steward is the coach of the famous Kronk boxing gym in Detroit (which has produced more than twenty world champions, including Thomas Hearns), and the man who guided Lennox Lewis to the heavyweight title. He explained to me that to create a culture in which people are expected to perform under pressure, he adopted a three-step approach, which not only reinforces this three-brains-in-one model, but also works at an empirical level:

'To teach you have to contain, entertain, explain. It doesn't work in any other order.'[23]

For the purposes of this chapter, let's look at the first two and how we can apply the principles within a non-sporting environment.

CONTAIN

Bad news, I'm afraid. The culmination of six million years' worth of neurological evolution is *not* the contents of this book, however much I hope you're enjoying it.

The human brain is the product of millions upon millions of adaptations and changes, which ensure that we are the ones best able to cope with what life will throw at us. And I am sorry to say much of what we deem important in our everyday lives is not among the eventual realities that natural selection has prepared us for. Perhaps if the consequences of not having done your annual appraisal had been far more stringent thousands of years ago, this might not be the case, but it is. Our civilization has outpaced our evolution, and we must train our brains to work differently.

At the end of the day the brain is designed for one thing: survival. It does all sorts of wonderful things, some of which we can barely begin to imagine, but the bottom line is that it is there to keep us and our progeny going. What coaches understand is that when young people come into the sporting cultures we are describing – remember D'Amato's test of whether they enter the gym – we are testing their ability to do something unnatural and biologically inconsequential. And if they fail to measure up, the implication is that there is something wrong with them.

Coaches understand that when we approach a learning situation, there is a part of our brain that posits the question: 'Do I need to know this in order to survive? Yes or no?' If yes, then we can get on with the learning in hand and start to tap into our potential. However, if the answer is no, it doesn't matter how good a coach you are, forget it.

If they create a culture where the people they are coaching

are scared, hungry, insecure, vulnerable or worried about being exposed, they have obviously got more important things going on in their heads than engaging their neurological resources to consider the finer nuances of their passing technique.

To start, in true Abraham Maslow style (the great American psychologist famous for his hierarchy of needs), all great coaches recognize the need to address the basics and have their charges warm, fed and free from fear.

EXERCISE – WIIFM?

The whole notion of the brain being designed for survival has been summed up in the neat phrase, 'What's in it for me?' affectionately known as the WIIFM.

In any situation, this question is always the same: what's in it for me? What is the point? Why should I bother to learn this? Often the phrase is unspoken. It simply lies there in the background.

Many leaders spend a great deal of time teaching others *how to*, but we need to ensure that the *why to* is addressed before we even approach the *how to*.

Think about a particular task – such as clearing away their desk at the end of a day – that you want them to do.

Answer the unspoken question of what is in it for them. How will they *benefit* from it?

Notice the use of the word 'benefit'? A good salesperson will always talk in terms of 'benefits' rather than 'features', so make sure that you do the same.

If you are not sure whether you have identified a benefit or a feature, try putting 'So what?' on the end. If you don't, they will!

3.v THE POWER OF RITUAL

Satisfying the reptilian brain involves working with territorial behaviour. To address this, many teams think in terms of an athlete's place, *their* seat, *their* locker, *their* name on the wall, as appropriate – all of which gives them a sense of belonging. The leading rugby league coach Tony Smith makes a point of shaking every player's hand when they arrive at work. 'It lets them know that I have seen them and I respect them,' he explains. Equally, he will never go into the players' dressing room unless invited. 'That is their private space and I have to respect that,' he explains.

Sir Clive Woodward adopted a similar approach in his half-time team talks. He called it Second-Half Thinking, and he used the time to influence the mindset of his players. Rather than worrying about whether they were winning or losing after the first half, he insisted on the players changing their shirts and putting on a fresh kit whilst he would think about his own words to influence their thinking and refocus them on winning. He describes how those crucial ten minutes should be used:

0000–0002 minutes

Absolute silence
Think about performance
Shirts off

Towel down
New kit
0–0 on scoreboard

0002–0005 minutes

Coaches' assessments
Take on food and fluids

0005–0008 minutes

Coach's final word

0008–0010 minutes

Absolute silence
0–0 on scoreboard
Visualize kick-off

EXERCISE – HALF-TIME THINKING

How many of us have thought (usually after something has gone disastrously wrong), 'If only I could rewind and do that again'?

To help avoid this, I often encourage coaches to plan their post-game interviews *before* the match. Whilst this may seem a strange exercise, it is a valuable method of avoiding making the greatest speech they will ever regret.

We know there are three outcomes to a game – win, lose or draw. If they plan what their message will be, they tend to avoid making knee-jerk assessments or reacting badly to events.

I have heard coaches blame a referee's poor performance for a loss and then struggle to get the players to listen to the lessons of the review in the days afterwards. They have already been handed an explanation.

So why not do a similar breakdown for the first few minutes of your own most important moments, such as the first few minutes of a meeting or the first few minutes of a conversation, and focus on the kind of behaviours which you want to demonstrate to others?

0001–0002 minutes
Behaviour:

_____

0002–0003 minutes
Behaviour:

_____

0003–0004 minutes
Behaviour:

_____

Such ritualistic behaviour is vital and allows us to focus on what works best for us through the medium of routine. In a world of chaos, rituals mean that we know what is going to come next. Chris Evans does a morning breakfast show which is essentially the same show at the same time with the same jokes delivered in the same way, day after day, five days a week throughout the year. Yet it is funny because of this. 'My aim is leave the listener in a better, more relaxed, or more thoughtful frame of mind,' he explained in his book, *It's Not What You Think*.

His method of establishing a regular rhythm to his show is worth understanding. 'To plan an hour of radio I actually draw a clock,' he explains. 'I use a CD to draw around – it's the perfect size. I then fill in all the things that *must* happen at the corresponding times, shade in those areas and then see how much room there is for anything else to happen. That's the *me* bit.'[24] Such rituals contribute to our feelings of stability and security in the midst of a world where anything can happen at any minute.

Phil Jackson, the legendary basketball coach, explained how at the start of every season he used to perform a ritual that he borrowed from the American Football great Vince Lombardi. He would make the players form a row on the baseline of the court and ask them to commit to being coached that season. He would announce, 'God has ordained me to coach you young men, and I embrace the role I've been given. If you wish to accept the game I embrace and follow my coaching, as a sign of your commitment, step across that line.

'Wonder of wonders,' Jackson says, 'every player, including Michael Jordan, Shaquille O'Neal and Kobe Bryant, always did it.

'I did it in a fun way but with serious intent,' he adds. 'The essence of coaching is to get the players to wholeheartedly agree to being coached, then offer them a sense of their destiny as a team.'[25]

One ritual that many coaches are religious about maintaining is the opportunity to eat together. Bill Sweetenham, one of the world's finest swimming coaches, uses breakfast times to start his coaching sessions. He insists that a 'barnyard breakfast' – a plate of bacon and eggs – is available to all of his swimmers when they sit down to eat, as it helps them to think about the animals that have helped produce the food. The chicken has been involved in producing the egg for breakfast, whilst the pig has been fully committed to providing the bacon.

Sweetenham then challenges his swimmers to decide whether they are going to be involved in or committed to the day's training session.

Brad Gilbert, the tennis coach who guided Andre Agassi to the world number one slot during their eight-year coaching relationship, however, preferred to use the evening meal. 'A big part of a great coaching relationship is never getting into a pattern of saying, at the end of the work day, "I'll see you tomorrow,"' he explains. 'Two guys, two cabs – no good. Some of the best coaching sessions I've done have been in the evening when the physical training was over. When we relaxed over dinner, we would start to discuss strategies and tactics.'[26] Professor Sir Tim Brighouse, a professor of education at Keele University, is equally vehement about this practice. He says, 'Eating together addresses a fundamental part of our evolutionary psyche that says, "If I eat with you, I like you."'[27]

EXERCISE – CHECKLIST CHARLIE

Pilots have checklists. Doctors and nurses have patient-care checklists. Not because they're forgetful but because they are smart enough to know that they're in a performance business. They know that a good checklist is not a crutch – it's a tool.

The real question is, if a checklist is good for pilots and doctors, why not for you? With that in mind, here's what it might look like, based on things I've learned from the great coaches with whom I've spent time.

1. **ARE YOU CONNECTED?** Before all else, establish the emotional connection. Show you are there, and that you care; take a moment to acknowledge your shared connection, to build togetherness and trust. Practice requires energy. This is where you turn the key and start the engine.
   Do: Make a joke, get personal, tell a story, ask a question.
   Don't: Launch straight into an activity.
   Gauge: Have you made good eye contact with everyone?

2. **ARE TODAY'S GOALS ULTRA-CLEAR?** Practice is about reaching, and to do it well, everybody needs to know exactly what they're reaching for. Not vague goals, like

'working hard' and 'getting better', but concrete, tangible, measurable targets like 'converting more sales from referrals', or 'nailing the sales pitch in twenty seconds'. You cannot be specific enough.

Do: Use models to show the target.

Don't: Set unreasonably high goals. Aim for something slightly beyond your current ability.

Gauge: Could a complete stranger walk up to practice, watch for a few minutes, and figure out the goal?

3. IS PRACTICE A STRETCH? Have you planned a practice that places people on the edge of their ability, making and then fixing mistakes?

Do: Celebrate struggle.

Don't: Celebrate success (it speaks for itself).

Gauge: Does your people's success percentage fit in the 50–70 per cent range – neither dispiritingly difficult nor too easy, but in that sweet spot on the edge of current ability?

What's interesting in part about this checklist is what's not there – inspiring speeches, pep talks, all the Hollywood stuff. This is not because they never occur, but because inspiring speeches are a terribly inefficient way to learn. Learning happens when you create a space where people work together, reach towards a goal; when you make the kind of human connection that keeps people coming back again and again, eager to reach a little further.

What will your checklist consist of?

3.vi   RELATIONSHIP ISSUES

There is a brilliant scene in Monty Python's *Life of Brian* which highlights the need for belonging. Brian, who is mistaken for the Messiah, speaks to a crowd who are gathered to hear his words. He urges them to think for themselves and tells them, 'Look, you've got it all wrong! You don't need to follow me. You've got to think for yourselves! You're all individuals!' The crowd then chant back in unison, 'Yes! We are all individuals!'

For a long time, it has been commonly agreed that food is the primary motivator behind our need for belonging; in other words, we remain in a group to ensure that we get fed. However, more recent studies on animals have found that this does not necessarily appear to be the case.

In a now famous study, animal learning theorists removed the mother from baby monkeys and replaced her with two different substitute mothers: one made from harsh wire and the other made from a soft cloth, but each was fitted with a feeding nipple. Despite our long-standing beliefs, it was found that the infant monkeys became more attached to the substitute soft cloth mother than the harsh wire mother, even when the researchers altered the experiment to ensure that only the harsh wire mother was supplying the food.

This study is part of a wider body of work on attachment theory. John Bowlby, the psychologist leading the work, believes that we develop attachment between the ages of

0–3 years old, based on our experience with caregivers. These are the people we look to for protection, comfort and support. From the way they respond to our needs we build up a picture of how belonging works and, based on these expectations, from a very early age we develop strategies and ways of ensuring that we belong.

One thing I have learned about great coaches is that it's all about relationships and bringing out the best in of your team. Once you get that right, players will leap through hoops of flames for you. Get it wrong – and it can feel like the other way round.

'A football coach who only understands football is not a great coach,' says Mourinho. 'I never forget: my players are men. Men with different personalities, different cultures.'

Mourinho recalls the environment where he began to understand the profound impact of this approach: his first job as a teacher working with children with Down's syndrome and mental disabilities. 'I wasn't technically ready to help these kids,' he said. 'And I had success only because of one thing, the emotional relation that was established with them. I did little miracles only because of the relationship. Affection, touch, empathy – only because of that.'

He says: 'Of course you need the knowledge, the capacity to analyse things. But the centre of everything is the relationship, and empathy, not only with the individual but in the team.'

Ask people what makes Mourinho unique, and one common response is this: his players almost universally adore him. In his autobiography, legendary Swedish striker Zlatan Ibrahimovic described him as 'a guy I was basically willing to die for'. And when Mourinho made the move from Milan's Internazionale to Real Madrid, Marco Materazzi was in tears as the pair said their farewells. Didier Drogba, the prolific

Chelsea striker, says he felt 'like an orphan' after Mourinho departed West London in 2007 following his successful first spell at the club. 'He's a great man,' Drogba says. 'You can see how close players are with him. He has a way of getting into players' minds as a manager – and as a man, the kind of man who's ready to give you all his confidence and trust because he expects that you'll give it back.'[28]

Zlatan Ibrahimovic describes how Mourinho forges such strong relationships. 'He formed an attachment to me before we had even met,' he said. 'I was told that Mourinho was going to phone me, and I thought, "Has something happened?"' Instead, Mourinho explained that he just wanted to chat and introduce himself. 'He said, "It'll be nice to work together, I'm looking forward to meeting you" – nothing remarkable,' Ibrahimovic recalled. 'However, he was speaking in Italian. I didn't get it. Mourinho had never coached an Italian club. But he spoke the language better than me. He'd learned the language in no time at all – in three weeks, people said – and I couldn't keep up. We switched to English, and already I could sense it: this guy cares.'

Ibrahimovic went on to help his coach win the league, contributing by scoring the most goals in the Italian League along the way. 'Following my final goal for him, which helped us win the league, as I ran back to the halfway line, I was only interested in catching his eye to acknowledge his impact,' he later recalled.[29]

Throughout life, the need for attachment continues to be an important part of our identity. Having warm and trusting friendships, feeling that you belong and that others care about you is fundamental. Our sense of personal identity and purpose stems largely from our various roles in life and how these roles relate to and depend upon others.

Howard Schultz, the chief executive of Starbucks, once took exception to his business being described as a coffee shop. 'We're in the people business serving coffee, not the coffee business serving people,' he clarified. It was an echo of Angelo Dundee's words. Muhammad Ali's coach once said, 'I am not a boxing coach. I coach people to box.' His logic was that human behaviour will out, and if I am going to spend time with you doing what you ask of me, then I need some sort of relationship with you for it to work.

I know that in a busy schedule asking people about how their children got on in the sports day, or whether they enjoyed their holiday, can be pushed to one side quite easily. Building relationships, however, is an *investment* of your time and energy that pays back many times and in many ways.

This is a technique which I use with coaches I support. Every few months, I ask them to answer questions about a player who will have been quizzed earlier in the day. These questions include the names and ages of their children, their last holiday destination and their favourite sports team. Points are awarded for each correct answer. It is a fun and simple way of finding out who they are connecting with and who they are not.

It's a similar approach to the format of the television quiz show *Mr & Mrs* – where couples were asked questions about the supposed minutiae of married life to test how well they knew each other.

EXERCISE – TIMPSON TEST

Working as a leader carries vast demands, so the requirement to get to know all of your people and take time for a regular chat can seem like one too many. But remember the wise words of

John Timpson, majority owner and managing director of the eponymous and successful high-street service business: 'Great bosses have great people.' The minute your people underperform it reflects on you, and more importantly, costs the business.

Think of an employee or customer who delivers great results. Think of one who doesn't. Now answer the following set of questions for both individuals. Add up the points for those you get right:

Do you know his or her	Score available	Your score
Age	5	
Address	5	
Partner's name	10	
Children's names, age, schools	20	
Last holiday	10	
Next holiday	5	
Main hobbies	10	
Partner's hobbies	5	
Career history	10	
Health record	5	
Make of car	5	
Parents' names	5	
TOTAL		

If you score more than 70, you are a people person. If you score less than 70, get to know your staff better before taking the test again.

When a coach tells me about a poor performer, my first instinct is to challenge the assertion by getting them to complete the test. It obliges them to look for their own contribution to such underperformance.

3.vii   THE WORLD SMILES WITH YOU

There is a technique that many coaches 'forget' to use, despite the fact that it costs nothing, takes no time to prepare or deliver and it makes *them* feel good at the same time. The technical term we use is – *smiling*.

A baby's eyes come into focus at around thirteen inches, roughly the distance between baby and mother during breast-feeding. One of the very first images we focus on is the smiling (if not a little tired) face of our mother. That image of two eyes and smiley face stays with us, deep down in our psyche. When someone smiles at us, an automatic response is triggered whether we like it or not. Something fires that distant memory and we smile back, we start to feel good whether we like it – or even notice it – or not. Research has found that the muscles around our mouth do react, albeit imperceptibly, when someone smiles at us. In other words, you really can turn that frown upside down.

The simple act of smiling can contribute to a winning mindset. I once heard Ben Zander, the conductor of the Boston Philharmonic Orchestra, explain how he responds to mistakes by using the 'F-word technique'. He stands tall, punches the air and says, 'How fascinating!' 'The ridiculousness of the response forces you – and others – to smile, before we begin the musical piece again.'

It can even help improve your memory. In one experiment

where studies were carried out to prove this assertion, psychologists asked volunteers to read two newspaper articles; one was a sad story and the other was a funny article written by the comedian Woody Allen. At the same time, they used a novel technique to make people feel happy and sad. Half of the group were asked to hold a pencil between their teeth without it touching their lips (go on, try it!). Automatically, your face is forced into a smile. The other half of the group were asked to put a pencil in their mouth and support it using only their lips (try that one, too). This forces the face into a frown. The purpose of these tasks makes an obvious point that when people smile or frown they immediately begin to feel happy or sad.

When both groups were asked to write down everything they remembered from the two articles, the 'happy' group remembered lots of details about both articles. The 'sad' group tended only to recall details about the sad article. The mood they had adopted had a huge impact on their memory.

EXERCISE – HOW THE BEST LEADERS BEGIN LESSONS

Here is a question for you: what's the single most important moment of a training session? Is it:

A. The initial explanation of the skill being taught?

B. The first couple of tries to implement the lesson taught?

C. The moment things click, when the learner 'gets it'?

I think the answer is D – none of the above.

There's a strong case to be made that the single most important moment of learning happens *before the lesson actually begins*.

We know that great coaches are extremely skilled at quickly

making a strong emotional connection with a learner, to create the bond of trust that is the foundation of all learning. But mere emotional connection isn't enough. The world is filled with extremely charismatic, fantastically entertaining leaders who are wonderful at creating a connection but not so great at actually improving performance.

Because it's not enough just to capture the learner's attention, you have to create intention: an urgent desire to work hard towards a concrete goal, towards some vision of a future self.

Science is giving us a peek inside that process. A group of researchers at Case Western University were able to look at the brains of learners in two situations. In the first, the coach was judgemental, and focused on negatives and the past. In the second, the coach was empathetic, and focused on the future.

With the judgemental coach, the visual cortex showed limited activity. With the positive, future-oriented coach, however, it lit up like a Christmas tree. The researchers concluded that this correlated with someone imagining their future.

The takeaway: when it comes to learning, brains work exactly like torches. It's not enough just to turn them on; they have to be pointed towards a target.

A few simple ways to do this:

Encourage visualization about future goals. Where do they want to be a month from now? A year? Five years?

Ruthlessly eliminate negative statements – especially judgements – that cause brains to shut down.

Count down towards some big future event. How many practices do we have left until the tournament? How many more lessons until the recital? How many days until the sales pitch? A calendar with Xs is a powerful tool.

When do you begin to think about your own impact on others?

3.viii FEELING, GOOD

In one exhaustive study of the English language, it was found that we have 558 words to describe emotions. 62 per cent of them are negative versus 38 per cent that refer to positive feelings. A pretty shocking discrepancy.

Test this yourself. When you next go into work, pick out some colleagues and simply say, 'Good morning.' What kind of response do you get? How do people respond to those two simple words? Typical examples are, 'Is it?', 'What's good about it?' or just a grunt. Then you must ask the one question you should never ask this type of person. 'How are you?' How do people respond to that question? For the next week, actively listen to people's responses. I have collected examples as varied as, 'Not so bad,' 'Surviving,' 'As good as they will let me be,' through to, 'I can't complain because no one listens to me anyway!' and my favourite, 'I've slipped into the seventh circle of Hell. You?' In contrast, notice how many positive responses you receive.

EXERCISE – BIDDING WARS

Managing your relationships with the significant people in your life is hugely important in helping you to create a winning mindset.

When I work with teams, I love to share the results of a study carried out in the early 1980s by psychologist John Gottman, who researched why some married couples stay together while others break up. Professor Gottman watched a series of couples closely as they went about their daily interactions and found that the answer he was looking for lay in the tiny details of those apparently inconsequential everyday exchanges. Banal as they seemed on the surface, at another level they were highly nuanced emotional exchanges.

Psychologists suggest that during the conversations we have with others, we make 'bids'. If that word makes you think of a poker game or an auction room, then you're on the right track. A bid is something that invites a response. Often, we don't notice how we are responding – until it is too late and the damage has been done.

The good news is that these microsignals (or 'bids') are very easy to spot and pretty easy to change if we know where to look and are willing to make the effort.

I once worked with a team that started poorly in the most important game of our season. The first ten minutes saw us come under a sustained attack and a number of players made repeated mistakes. Later, when we watched the game back, we heard the television commentators make a disparaging remark about the players' tendency to give high fives and slaps on the back after such errors. They mistakenly perceived this behaviour as a sign of weakness – betraying our nerves. We recognized it as a strength, which helped us to recover eventually and win.

Picture the scene. You see one of your teammates make a silly mistake, which costs the team a goal. The player acknowledges the mistake. At this moment, you have the chance to respond in one of three ways:

1. You could acknowledge the mistake and reply to it in a positive way: 'Come on. You're better than that.' Or, 'Don't

worry. Let's put it right.' In psychologist-speak, this is called a 'turning-towards response' or a 'response bid'.

2. You could acknowledge it in a negative way: 'You are useless. What are you doing?' or, 'How can you be so stupid?' Unsurprisingly, this is called an 'against bid'.

3. Or you could just stay silent: '!'. This is called an 'away from' bid. You don't engage with what they've done. In effect you ignore their bid.

Whatever response you choose will determine what they do next. But only the first one is likely to encourage them to make another bid. Faced with an 'against' or 'away from' response we are more likely to make an unconscious mental note not to bother next time.

The research shows that, when we use plenty of the 'turning towards' bids, the effects are enormous. Couples where the exchanges are predominantly 'towards' stay together. In fact, there is even a magic ratio. If we manage a ratio of 5:1 positive ('towards') responses to negative ('away from or against') responses, we are likely to have a healthy, long-lasting partnership.

Pay attention to the most important relationships that help you build a winning mindset. What is the ratio of bids?

This negative focus is not solely confined to our emotions, either. We generally seem to be wired to focus on the negative. A group of psychologists reviewed over two hundred newspaper articles and concluded that, for a wide range of human behaviour and perception, a general principle holds true: bad has a stronger influence than good.

This shouldn't be a surprise. In the world of the newsroom, the phrases 'good news' and 'bad news' pretty much have the opposite meanings to those they do in the real world. For a journalist, a 'good news' day is a day filled with mayhem, murder and mischief. A 'bad news' day is a day is when nothing in particular happens.

Understanding our 'bad is stronger than good' bias is critical for creating a winning mindset. Let's call it a problem focus. To see it, consider this situation:

Your child comes home with their school report. They show you the following grades:

English – A
Social Studies – A
Biology – C
Algebra – F
Maths – C
French – B

Is there a grade which immediately jumps out at you?

A recent Gallup poll looked at this very issue, in particular parents' focus on their children's best grades compared to the focus on their worst grades. The survey, carried out across multiple countries and cultures, found that the vast majority of parents in every country immediately focused on the F.

COUNTRY	Focused on As	Focused on Fs
UK	22%	52%
Japan	18%	43%
China	8%	56%
France	7%	87%
US	7%	77%
Canada	6%	83%

This brings us back to the importance of the 'turning-towards response'. When your brain sees that things are going well, it doesn't think much about them. But when things break, it snaps to attention and starts applying its problem-solving skills. So when your kids are achieving A and B grades, you don't think much about their good results. But when they receive a D or an F, you spring into action. It's weird when you think about it, isn't it?

Our ability to analyse problems can be extremely helpful, obviously – many issues get solved through such thorough analysis – but in situations where change is needed, too much analysis can doom the effort before it ever gets started. The human brain simply sees too many problems and spends too much time sizing them up.

'Positive response bids' are key here. When times are tough, our brains will instinctively see problems everywhere, and this is when analysis paralysis often kicks in. The thinking brain will mull over these issues indefinitely unless you give it a clear direction. That's why, to start to make progress on inspiring change, you need ways to direct it. Show it where to go, how to act, what destination to pursue. And that's why your language is so essential.

So how do you do this? The answer may be easier than you think.

In the kind of classical psychotherapy which television's greatest mobster Tony Soprano enjoyed, you and your therapist will explore your problem in great detail. What are its roots? Does it trace back to something in your childhood? You dig around your mind for a buried nugget of insight, something that may explain why you behave the way you do. This approach can take some time. A standard Freudian psychoanalysis might take five years' work with sessions once or twice a week before you finally establish that it was all your mum's fault.

In the late 1970s, a husband-and-wife therapist team, Steve de Shazer and Insoo Kim Berg, developed a different approach, called solutions-focused therapy. This new approach couldn't care less about your past. It doesn't dig around for clues about why you act the way you do. It doesn't delve into your childhood. All it cares about is the solution to your problems at hand. Solution-focused therapists use a common set of techniques for discovering potential questions which all change-inspirers would do well to note.

Early in the first session, after hearing the client explain their problem, the therapist will ask them to rate where they are on a scale of 0–10, nought being very unhappy and ten being perfectly content. After the client provides an answer, they will pose the Miracle Question: 'Can I ask you a strange question? Suppose you go to bed tonight and sleep well. Some time in the middle of the night, while you are sleeping, a miracle happens and all the troubles that brought you here are resolved. Your world is now a ten. When you wake up in the morning, what's the first small sign that would make you think, "Well, something must have happened – the problem is gone?"'

Solution-focused therapists teach their patients to focus on the first hints of the miracle – 'What's the first small sign you see that would make you think the problem was gone?' – because they want to avoid answers that are overly grand and unattainable, such as, 'My life is now wonderful, my bank account is full, I love my job and my marriage is great.'

Once they have helped patients identify specific and vivid signs of progress, they pivot to a second question, which is even more important. It's the Exception Question: 'When was the last time you saw a little bit of the miracle, even for just a short time?'

It's an effective tactic. What the therapist is trying to demonstrate, in a subtle way, is that the client is capable of solving their own problem. As a matter of fact, the client is offering proof that they have already solved it, at least in some circumstances.

Solution-focused therapists believe that there are exceptions to every problem and that those exceptions, once identified, can be carefully analysed, like the film footage of a sporting event. Bill Sweetenham, the man behind a clutch of swimming champions, uses this same technique when he works with young athletes. After a race, they will first study the athlete's best ever performance and then compare the last race with this, whilst Bill asks questions like, 'Let's replay that scene, where things were working well. What was happening? How did you behave?' And that analysis can point directly towards a solution that is, by definition, workable. After all, it has worked before.

A fitting contrast with this considered approach was demonstrated in December 2008, when Phil Brown was being hailed as the architect of Hull City's first ever promotion to England's top flight. His successes will always be recalled along with a now infamous half-time team talk he administered to his players at Manchester City's Etihad stadium.

After forty-five minutes, with his team already 4–0 down, Brown decided to dispense with convention. Rather than seeking out the safety of the dressing room in which to conduct his inquiry into his team's inadequacy, he instead joined his players on the pitch. Signalling them to follow him, he marched over to the corner where the Hull supporters were gathered and – after applauding the fans – sat the players in a circle and proceeded to conduct the sort of on-pitch dressing-down more generally associated with a Sunday-morning hangover-busting pub team than a bunch of professionals. As his face turned puce, he hectored and lectured, jabbing his finger ostentatiously to make his point very public indeed.

'Our 4,000 travelling fans deserved some kind of explanation for the first-half performance and it was difficult for me to do that from the confines of a changing room,' Brown said.

'We owed them an apology. I thought it was nice and cold and I thought I would keep the boys alive because they looked as if they were dead. It wasn't a knee-jerk reaction. It was definitely the right thing to do. If it meant bruising one or two egos so be it.'[30]

The problem for Brown was that few others observing his unusual man-management technique agreed. Most notably, his players.

Up until that point, those same players had performed well above expectations. Hull's record was: played 18, won 7, drawn 5 and lost 6 – a total of 26 points. In their next twenty games, they went on to win one more game, losing 14 and drawing 5. That's just 8 points. They escaped relegation by a single point.

The team captain, George Boateng, was unequivocal about the damage caused by this unconventional approach. 'That's when all the problems started. The team felt disrespected, didn't feel appreciated. We were sixth and we had lost two consecutive games,' he said. 'It did affect the team. We covered up the cracks but from that moment on we never seemed to recover. We didn't feel like we deserved to be treated like that. We were treated like a bunch of kids.'[31]

What Brown appeared to do was create a culture where he was spending a great deal of time trying to coach players who had gone reptilian. The player who feels vulnerable or exposed has got more important things going on in his mind than listening to an analysis of his mistakes in front of a captive audience.

Brown broke almost all the rules in this book and it ultimately cost him his job.

Once you have worked to satisfy the reptilian brain you can then move towards the limbic system.

EXERCISE – HOW TO FIND A SOLUTION

Get a partner to help you with this. One of you should think of an issue (a mild one – nothing too intense!) whilst the other acts as the interviewer.

The interviewer gets a copy of the questions below and asks them as set out in the script, with no additions or alterations. Both interviewer and interviewee should focus on how the questions make them feel. Then repeat the whole exercise using the questions in Set B.

Question Set A

Rate where you currently are on a scale of 1–10.
What is the problem?
Why are you not at ten?
How long have you had this problem?
Where does the fault lie?
Who's to blame the most?
What's your worst experience of it?
Why haven't you solved it?

Question Set B

Rate where you currently are on a scale of 1–10.
What do you want instead of the problem?
How will you know you've got this?
What else will improve as a result?
What resources do you already have to help?
What's something similar you've achieved?
What's the first step?

3.ix   LOSE YOUR ILLUSION

ENTERTAIN

'Entertain' is a useful word because it rhymes with 'contain' and 'explain', but it involves a lot more than simply doing a good old song-and-dance routine (although that helps sometimes). What we are talking about here is the use of positive emotions in a culture – *not as an optional extra* – but for very valid reasons.

We have already looked at the studies which show that the vast majority of us consider ourselves above-average drivers. In psychological terms, this belief is known as positive illusion. Our brains are positive illusion factories: only 2 per cent of middle managers believe that their leadership skills are below average. A full 25 per cent believe that they are in the top 1 per cent in their ability to get along with others. 94 per cent of college professors report doing above-average work. People think they are at a lower risk than their peers from heart attacks, cancer and food-related illnesses such as salmonella. Best of all, 60 per cent of people say that they are more likely than their peers to provide accurate self-assessments.

Positive illusions pose an enormous problem with regard to change, and thus a significant obstacle to creating a winning mindset. Before people can change, before they can move in a new direction, they have got to have their bearings. But positive illusions make it hard for us to orient ourselves – to get a clear picture of where we are and how we're doing. Yet how can we dispel people's illusions about themselves without raining down negativity on them?

The first thing to understand is that it's emotion that motivates us. In fighting for a winning mindset, we've got to find the feeling. But which feeling? Anger, hope, dismay, enthusiasm, fear, happiness, surprise? Will connecting with any old feeling do?

We often hear that people change only when a crisis compels them to, which implies that we have to create a sense of fear, anxiety or doom. This is the kind of belief that once prevailed amongst therapists, many of whom believed that alcoholics or drug addicts couldn't be helped until they hit rock bottom. This perceived need for a crisis has manifested itself in the term 'burning platform', a familiar phrase in organizational literature.

It refers to a horrific accident that happened in 1988 on the Piper Alpha oil platform in the North Sea. A gas leak triggered an explosion that ripped the rig in two. One newspaper report recounted, 'Those who survived had a nightmarish choice: to jump as far as 150 feet down into the fiery sea or face certain death on the disintegrating rig.'

Out of this human tragedy has emerged a rather ridiculous business cliché. When executives talk about a need for a 'burning platform', they mean, basically, that they need a way to scare their employees into changing. To create a burning platform is to paint such a gloomy picture of the current state of things that employees can't help but jump into the burning sea. In short, the 'burning platform' is supposed to be a great, uplifting tale for people!

Health educators have been using this act for many years.

Remember the adverts showing photos of smokers' black, gnarled lungs? There is no question that negative emotions are a motivational force but what, exactly, are they motivating?

In 1998, after psychologists had spent decades studying negative emotions, the psychologist Barbara Fredrickson wrote a provocative paper called 'What Good Are Positive Emotions?' The paper became a classic. It has been referenced far more often than a typical psychology paper and it helped to fuel the rise of the discipline of positive psychology, which has yielded many popular books on happiness.

As the title suggests, positive emotions are a bit of a puzzle. Unlike negative emotions, they don't seem engineered to produce particular actions, such as punching or fleeing or avoiding. If your body is tensing up as you walk through a dark alley, your mind isn't likely to wander over to tomorrow's to-do list. Fear, anger and disgust give us sharp focus – which is the same thing as putting on blinkers.

Fredrickson argues that, in contrast with the narrowing effects of negative emotions, positive emotions are designed to 'broaden and build' our thoughts and actions. Joy, for example, makes us want to play. Play doesn't have a script, it broadens the kind of things we consider doing. We become willing to fool around, to explore or invent new activities. And because joy encourages us to play, we are building resources and skills. For instance, kids learn physical skills through the rough-and-tumble of play; they learn to work with objects by playing with toys and blocks and crayons; they learn to get along with others by pretending to be animals or superheroes.

The positive emotion of interest broadens what we want to investigate. When we are interested, we want to get involved, to learn new things, to tackle new experiences. We become more open to new ideas. The positive emotion of pride, when we achieve a personal goal, broadens the kind of tasks we contemplate for the future, encouraging us to pursue even bigger goals.

Most of the big problems we encounter in organizations or society are ambiguous and evolving. They don't often look like burning platform situations, where we need to buckle down and execute a hard game plan. To solve bigger, more ambiguous problems, we need to encourage open minds, creativity and hope.

3.x   FUN, FUN, FUN

Have you ever had a look at the lonely hearts adverts at the back of your local newspaper? Next time you get an opportunity, have a quick look at them. (If you're in a relationship, make sure that you are alone when you do this – or at least explain to your partner what you are doing.)

One common term you will find in the majority of the adverts is a request for potential partners to be in possession of a GSOH. For those of you not familiar with dating jargon, this stands for a Good Sense of Humour and it tends to be a quality which most people look for in an ideal mate. Most of us don't like people who are too stuffy or serious as they tend to put a dampener on everything, yet when was the last time you saw a request for a GSOH included in a job advert?

Did you know that, on average, a child laughs about 400 times a day? In contrast, an adult will only laugh about fifteen times. Did that just wipe a smile off your face? Sorry.

What happens to the other 385 laughs? Why is it that when we step into the grown-up world, a sense of humour becomes a rare commodity? Too often, we are preoccupied with our own worries, stresses and the pressures of our lives and so the importance of fun doesn't even merit a mention, yet the relationship between high performance and fun is critical.

Research carried out at Colorado University suggests that playing is more than just about having fun. It is through playing that all animals, including humans, learn to take on and master life's challenges.

Fun is just one of the positive emotions that we can use in a high-performing culture (although it is a hugely important one for young people). Whenever researchers ask children what they are looking for in a teacher, two things always seem to come up: 1) a sense of humour; 2) consistency.

Suspense, intrigue, curiosity, novelty, surprise, awe, passion, compassion, empathy, hitting goals, discovery, competition, overcoming obstacles, achievement, a sense of growth – all of these have a vital part to play in opening up the learning brain.

Normally our brain provides us with structure and places barriers between ideas and concepts. This is essential because it keeps us safe and allows us to operate efficiently. When you have fun and are relaxed and playful, your brain starts connecting seemingly detached ideas and starts to see situations from a different perspective. This is the best state to be in when you want to begin creating the unexpected.

Try to guess which common phrases these picture word-puzzles suggest. For example:

YOU JUST ME – represents the phrase 'just between me and you'. Now that you have the general idea, try these:

HEAD
HEELS

R|E|A|D|I|N|G

. _____ RANGE

In case you haven't solved them, the answers are 'head over heels', 'reading between the lines' and 'point-blank range'.

These puzzles were used in a study to understand how play

can impact on performance. Volunteers were presented with the word-puzzles and asked to solve them as quickly as possible. After a fifteen-minute break where they could relax, the same volunteers were able to improve their scores by 30 per cent. They hadn't been consciously working on the problems during their break but this rest period had helped their brains to view the puzzles in a new and helpful way.

Even in times of crisis, having fun should be encouraged as it helps release tension. Sir Ernest Shackleton, one of the greatest adventurers of all time, knew this and used games which were designed to promote camaraderie, hope and fortitude when his ship *Endurance* became stuck in the Antarctic ice. Competitions involving racing dogs and the organizing of variety shows all helped maintain morale during the nine long, dark months they were trapped, and were later cited as an important reason why all twenty-two members of his crew survived.

EXERCISE – HOW TO MAKE LEARNING FUN

If you are a parent, you have probably pondered how great it would be if we could get both children and adults to learn everything as fast and efficiently as we learn video games. Imagine if your team could learn the new sales process as quickly as they get to grips with *Angry Birds*.

With that in mind, here's a video-game term that might apply: replay value. It refers to how much a user wants to play a game over and over. You know the feeling – the irresistible itch to repeat a game just one more time, and just one more time after that.

Though the motivation feels internal, in fact replay value doesn't come from the user; it comes from the design of the game itself. Games that provide lots of roles, lots of paths, lots of possible outcomes, have high replay value – people love to play them, and get addicted. Games with few roles, few paths, few outcomes have low replay value; people play them once and then quit.

If you look at the practice routines of those who possess the winning mindset, you'll find they have high replay value. They are designed in such a way that you naturally want to do them again, and again, and again. For example:

- Bubba Watson, who won the US Masters golf tournament with an 'impossible' curving shot from the woods, learned to control the ball by hitting a small plastic ball in his yard when he was a small boy. The game young Bubba invented was to see if he could go around his house clockwise, then turn around and do it anticlockwise.

- Earl Scruggs, one of the greatest banjo players who ever lived, practised his sense of timing by playing with his brothers. The game went like this: the brothers would all start a song, then walk off in different directions, still playing. At the end of the song they'd come together to see if they'd stayed in time. Then do it again. And again.

- Pretty much any skateboarding or snowboarding practice has a high replay value: think of how the sides of a half-pipe or ramp literally funnel the athlete into the next move. No wonder they learn so fast: the replay value in most gravity sports is off the charts.

The larger pattern here is that practices with high replay value tend to be practices the learners design themselves. One of the reasons the learners can't help but repeat them is that they have a sense of ownership and investment – they're not robots executing someone else's drill; they're players immersed in their own fun, addictive game.

Which leads to an interesting question: how else can we raise the replay value in our world to create a winning mindset? Here are a few ideas.

1. *Keep score* – and I don't mean on the scoreboard. Pick exactly what you want to learn, and count it, or time it. Sales people could count the number of times they deliver a pitch perfectly; accounts team could count the time it takes to do the books.

2. *Provide multiple roles.* Basically, switch places a lot. Everybody should periodically trade positions, to experience it from a new angle and come to a deeper (and more addictive) understanding. Salesperson becomes client; presenter becomes listener.

3. *Set near/far goals.* The most effective goals have two levels, one near and one far. The near goal is today's immediate goal; the far goal is an ideal performance far in the future which serves as a North Star. Putting both goals out there, as video games do so well, adds a dose of sugar to the practice process, and keeps people coming back for more.

3.xi   CURIOUSER AND CURIOUSER

Whether we like it or not, we can't help but be curious. It is a survival instinct. Put a laboratory rat in a new environment (that is, take it from one cage and put it into another) and it will naturally explore. Where is the food, where are the exits, where might danger come from? We work in a similar way and we can draw students out of themselves, whether they like it or not, by actively engaging their curiosity.

Imagine it's your job to educate incoming rookies to America's National Basketball Association about the dangers of AIDS. NBA players are young men – often under twenty-one. And they are sudden celebrities, with all the attention that accompanies this new-found fame. They've heard about AIDS their whole lives and so the risk is not that they are unaware of AIDS, the risk is that the circumstances of their lives prompt them to drop their guard for a night. How do you make the threat of AIDS credible and immediate?

A few weeks before the NBA season begins, all the rookie players are required to meet in New York for a mandatory orientation and induction session. They're essentially locked in a hotel for six days with no access to the outside world. The rookies are taught about life in the big leagues – everything from how to deal with the media to how to make sensible investments with their new wealth.

One year, despite the intense secrecy surrounding the

induction, a group of female fans staked out the location. On the first night of the orientation, they were hanging out in the hotel bar and restaurant, dressed to be noticed. The players were pleased by the attention. There was a lot of flirting, and the players made plans to meet up with some of the women later in the week.

The next morning, when the rookies showed up for their session, they were surprised to see the female fans at the front of the room. The women introduced themselves again, one by one. 'Hi, I'm Sheila and I'm HIV positive.' 'Hi, I'm Donna and I'm HIV positive.'

Suddenly the talk about AIDS clicked for the rookies. They saw how life could get out of control, how a single night could cause a lifetime of regret.

In contrast, the National Football League's orientation in the same year saw every rookie put a condom on a banana. Later, two women – former football groupies – talked about how they would go about seducing players, hoping to get pregnant.

The women's sessions were powerful but which would be more likely to change your behaviour? Hearing about someone who fooled someone else or feeling fooled yourself? People's feelings can have a disproportionate impact on their behaviour, which psychologists refer to as 'the *aha* moment'.

3.xii   THE POWER OF NOVELTY

Who was the first American president?

Most people would be able to answer, George Washington.

But if I ask who was the forty-fourth American president, a lot of people wouldn't be able to answer. You can't remember all the American presidents, and what order they came in. Why would you?

You can certainly remember the names of a few American presidents: Lincoln, Roosevelt, Kennedy, Nixon, Bush. But who cares what number they were?

Most people don't know and can't be bothered to know who was the forty-fourth American president.

Now suppose I asked who was the first black American president? Everyone would answer, Barack Obama. You know that immediately because he has a definite point of difference.

So he stands out.

Actually, Barack Obama is also the forty-fourth president, but no one remembers that because that positioning has no point of difference.

The advertising guru Dave Trott uses this example to illustrate how novelty is another element of an entertaining culture. Because we have no memory of something novel, the brain has to use higher areas in order to make sense of it. For us to remember things, they need to be 'novel' and 'high contrast'.

When things stand out they lure us in and they stick in our memories whether we like it or not.

The galvanizing effect on our motivation and memory of outstanding events is a phenomenon known as the Von Restorff effect, named after the psychiatrist and paediatrician Hedwig von Restorff. When faced with something that we don't expect, the brain seems to take a snapshot of what was happening just before it and immediately after it.

Examples of the Von Restorff effect can be seen in the death of Princess Diana, or the 9/11 attack on the World Trade Center. The emotional reaction caused by the nature of an event is what is involved in making an event memorable. Short-term memory (making it to the telephone from the directory with the number still in your head, the fact that it's your turn to take out the wheelie bin, or the bit of background music you heard five minutes ago) is predominantly a fleeting chemical-electrical flash in our brains, certainly transitory to our conscious brain. A long-term memory, however, is an actual physical change in the very structure of our brain. How does the brain know what to make into a long-term memory and what to let pass as a brief flash? The answer would appear to be the chemical triggers released by our emotions. Without emotions there are no – or at least far fewer – triggers to send the message to the brain: this stuff is important, remember it.

3.xiii   THE FOUR PRINCIPLES

In summary, many leaders focus first on skills and ability to perform. Emotionally intelligent leaders, on the other hand – those who build a winning mindset – focus first on creating a sense of belonging. A conventional leader asks: what can I do to help them win? An emotionally intelligent leader asks: what can I do to help us nurture connections and create a culture? A conventional leader views his team through the lens of performance. An emotionally intelligent leader views his team through the lens of relationships – which, not coincidentally, tends to make the lessons all the more effective. People work hard for a team. They work even harder for a team that truly feels like family.

You may call these 'soft skills' but, as this chapter shows, they are anything but 'soft' in their application. They're the product of an emotionally intelligent approach that has four core principles:

1) seeking to create belonging by establishing a clear, vivid identity;

2) creating an environment of safety and trust by talking openly about emotions;

3) giving value and connecting in ways beyond the business, field or classroom by leading the whole person, not just the athlete;

4) strengthening relationships by sharing control of results through honesty and trust.

So simple, and so powerful.

It is then, and only then, that we can complete our journey from 'contain' to 'entertain' to 'explain'. Here, arriving at the neocortex, we can now work with the intellectual processing required to creating a winning culture.

THE FOURTH STEP

PRACTICAL

If you can't explain what you're doing to a six-year-old, you probably don't understand it yourself.
Albert Einstein

4.i   A BUSY MAN

For many football fans, it's a difficult task to describe Gary Neville in one word. For nineteen years, when he occupied the right full back berth at the all-conquering Manchester United, he was widely considered by non-United fans as a villain, an irritant or, more likely, something requiring an excessive use of the asterisk key.

However, since he has retired from playing, his analysis and commentary for television has been widely acclaimed and has helped to change the public perception of him.

Other TV pundits have often been criticized for, as one reviewer put it, 'offering little more than bad shirts and tired clichés', stating the obvious and adding little new to the football discussion.

Neville, who is also England's assistant manager, says: 'People don't just want telling that the ball has ended up in the back of the net, they want to know why it has ended up in the back of the net. They want to know who made the mistake, why they made the mistake, how they made the mistake and how to rectify the mistake.'

This is where Neville has excelled, offering passionate opinion, considered insight and the finest deadpan one-liners. 'Sunderland haven't made one run forward,' he muttered during a recent match. 'It's winding me up and I don't even want them to win.'

Neville prepares for each game by focusing on a few ideas taken from the weekend's games that he'll pitch as discussion topics for the evening's show. 'I've always been a "talker",' he grins. 'That's no secret. Sir Alex Ferguson once said to me: "I bet your tongue says a prayer when you go to sleep at night."' He adds an important caveat: 'I'm interested in substance. Everyone has an opinion in football, but to make people trust you, you've got to have the facts to back that opinion up.'[1]

A big part of Neville's appeal as a pundit is his frankness. In a sport renowned for its superhumanly tedious sound bites, where 'The lads gave 110 per cent' constitutes a broadcast-worthy interview, his tendency to say what he really thinks is refreshing.

When Stuart Lancaster took over as England Rugby Union head coach in 2012, he invited guest speakers in to enlighten the players about how a world-class environment can be created. Gary Neville addressed the squad and asked them to look at the person sitting next to them.

'Think about whether they are simply happy to be here. If you don't believe that they want to win as much as you, get up and go and sit next to someone who does,' he challenged them. 'Playing for my country was not enough for me. Winning for my country was.'

One current England international footballer told me that Neville's dual role of commentating on players he then trains for England is not an issue. 'He is transparent. He won't change what he said on telly when he meets you. He sits down and explains what his reasons were and how to fix the issue.'

Neville embraces this transparency. 'With me, how I am on telly is how I am in normal life. I'm just . . .' He breaks off, searching for the right word. 'Northern.'

Sometimes a straight answer or an unflinching analysis

of a situation, be it positive or negative, is essential for the creation of a winning mindset. You don't have to be a bluff northerner to perfect this technique.

4.ii   ABSTRACT VERSUS PRACTICAL, EXPERT VERSUS NOVICE

But if, as Gary Neville has demonstrated, practical language is so powerful, why do we so easily slip into abstraction?

The reason is simple: because the difference between an expert and a novice is the ability to think abstractly. Because, by definition, experts know their subject in intimate detail, it is easy to lose awareness that we are actually talking like an expert. It can start to feel unnatural or patronizing to speak in basic terms and metaphors about subject matters we've known intimately for years. But if we are willing to make the effort, as Gary Neville has demonstrated, we'll see the rewards: our audience will understand what we are saying and remember it. Imparting knowledge without jargon or overcomplication is one of the key skills any expert must acquire if they are to pass on their expertise. And doing so in a practical way is imperative – because what we want are practical results. The good news is that embracing simplicity and practicality can in itself be a very simple and practical matter – a habit easily acquired and highly valuable.

Research has shown that in a courtroom setting, jurors are often struck by lawyers' personalities and factual details and the courtroom rituals. Meanwhile, a judge's role is to avoid being swayed by such matters and weigh the current case against the abstract lessons of past cases and legal precedent.

It's the same in the world of elite sport. Great coaches are the bridge between these two worlds. They understand the nuances but are capable of explaining it in simple terms. Think of Jürgen Gröbler's one-word commands – 'He would say very little during outings. Out of the river, he might utter one prized word, such as "Acceleration,"' recounts Tim Foster – or Alex Ferguson's three-word team talks.

Bruce Abernethy, an associate dean for research at the University of Queensland, has researched elite athlete decision-making processes and his findings show that elite athletes need less time and less information to know what will happen in the future. Almost without knowing it, they zero in on critical information.

'We've tested expert batters in cricket where all they see is the ball, the hand and wrist, and down to the elbow, and they still do better than random chance,' Abernethy says. 'It looks bizarre, but there's significant information between the hand and arm where experts get cues for making judgements.'[2]

Top tennis players could discern from the minuscule preserve shifts of an opponent's torso whether a shot was going to their forehand or backhand, whereas average players had to wait to see the motion of the racket, costing invaluable response time. Ivan Lendl claims that much of his input in helping Andy Murray record a Grand Slam success was like fine-tuning a car. Rob Castorri – director of Lendl's tennis academy in the US, whose sister Alexis is Murray's sports psychologist – says, 'I have witnessed their training and what I saw was very simple. Ivan takes a very backseat approach. He lets Andy hit and his input is very subtle, but very positive. He is a man of very few words. He chooses them carefully, and he embodies them in a positive outlook. He points out the good things and then coming in with his subtle suggestions of ways to do things.'[3] Not only does Lendl's coaching echo our tripwire technique of 'guided discovery', it also shows that even a fellow expert – a top tennis player – benefits from relative simplicity in the imparting of expertise.

When Murray won at Wimbledon in 2013, Lendl communicated to him by doing nothing, or almost nothing. Murray even claims to have learned to differentiate between one version of 'nothing' and another. 'Ivan is so poker-faced, so stoic and he never claps,' Chris Evert, a tennis star of the 1970s and 1980s, has said. 'If Andy played a good shot and looked over at Ivan, he would receive a look that said, "OK, keep going." If Andy was down, Ivan would look at him in a way that said, "You can get out of this."'[4]

Pro boxers have a similar skill. A Muhammad Ali jab took a mere forty milliseconds to arrive at the face of a victim standing a foot and a half away. Without anticipation based on body movements, Ali's opponents would have been down in round one, hit flush by every punch. Ali's skill at disguising the trajectory of a punch, and thus confounding the opponent's anticipation, often meant they were finished a few rounds later anyway. Angelo Dundee, Ali's coach throughout his whole professional career, told me that during the minute-long break between rounds, he would never use the time to communicate more than one message.

As these examples illustrate, often a simple, practical message is all it takes.

No one is born with the anticipatory skills required of an elite athlete. When Bruce Abernethy studied the eye-movement patterns of elite and novice badminton players, he saw that novices were already looking at the correct area of the opponent's body, they just did not have the cognitive database needed to extract information from it. 'If they did,' Abernethy says, 'it would be a hell of a lot easier to coach them to become an expert. You could just say, "Look at the arm." Or for a baseball batter the real advice wouldn't be, "Keep your eye on the ball," it would be, "Watch the shoulder." But actually, if you tell them that, it makes good players worse.'[5]

This database can only be built through years of rigorous practice. This is why many pro cricket teams are moving away from using bowling machines, because they don't train the body recognition skills that hitters need for anticipation. Without this database, every athlete is a chess master facing a random board, stripped of the information that allows them to predict the future.

Novices perceive practical details as exactly that, practical details. Experts perceive practical details as symbols of patterns and insights into what they have learned through years of experience. And, because they are capable of *seeing* a higher level of insight, they naturally want to talk on a higher level. They want to talk about chess strategies, not about bishops moving diagonally. Great coaches resist that urge when they are talking to their teams. This is the key point for us to remember here: what matters is not only what we know, but how simply and clearly we can communicate it to those who need to grasp it in order to succeed.

Great coaches understand that while they themselves are able to understand what they mean, abstraction makes it harder to understand an idea and to remember it. It also makes it harder to coordinate our activities with others, who may interpret the abstraction in very different ways. Practical language helps us avoid these problems. This is perhaps the most important lesson of all.

Let me show you how abstraction works.

In June 1956, Horace Miner, Professor of Anthropology at the University of Michigan, published an article that sent a shockwave through the anthropology community.

The journal in which he wrote, the *American Anthropologist*, was already accustomed to colourful studies of exotic tribes: the same issue contained articles about kinship networks among the Araucanian Indians of Chile and lineage in the Mundurucu society of Brazil. But Miner's latest study was something else. He was describing a tribe, the Nacirema, for the very first time.

No one, it seemed, had written or even heard about this tribe before.

It wasn't just that the Nacirema were new to the study. Their tribal practices seemed particularly bizarre, too; practices that were so unusual, and so shocking, said Miner, that they might even be described as 'an example of the extremes to which human behaviour can go'.

The Nacirema were gripped by magic. Their days were marked by a parade of rituals based on the human body. This in itself was not exceptional: countless tribes performed body rites, from fasting to tattooing. But what stood out about this tribe was their wacky belief about bodies.

To the Nacirema, the human body was fundamentally ugly and prone to decay. Their every ritual was dedicated to reversing the process at all costs. Some of the steps they took to do this verged on the barbaric. The men lacerated their faces with sharp instruments; the women baked their heads in small ovens. They also displayed a curious preoccupation with the mouth, which they would ritually fill with hog hairs and holy powders. It followed that the Nacirema society conferred special status on the wise elders – the medicine men, the herbalists – who provided them with the charms and magical potions to stave off decay.

The spectre of physical deterioration was not the only thing that preoccupied the tribespeople: their very peculiar take on aesthetics also seemed to dominate their lives. The Nacirema were consumed by disgust for the body's natural state. When a member of the tribe was too fat, they performed a ritual fast to become thin; when a member of the tribe was too thin, they held a ceremonial feast to become fat. The female breast was singled out for particular concern: the Nacirema used outlandish body-modification techniques to make women's breasts 'large if they are small, and smaller if they are large'.

Given the burdens they have imposed on themselves, Miner concluded, it is astonishing that the Nacirema have survived for so long.

What have you learned about the Nacirema?

That they are barbaric, masochistic? That they have questionable values? Do you see them as primitive, foreign, strange?

If these are the words that spring to mind, you're on the same page as anthropology students today when they are given the study.

The thing is – and forgive me if you've already cottoned on to this – the Nacirema isn't actually some weird, primitive tribe: it is 'American' spelt backwards.

Now that you are in on Miner's joke, you can see that the behaviour and practices you found so strange are actually rather ordinary. When the men lacerated their faces, they were shaving; when the women put their heads in small ovens, they were under hairdryers in a salon (this is the 1950s we're talking about). When the Nacirema filled their mouths with hog hairs and magical powders, they were brushing their teeth; when they performed ritual fasts or feasts, they were watching their weight.

So why have so many people from the 1950s to the present been tricked by Miner's study?

In part this relates to how deferential we are to those who are labelled as 'experts'. Miner was President of the American Anthropological Association, his article appeared in its house journal, and in it he deployed fellow academics to add weight to his assertions: Professors Linton, Malinowski and Murdock were all cited. But it was also down to something else.

The answer lies primarily in the power of language, the ability of carefully chosen words to shape our reactions, change the way we think and influence our decisions. From Gary Neville's punditry to the great coaches' team talks, we can see that it is crucial always to remember that effective guidance is marked out by a kind of intelligent simplicity, where knowing what to leave out is just as important as knowing what to say.

One coach suggested to me that when planning his sessions, he channels his 'inner Basil Fawlty'. 'Do you remember the scene in *Fawlty Towers*,' he reminded me, 'where Basil suggests that if his wife, Sybil, should ever participate on *Mastermind*, her specialist subject should be "the bleeding obvious"?'

Think about Professor Miner's choice of language. He introduced his subjects using the word 'tribe'; and not any old tribe, but one with 'particularly unusual aspects'. Throughout the text he used words like 'rites', 'exorcism', 'natives', 'body rituals' to further convey a sense of otherness, primitiveness and foreignness, when what he was really describing was the American citizen.

It's a simple technique, but it's very powerful. With just a few words, Miner takes the reader a long way from Manhattan or Kansas City. Unfamiliar language, unfamiliar reference points make the local and known feel distant and alien. To show us what we already know from a new vantage point is a very effective device for achieving this intelligent simplicity.

How easily manipulated we are. And with the right guidance, how usefully so, to our own benefit.

EXERCISE – THREE MOST IMPORTANT WORDS

Kids love to declare that they're not good at something. They usually do it just after they try something new and challenging, and they say it with finality, as if issuing a verdict.

'I'm not good at maths!' or, 'I'm not good at football.'

At that moment, our normal parental/teacher/coach instinct is to fix the situation; to boost the child up by saying something persuasive like, 'Oh yes you are!' which never works, because it puts the kid in the position of actively defending their ineptitude. It's a lose–lose situation.

It's the same with adults. I have been in so many businesses where the resident cynics announce that a new change is doomed to failure. 'We don't do change here,' I was once told.

So here's another idea: ignore the instinct to fix things. Don't try to persuade. Instead, simply add the word 'yet'.

You add the 'yet' quietly, in a matter-of-fact tone, as if you were describing the weather or the law of gravity.

'I'm not good at maths' becomes 'You're not good at maths yet.'

'I'm not good at football' becomes 'You're not good at football yet.'

'I'm not good at IT' becomes 'You're not good at IT yet.'

The message is: of course you're not good – because you haven't worked at it. But when you do, you will be good.

At first glance, it seems silly – how can just one word make a difference?

The answer has to do with the way our brains are wired to respond to self-narratives. That's where Dr Carol Dweck and her work on mindset come in. Through a series of remarkable experiments, she's shown how small changes in language – even a few words – can affect performance.

Her core insight is that the way we frame questions of talent matters hugely. If we put the focus on 'natural ability', kids tend to be less engaged and put in less effort (after all, if it's just a genetic lottery, then why should I try?). When we place the focus on effort, however, kids — and adults — tend to try harder and are more engaged.

How about you? Is your language fixed or do you leave yourself open to the possibility of change?

4.iii   HOW TO LEAD LIONS

Sir Ian McGeechan is regarded as a coaching legend, not just in his chosen sport of rugby union.

He started his career as a PE teacher whilst playing for Headingley and Scotland but his name is synonymous with the British Lions, for whom he played in the two unbeaten tours of South Africa in 1974 and New Zealand in 1977. Switching to coaching, he led the Lions to victory in 1989 against Australia, 1993's series defeat to New Zealand and the magnificent victory of 1997 over world champions South Africa, whilst also leading his native Scotland to the Grand Slam in 1990 – a feat that has not been equalled for a quarter of a century since.

In *The Grudge*, Tom English's book on that 1990 triumph, McGeechan describes himself as a Yorkshire Scot – 'Mean twice over!' English observes that he speaks without embellishment, like any good Scot, like any good Yorkshireman. He's both.

Sir Ian McGeechan presided over what is widely regarded as the best British Lions touring party, the 2009 British Lions. Before they set off for the eight-week tour of South Africa, McGeechan gathered his forty-four players together.

'There were players in the room that had spent the previous couple of years in competition with each other,' McGeechan recalls. 'There is always a certain level of wariness when they enter the room, still sticking to their own familiar colleagues.'

As they sat down, McGeechan welcomed them and then immediately directed a question to them.

'You've all been members of great teams,' he began. 'That is partly why you have been selected for the honour of playing for the British and Irish Lions.' The players' eyes bored into the head coach as he spoke. 'I have my own experiences of this too but I am interested in learning from you. What kind of behaviours do great teams demonstrate?' he asked.

His words hung in the air. There was an initial reluctance to break the silence. McGeechan smiled warmly. He looked his players in the eye and nodded, encouraging them to participate.

Slowly, warily a hand went up. 'Er, hard work,' said one. McGeechan immediately scribbled the words in his notepad. 'Good,' he said, 'any more?'

'Focus,' shouted another voice. 'Working together,' the next. 'A common goal.' Slowly, and then with greater confidence, players began to offer their own assessment of the behaviours which separated the winners from the losers. 'Trust', 'Toughness', 'Discipline', came next. McGeechan dutifully noted them all.

When the words started to repeat themselves and then come more slowly, the Scottish coach raised his hands to signal that the question had been answered satisfactorily. 'That is good,' he acknowledged. 'I'd like to look at them in more detail, if I may?'

The players stared back at him and offered their wordless assent.

'If we are going to perform at our best during this tour, it's important that we define what our best looks like and the behaviours you have offered are very helpful to start with,' he began. 'I'd therefore like to look at some of those behaviours in greater detail. Let's start with, "Trust".'

The players continued to look at McGeechan with a quiet intensity, eager to make a strong first impression through their respect and concentration on his opening address.

'How important, on a scale of 1–10, would you rate "Trust" in a high-performing team?' he asked.

There was a buzz of discussion amongst the players before they began to offer their assessment. All of them gave it the maximum rating of ten.

McGeechan jotted the responses down before he looked up, directing his gaze around the gathered athletes. 'I would like you to take a moment to have a look at your forty-four playing colleagues gathered here in this room,' he instructed, 'and then decide which is the person whom you trust' – he paused for a beat – 'the least.'

There was a long moment of silence as the words began to sink in. McGeechan allowed it to settle and then continued. 'It doesn't matter why. You may not know them or you may know them too well. Decide who it is, because I am going to give you two minutes to approach them and look them in the eye before explaining your reasons.'

The quiet concentration which had enveloped the Penny-hill Park meeting room was broken by nervous laughter, uncomfortable shifting in seats and a low rumble of hushed conversation. No one moved from their position to complete the task. The discomfort was palpable.

Eventually, McGeechan called the room to order. 'Gentlemen,' he began, 'let me just remind you of what we have, so far, discussed.

'I asked you for the behaviours of high-performing teams and you told me that trust was important. In fact, you rated trust as essential. Do you agree?' The players nodded their agreement. 'All I have done,' he said, 'is to think of the most extreme manifestation of testing this behaviour.

'At the start of this camp, it is evident that we don't have the levels of trust required to be a great team, yet.' He added, 'But over the next few weeks, we are going to create an environment where trust is central to our success. An environment where you can offer direct feedback to those who are threatening it and an environment where it will be accepted.

'Trust isn't merely a word,' he concluded. 'It is a real behaviour that will be central to our success.'

He later reflected on his approach. 'It's not rocket science, winning big Test matches. I've never got very complicated because players under pressure don't remember too many instructions and I wasn't about to start now.'[6]

EXERCISE – MASTERY LANGUAGE

If you were to survey a million leaders, parents, coaches and teachers about their biggest barrier to creating a winning mindset and improving performance, most would mention motivation.

Because, while science has made many advances in recent years, motivation remains an area of profound mystery. How does it start? Why does it vanish? How do we sustain it in our families, our teams, our businesses?

Part of the problem could lie in one word: practice.

Words are signals, and the signal that the word 'practice' sends is 'THIS WILL PROBABLY BE BORING'. 'Practice' tells a story of dutifulness, obligation, of putting in required hours. It's vague, devoid of spark or specificity.

Now go and do your practice. I've got to go to practice. We have practice all week.

That's why I think many smart leaders are starting to avoid

the word 'practice' and replace it with words that tell a more precise, motivating story.

Many music teachers avoid the word 'practice', and recommend using the word 'play' instead. So instead of saying, 'It's time for you to practise piano,' you say, 'Time to play piano.' A small change, perhaps, but an important one, because it puts the focus on the action itself.

Jim McGuinness, the coach of Ireland's outstandingly successful Gaelic football team, County Donegal, also avoids the P-word and instead talks about his team's 'rehearsals'.

I love that. McGuinness's team doesn't aim to 'practise' in some general way – they rehearse specific plays over and over, so that they can hit their marks with timing and precision, exactly as an actor or musician might. Exactness is the goal; so 'rehearsal' is the right word.

I've heard some musicians refer to their practices as 'workouts', which I like because it implies a muscular specificity. 'I need a couple more workouts on the new guitar solo,' is far better than, 'I need to practise that new guitar solo.'

All these terms work because they refocus the soft generality of 'practice' on something more precise and useful.

They also underline a larger fact: motivation isn't about handing out group hugs and high fives, or telling people that they're awesome. It's about finding the right words to convey the harder, more precise truth about the process, the goal, and where to put the effort.

How could you begin to describe your preparation?

4.iv   PRACTICAL SCIENCE

So how do we avoid falling into the trap of abstraction?

On the Internet, one satirical site features a 'business buzz-word generator', where readers can produce their own business buzzwords by combining one word from three columns, which yields phrases like 'reciprocal cost-based re-engineering', 'customer-oriented visionary paradigm', and 'strategic logistical values', which all sound eerily plausible. When we visit our doctor, we may come away equally baffled; but medical jargon at least refers to something specific and technical, even when we don't understand. The trouble with business buzzwords is that they are often so vague as to be meaningless, and we cannot build tangible results on incomprehensible ideas.

Language is often abstract, but life is not abstract. Teachers teach students about battles and animals and books. Doctors repair problems with our stomachs, backs and hearts. Companies create software, build planes, and distribute newspapers; they build cars that are faster, cheaper or fancier than last year's.

Even the most abstract business strategy must eventually show up in the tangible actions of human beings. It is easier to understand those tangible actions than to understand an abstract strategy statement – just as it is easier to understand a children's fable than some abstract commentary on the human psyche.

But the evidence isn't just anecdotal. There's science in the mix as well.

Research on the psychological principle of cognitive fluency, for example – how easy or difficult an object, argument or concept is to think about – demonstrates something time and again. The easier something is to understand, the more profitable, the more pleasurable, the more persuasive – in general, the more *positive* – we seem to find it. This principle has been shown to work on the stock market.

One famous study conducted several years ago found that if you invest in companies with pronounceable ticker codes (like GOOG for Google), you stand to make 10 per cent more profit after *just one day's trading* than if you invest in companies with unpronounceable codes (e.g. RDO).

In a similar vein, another study listed the features of a product in either an easy-to-read or a difficult-to-read typeface. Guess what the researchers found? Easy-to-read typefaces pretty much doubled the number of people willing to purchase the product. Again, this underlines the importance of two of our steps – simplicity and emotion – and the link between them.

When we look at objects that are easy to pick up, for example, we produce microscopic smiles invisible to the naked eye. These imperceptible changes in facial muscle tone can be measured by a technique called electromyography and are *not* present when we look at objects that are difficult to pick up.

The key, therefore, is to make sure that your words are related to tangible, practical actions.

What makes something 'practical'?

If you can imagine something with your senses, it is practical. A Rolls-Royce engine is concrete. 'High performance' is abstract. Most of the time, practicality boils down to specific people doing specific things. When Fred Smith, the founder of

FedEx delivery service, thought that the slogan 'World-class customer service' was abstract, he introduced speed-walking training for all his drivers, to create a practical idea of the sense of urgency with which they should treat all customer parcels.

It was Colin Powell, the former US secretary of state, who said that, 'If you can't explain what you are doing to your mother, maybe you don't really understand it.'

Practical language helps people, especially novices, understand new concepts. Abstraction is the luxury of the expert. If you've got to teach a roomful of people and you aren't certain what they know, practicality is the only safe language.

Maybe you've experienced the frustration of cooking from a recipe that was too abstract: 'Cook until the mixture reaches a hearty consistency.' Huh? Just tell me how many minutes to stir! Show me a picture of what it should look like. After we have cooked the dish a few times, the phrase 'hearty consistency' might start to make sense. We build a sensory image of what the phrase represents. But the first time it's as meaningless as 3 + 2 + 1 would be to a three-year-old.

Using tangible examples as a foundation for abstraction is not just good for your cooking; it is the basic principle of understanding. Novices crave practicality. Have you ever read an academic paper or a technical article or even a memo and found yourself so flummoxed by the fancy abstract language that you were crying out for *an example*?

Michael Henderson described rugby league as 'the last true working-class game', and it's a sport where bullshit doesn't last long. 'Say what you mean,' was the advice one player gave me when I first started working in it.

I once asked a highly decorated rugby league player what career he hoped to pursue after retiring from the sport. 'I'd like to work for Sky TV,' he replied. I was pleasantly surprised by his certainty and the fact that he appeared to have given some serious consideration to working for 'the home of rugby league'. 'What kind of role would you like?' I asked. 'Presenting or doing the analysis?'

He looked at me with a quizzical expression, unsure whether my question was genuine or whether I was being deliberately stupid. After he'd ascertained that I was sincere, he explained his plans to me very slowly. 'I'd like a job fitting the Sky TV boxes in people's houses.'

Matt King, one of the central characters behind Melbourne Storm's success, believes that their practical demonstration of 'hard work' was an important factor. Led by Craig Bellamy, all new recruits must start their career at the club by working full-time for one of the club's sponsors and training in the evening. 'You could be working as a dust collector or on a construction site,' King explains, 'and then you have to come and train in the evenings.' King reasons that this approach 'makes you realize how fortunate you are to do this for a living. Staying behind to do extra work never seems so bad afterwards.'

Jamie Peacock, the England captain and winner of nine Grand Finals, combined these approaches when demanding high standards from his Leeds Rhinos teammates. 'All great teams are committed,' he explains, 'but what does commitment actually mean?'

Peacock calculated how many times a year he is requested to run between cones in training and estimated how much time you shaved off. He equated this to time in games and realized that avoiding running the extra yard added up to stopping playing an eighty-minute game after seventy-five minutes.

He explained this by starting from the players' goal, which was to win the Grand Final. If they stopped short of the cone, they would lose their discipline. If they lost their discipline, they would lose penalties. If they lost penalties, they would lose points. If they lost points, they would lose games. If they lost games, they would lose the Grand Final. 'You run to the cone every time,' he demanded. This may seem a trivial demand, but it is – crucially – a simple and practical one which helps to bring about important results.

This is how practical language helps us to understand – it helps us construct higher, more abstract insights on the building blocks of our existing knowledge and perceptions. Abstraction demands some concrete foundation. Trying to teach an abstract principle without concrete foundations is like trying to start a house by building a roof in the air.

EXERCISE – THE COACH IN YOUR HEAD

Self talk is the world's most mysterious language. We all do it constantly – you know, that whisper that comes into your head at key moments, the one that says, OK, take a deep breath . . . keep your calm . . . now go! – but it happens mostly unconsciously, and nobody talks about it.

Which is strange, because when it comes to performance, self talk is a massively useful tool. For example, studies show that skilled athletes tend to self-talk more often, and in a more planned and consistent manner (less skilled athletes tend merely to react). Sprinters who self-talk run faster. Good self talk functions like an early-warning radar system, helping us to identify key moves and navigate problems. Done well, it's like having a coach inside your head.

But here's the question: if self talk is a good thing, how do we get better at it and more able to share our insights with others? Is it possible to teach it, the same way you'd learn any language? With that in mind, here are a few tips.

1. Keep it short and chunky.
Good practical self talk is never chatty or complicated.
It divides the skill into its key moves, and uses those
as clear cues. For example, with a golf swing:
Say this: 'Smooth arms, still head.'
Not this: 'OK, let's keep the takeaway smooth, relax your
posture, make sure to keep your head still through the
backswing.'

2. Make it vivid.
The more vivid the image, the easier it is to remember,
and to do. For example, with a leader about to deliver
a presentation:
Say this: 'Stand like a tree.'
Not this: 'Make sure you stand up straight.'

3. Keep it positive.
Don't focus on what you want to avoid, but on what you
want to accomplish. For example, before meeting an
important client:
Say this: 'Take your time; listen to them.'
Not this: 'Don't rush; don't forget the main points.'

Finally, and maybe most usefully, fluent and practical self-
talkers don't just talk to themselves during their performance;
they also do it before and after. Self talk is like a game tape: you
use it to preview what's going to happen, and then afterwards
you use it again to relive what happened, and figure out how
you might do it better the next time.

4.v   VELCRO MEMORY

What is it about practical language that makes ideas stick? The answer lies with the nature of our memories.

Many of us have a sense that remembering something is a bit like putting it into storage. To remember a story is to file it away in our cerebral filing cabinets. There is nothing wrong with that analogy. But the surprising thing is that there may be completely different filing cabinets for different kinds of memories.

To understand this better, think of learning as the game of Skatch in which a tennis ball is thrown to be caught by someone wearing a Velcro glove to which it sticks – catch for people who can't catch. Think of the tennis ball as the new knowledge and the glove as our existing knowledge. We learn best by hooking new knowledge on to things for which we already have connections.

This is one of the reasons why similes and metaphors work so well. If I am told, 'He's as brave as a lion,' then I can quickly take on board the sort of person he is, as this new fact hooks into my existing knowledge about lions. Or, if you say an acre is 4,840 square yards, I look blankly at you. But if you say, 'That's about the size of a football pitch,' I can immediately comprehend the size. How your memory works requires the rephrasing of an old saying: it's not, how clever are you? but, how are you clever?

You can test this idea for yourself. The following set of sentences will ask you to remember various ideas. Spend five or ten seconds lingering on each one – don't rush through them. As you move from one sentence to another, you'll notice that it feels different to remember different kinds of things.

- Remember the capital of France.
- Remember the first line of the Beatles' 'Hey Jude'.
- Remember the *Mona Lisa*.
- Remember the house where you spent most of your childhood.
- Remember the texture of an orange.
- Remember the definition of 'truth'.

David Rubin, a cognitive psychologist at Duke University in North Carolina, uses this exercise to illustrate the nature of memory. Each command to remember seems to trigger a different mental activity. Remembering the capital of France is an abstract exercise, unless you happen to live in Paris. By contrast, when you think about 'Hey Jude', you may hear Paul McCartney's voice and piano-playing.

No doubt the *Mona Lisa* memory conjured up a visual image of that famously enigmatic smile. Remembering your childhood home might have evoked a host of memories – smells, sights, sounds. You might even have felt yourself running through your home, or remembering where your parents used to sit.

The definition of 'truth' may have been a bit harder to summon – you certainly have a sense of what 'truth' means, but you probably had no reformulated definition to pluck out of memory, as with the *Mona Lisa*. You might have had to create a definition on the hoof that seemed to fit with your sense of what 'truth' means.

The definition of the texture of an orange might also have

involved some mental gymnastics. The word 'orange' immediately evokes sense memories – the thick, orange rind, the smell and the sweet taste. Then you might have found yourself shifting gears as you tried to encapsulate these sense memories into a definition.

Memory, then, is not like a single filing cabinet. It is more like Velcro. If you look at the two sides of Velcro material, you'll see that one is covered with thousands of tiny hooks and the other is covered with thousands of tiny loops. When you press the two sides together, a huge number of hooks get snagged inside the loops, and that is what causes Velcro to seal.

Your brain hosts a truly staggering number of loops. The more hooks an idea has, the better it will cling to memory. Your childhood home has a gazillion hooks in your brain. A new credit card number has one, if it's lucky. This is a key reason why practical language and novel communication are so important: the practical and the novel are full of such hooks; outside of organized crime or petty fraud, no winning mindset was ever constructed on expecting anyone to memorize a credit card number.

4.vi   LESSONS FROM LOUIS

Louis Van Gaal's career followed the two-track approach of player-cum-teacher that has been taken by Ian McGeechan and by Van Gaal's fellow Dutch coaching greats, most notably his hero, Rinus Michels, and Guus Hiddink. The experience of working with often unmotivated or emotionally troubled youths at school has given these trainers a cutting edge, a degree of psychological insight some of their colleagues lack.

Van Gaal maxims such as, 'All people have talent – but they often don't know which,' and, 'I can be a medium to help a player manifest his talent,' originated in his twelve-year teaching career and have taken him to Ajax, Barcelona, Bayern Munich and Manchester United – a CV of which José Mourinho admits, 'I am jealous of such a list of prestigious teams.' Along the way, Van Gaal has also led his country's national team to third place in the 2014 World Cup and taken the unfancied AZ Alkmaar to a national title in his homeland.

Along with his successes, there have been a number of high-profile 'failures'. The most notable happened in November 2001 when Van Gaal resigned publicly as Holland manager at a positively surreal press conference. He said a great many things that deserve to be translated into English, but the most relevant is: 'My greatest ability is that I can get an extra 10 per cent out of a player. But only if everyone subscribes to the same idea.'

Economists agree with Van Gaal's analysis. In *Soccernomics*, the economist Stefan Szymanski and the journalist Simon Kuper wrote that money determines somewhere between 80 and 90 per cent of the performance of football clubs. That leaves 10 or 20 per cent for other factors, one of which may or may not be the manager. Bas ter Weel, a Dutch economist who also studied the effect of managers on their football teams, compared their influence to that of prime ministers on the economy: probably no other single individual has more influence, but it's still marginal.

To develop Van Gaal's theory further, if he is to coax this extra 10 per cent out of his players, if he is to matter at all, he is prepared to do nearly anything to get his ideas across effectively. He told the trade journal *De Voetbaltrainer* that he had a floor of the Dutch team hotel in Noordwijk rebuilt in a way that he believed would help the players communicate better. He also had the hotel's Internet access rewired for higher broadband speeds to save his players who play online games from annoyance. As we observed in the 'Emotions' chapter, annoyed players have Elephants who are unwilling and unable to learn, and only once they are prepared to learn can they become better, so runs his thinking. Only if everything is perfectly tailored to the goal of transferring knowledge from Van Gaal to his players can he have a significant effect on his team's results. He prizes not only simplicity of communication, but also the means by which his players can be made most receptive to this simplicity. The fewer other things they have to think about, the more space those Velcro hooks will have to stick.

Central to all this is what Van Gaal calls the 'learning process'. In 2009, his video analyst Max Reckers explained how Van Gaal uses video to aid the learning process. 'Why people think he is so dominant over others is that he wants to control the whole process [of learning]. He wants to know about all the feedback players get about their performance: from friends and family but particularly from journalists. If he knows this, he can decide what video images and commentary he gives to the player. Every stimulus he gives is tailor-made to the player's needs.'

Van Gaal tries to reduce interference with the learning process by minimizing his players' contacts with what he often calls 'the outside world'. Until he became Ajax manager in 1991, former players and journalists habitually hung out in the *spelershome*, the 'players' home'. He ended this immediately; access was to be denied to everyone except the players. 'Only the people who worked at achieving the same goal were allowed in,' he writes in his autobiography, *Louis Van Gaal: Biography and Philosophy*.[7] In short: Van Gaal fully appreciates that his theoretical influence as a manager is limited and so does everything to maximize it.

In order to influence his players' minds, Van Gaal, when managing AZ, called in the help of psychologist Leo van der Burg, who ran a consultancy business in 'scientific business humanities'. Van der Burg – who wrote a book titled *Do What You're Good At* – taught Van Gaal and his staff two lessons:

1. It's better to work on a player's strong suits.

He explains, 'In Germany they once did research amongst left-footed players, they were asked to only shoot with their right. The result was that the right leg of those boys improved by 3 per cent after those three months. But the left leg had declined by 30 per cent. You should let players do what they are good at.'[8]

2. Every player is different and warrants a different approach.

To properly tailor his efforts, Van Gaal needed to know what his players were like outside of their football identities. Before he met Van der Burg, he used to visit most of the players he wanted to sign at their homes, took notes, and then made reports on what he registered. But these reports turned out to be useless, he writes in his book. 'They turned out to be too much of a snapshot [rather than a rounded profile]. So I called in the help of a professional agency that, together with me, profiles the players.'

Using these profiles, Van Gaal divided his players into three colour categories that Van der Burg devised: blue players, who are 'intellectually orientated'; green, 'emotional' players; and 'creative' red players – although it's not known what colour he would ascribe to the method of communication he once used when he was readying Martin Demichelis to come on as a substitute for his Bayern Munich team. The player was still grumbling about not being picked to start; Van Gaal simply planted a kiss on the Argentine's cheek.

These categories differ in the way the players process information, which guides Van Gaal's communication with them. For example, at half-time, he uses different pitches in his voice for the different kinds of players. The same principle applies to the post-match feedback. As Van Gaal's video analyst Max Reckers explained, players are always shown successful passages of play because positive images stick in people's heads more easily and make for faster learning.

All feedback is tailored to the individual and depends on the circumstances. Did a player get critical questions about a certain play? Or perhaps a journalist was very positive about a particular decision a player made that Van Gaal and his staff were actually critical of? Red players will get different video and commentary from Van Gaal to blue players.

EXERCISE – COMMUNICATE WITH COLOUR

In the first horizontal row of four squares, decide which group of three words seems most like you and put a 4 in that square.

The group or words in the same row that seems next most like you will rate a score of 3, the next again will get a 2, and the group which seems the least like you should be given a score of 1.

Then go to the second horizontal row and score those squares in the same way: 4 for the group that's most like you, 1 for the group that's least and 2 and 3 for the ones in between.

FIRST ROW	Spontaneous Impulsive Impetuous	Stable Methodical Planner	Co-operative Idealistic Wants harmony	Rational Curious Complex
SECOND ROW	Adventurous Daring In a hurry	Traditional Responsible Dependable	Catalyst Compassionate Inspirational	Logical Analytical Loner
THIRD ROW	Love excitement Explorer Unpredictable	Dutiful Teacher Industrious	Authentic Empathic Motivator	Intellectual Inventive Problem solver
FOURTH ROW	Energetic Expedient Jokester	Makes rules Orderly Prepares	Supportive Self-aware Caring	System-thinker Independent Perfectionist
FIFTH ROW	Bold Witty Risk-taker	Loyal Reliable Likes structure	Romantic Flexible Self-actualizing	Theoretical Ingenious Individualist

Now add the numbers in each of the vertical columns and put the totals in these squares.

Number				
Colour	RED	YELLOW	BLUE	GREEN

COMMUNICATING WITH REDS

Get to the point quickly – headlines are important.

Sell immediate benefits of decision.

Make outcomes clear and vibrant.

Emphasize action in what you are proposing.

Talk about new ideas and creative approaches.

COMMUNICATING WITH YELLOWS

Be clear, direct and structured.

Give the detail, not just the headline.

Think about long-term implications.

Be on time and prepared.

Ensure ideas support our policies and mission and are financially sound.

COMMUNICATING WITH BLUES

Demonstrate active listening to establish a good rapport.

Use eye contact and positive body language.

Where possible, make your ideas people-related.

Focus on cooperation and team work.

COMMUNICATING WITH GREENS

Enjoy talking about theories and models.

Be logical and factual.

Be ready to back up your theories and suggestions, as GREENS will have lots of questions.

Avoid 'small talk' or idle conversation.

4.vii IN PRACTICE

The moral of the story is not to dumb things down. Rather, the moral of the story is to find a universal language, one that everyone speaks fluently. Inevitably, that universal language will be practical.

Of all of the traits that great coaches use, practicality is perhaps the easiest to embrace. It may also be the most effective of the traits.

To be simple – to find our core message – is quite difficult. It is certainly worth the effort but let's not kid ourselves that it's easy. Crafting our ideas in an unexpected way takes a fair amount of effort and applied creativity. But being practical isn't hard, and it doesn't require a lot of effort. The barrier is simply forgetfulness – we forget that we are slipping into abstract-speak. We forget that other people don't know what we know.

THE FIFTH STEP

STORIES

If history were taught in the form of stories,
it would never be forgotten.
Rudyard Kipling

5.i THE LEGEND OF PEP GUARDIOLA

In the spring of 2008 Barcelona Football Club was a big-name global brand that was losing its lustre. The ideas were running out, the competitive edge had faded, morale was low. New leadership was called for.

The board had a range of options. Among them was José Mourinho, a serial winner whose record offered the closest thing to a guarantee of success in a game where, more often than in most other sports, outcomes turn on fortune's tricks. To the dismay of the majority of Barcelona's shareholders, or, rather, their 180,000 paid-up members, they chose Pep Guardiola, a novice with one year's experience as a lower-division coach and none in the game's upper reaches. Guardiola had been a great player and captain of Barcelona, but in terms of the new responsibility on his shoulders and the uncharted waters he was being asked to navigate, 'it was,' suggested the writer John Carlin, 'like Sony selecting the manager of a medium-sized regional office to take over as company CEO.'[1]

At a pre-season gala when he was reintroduced to a packed Camp Nou stadium – which has a capacity of 98,000 – Guardiola announced, 'Fasten your seat belts.' Microphone in hand, from the centre of the pitch he cried out, 'You're going to have fun!'

A year and a half later, Barcelona had won all six trophies they had competed for, including the European and world club championships. In the four years that Guardiola remained at the club, they won fourteen out of nineteen possible cups and league titles, a feat unequalled in the history of the game. Barcelona achieved something else too, something more difficult to win than any official prize: the admiration of the football world. Guardiola's team revolutionized the 150-year-old sport. Coaches from clubs large and small made pilgrimages to Barcelona's training camp, notebooks in hand, hoping to glean some of the Guardiola gold dust.

In May 2012, Guardiola quit Barcelona and took a sabbatical in New York. He decided he had had enough. A severely self-critical perfectionist, he needed a break from the demands he imposed on himself and the weight of expectation placed on him by the club faithful, for whom Barça is not merely a football team, but the flagship of Catalan pride.

During his absence, he was gone but certainly not forgotten. Inquiries came from England, Italy, Germany, Russia, France and China. Finally it was announced that he would return to coach Germany's biggest club, Bayern Munich.

What is Guardiola's secret? How did a man who began his coaching career aged thirty-seven achieve so much, so soon? A large part of the answer is that he spent twenty-four years, from the day he arrived at the club, preparing himself for the job. Johan Cruyff, Holland's greatest ever player, who, as coach of Barcelona, laid the foundations for the temple Guardiola built, plucked him from the club's youth ranks into the first team. Cruyff saw an avid learner. The Dutch master, a magnificent player in his day, never had a more attentive pupil. Cruyff's core message remains Guardiola's today. Lessons one, two and three of football: keep possession of the ball. It may be tempting to treat the message itself as a metaphor, but remember the perils of abstraction; it is hard to know, in a business situation, what the 'ball' actually is. But whatever our job, our responsibilities and our level of expertise, we can learn from the nature of the message itself, as a foundation for Guardiola's own winning mindset: he has a core idea, simple, practical and clearly communicated.

Eusebio Sacristán, a former Barcelona player who was on the pitch on the day of Guardiola's first-team debut, said that Guardiola possessed 'a brain which worked so fast he could make those around him play at the speed of light'.[2] He processed every game in his mind, every training session, every lesson Cruyff imparted. It was a habit of mind that extended to his life beyond football. He read books, he took an interest – ever greater the older he got – in film, music and politics. One of his closest friends is David Trueba, a Spanish novelist and film director whom he met at a poetry reading in 1995, when he was twenty-four. Trueba wrote this about him: 'He is curious about a lot of things beyond football. But you get the sense sometimes that he codifies them in his own special way. That he "footballises" them.'[3] In other words, that everywhere he finds a lesson applicable to football. Such are the obsessive thought processes of a top football coach, a destiny which Sacristán, who played alongside him for six years, says he never doubted he would fulfil.

Juan Carlos Unzué, the goalkeeping coach for three of the four years Guardiola coached Barcelona, watched this development up close. 'In terms of tactics, in terms of motivation, in terms of every single facet required in a coach,' Unzué said, 'Guardiola is outstanding, in a class of his own.'[4]

Towards the end of his fourth and final season Barcelona began to lose their edge. It appeared that his team remained, to the end, a mirror of their coach. Guardiola had dedicated every waking moment for four years to devising new tactics, new ways to motivate his players, new responses to new challenges. His batteries were drained. 'He always said success wears you down and in his case he was right,' said Evaristo Murtra. 'He needed a rest.'[5] For his own good and, as he saw it, that of the team, which he felt he could no longer improve, he quit and headed to New York for a year-long sabbatical.

Apart from recharging his batteries and spending more time with his family, he spent the year absorbing and processing information in preparation for the next challenge. According to David Trueba, he spent hours studying European football at home. Less obviously, as Trueba says, he sought out new stimuli by devouring all New York has to offer. 'I went over to see him and we went to shows and museums – we even had dinner with a famous economist,' Trueba said. 'For the American elections he stayed up until the final result was in, peppering me with information all night on the phone, following Obama.'

Guardiola has no doubt been 'footballising' Obama too; learning what he can from an expert in another field, to apply within his own – which is, of course, exactly what I want to help you do here. He surely took lessons in leadership, and in particular the storytelling ability which allowed Obama to connect so effectively with voters, that he would apply to coaching the most successful German football club, Bayern Munich – a club run, in the main, by former players with long histories of attachment to it, and with a clearly defined identity on and off the field. In recent years the football they and the German national team have played has converged with the philosophy of attractive, possession-based attacking football that Guardiola refined and perfected at Barcelona. In fact, they won a unique German treble – league, cup and European Cup – in the season before he arrived. Bayern's expectations were for him to evolve their approach, take it to a higher plain.

A question lingered, however. Would Guardiola be able to repeat his success at his latest club? The doubters' argument rested on the notion that he was lucky at Barcelona to have stumbled upon a spectacularly talented set of players. 'With that lot, who couldn't succeed?' goes a familiar jibe in football circles.

His first test came within the first month of competition. Bayern, as European Cup holders, were pitted against his rival José Mourinho's Europa League-winning Chelsea in the European Super Cup Final played in Prague.

In a tense, agonizing final, Bayern equalized fifty-one seconds after the official 120 minutes had been played. Swedish referee Jonas Eriksson had added one minute for stoppages, and there were nine seconds to go when Javi Martínez scored for Bayern.

This was the second time in fifteen months that the two teams had gone head-to-head in a penalty shoot-out. Just over one year earlier, the English team beat Bayern in the Champions League Final, in a penalty shoot-out in Bayern's own stadium. All German eyes turned towards the new coach.

The author Marti Perarnau was given total access to Bayern Munich during Guardiola's first big match in charge of the Bundesliga giants. His book, *Pep Confidential: The Inside Story of Pep Guardiola's First Season at Bayern Munich*, gives a unique insight into what the charismatic coach did next.

In the middle of all the euphoria, Guardiola called his people together in one big huddle. 'Everyone is there: doctors, physios, assistant coaches, players, substitutes and even the injured men. This is Pep at his brilliant best. The guy who rises to the big occasions and dazzles his men,' recounts Perarnau. 'Just as everyone is expecting him to mobilise his players with a call to arms of epic proportions, Pep tells them a simple story . . . About water polo.'

'Lads, I don't know how to take penalties myself,' Guardiola confessed. 'I've never taken one in my whole life. But here's the best penalty taker in the whole world.' And he pointed to a figure half hidden, right at the back of the huddle.

'I'm talking about Manel Estiarte,' the Catalan coach clarified. 'He was the best water polo player in the world. He took penalties better than anyone. Hundreds of them. Water polo is like football. Only four out of every five penalty kicks hit the target, but Manel put them all away! He is a world expert on penalties.'

Perarnau observed that Guardiola 'hadn't just managed to get the players' attention. He had completely changed the expressions on their faces. They had been waiting for war cries and motivational oratory, an adrenalin boost.' What they received instead, standing in the middle of the clamouring, heaving mass of humanity that rocked the stadium, was a simple tale.

'I've learned two things from Manel and his penalties, so listen up,' Guardiola continued. 'These are the only two things you need to do now. Firstly, make up your mind immediately as to where you're going to put the ball and stick with that decision. I'll say it again. Decide now and don't change your mind no matter what happens. Secondly, keep telling yourself that you're going to score. Repeat it a thousand times and don't stop until after you've taken the penalty. Don't worry and don't change your minds.'

'What a team talk. Incredible!' the Bayern sporting director Matthias Sammer later said.

Before he concluded, Guardiola offered the ultimate example of the kind of autonomy of thinking he demanded from his players. 'Lads, there's no list. You can choose whether or not to take one. You choose. You're all going to score anyway, so you decide who is taking them. Who's up for it?'[6]

All five volunteers scored to help Bayern become the first German team to win the trophy and claim Guardiola's third European Super Cup.

Guardiola later admitted that this first trophy with Bayern was crucial. He told Perarnau, 'The team needed this win. If we hadn't won, I don't know how we would have moved forward.' Indeed, the team did continue to move forward. By the end of the season, Guardiola added the league and cup to his increasingly stocked trophy cabinet. And it all began with a moment when he combined a number of the crucial elements for a winning mindset that we have discussed so far in the book: storytelling; the unexpected; simplicity; a practical message.

5.ii WHAT STORIES ARE FOR

Gary Klein is a psychologist who studies how people make decisions in high-pressure, high-stakes environments. He spends time with firefighters, air-traffic controllers, power-plant operators, and intensive-care workers. His book, *Sources of Power*, contains a chapter called 'The Power of Stories'.

Klein says that in the environments he studies, stories are told and retold because they contain wisdom. Stories are effective teaching tools. They show how context can mislead people to make the wrong decisions. Stories illustrate causal relationships that people hadn't recognized before and highlight unexpected, resourceful ways in which people have solved problems.

A story's power is twofold: it provides stimulation (knowledge about how to act) and inspiration (motivation to act). Note that both benefits, stimulation and inspiration, are geared to generating *action*. We have seen that a *practical* idea can make people believe. An *emotional* idea can make people care.

In this chapter, we'll see that the right stories make people act.

5.iii   THE VIRTUES OF SIMULATION

Stories are strongly associated with entertainment – movies and books and TV shows and magazines. When children say, 'Tell me a story,' they are begging for entertainment, not instruction. Yet the fact that they are requesting it in the first place, and eager to hear it, makes a story the perfect medium for a strong, clear message – as educators have long known.

Being the 'audience' for a story seems like a passive role – audiences who get their stories from television are called 'couch potatoes', after all. But 'passive' may be overstating the case. When we read books, we have the sensation of being drawn into the author's world. When friends tell us stories, we instinctively empathize. When we watch movies, we identify with the protagonists.

But what if stories involve us in less intuitive, more dramatic ways?

One team of researchers has produced some exciting evidence suggesting that the line between a story's audience and a story's protagonist may be a bit blurry.

Three psychologists interested in how people come to understand stories created a few for their study participants to read on a computer. They divided the participants into two groups. The first group read a story in which a critical object was *associated* with the main character in the story – for instance, 'John *put on* his sweatshirt before he went jogging.'

The second group read a story in which the same critical object was *separated* from the main character: 'John *took off* his sweatshirt before jogging.'

Two sentences later, the story threw in a reference to the sweatshirt, and the computer was able to track how long it took people to read that sentence. Something strange happened: the people who thought John had taken off his sweatshirt before the jog *took more time to read the sentence* than the people who thought John had it on.

The result is subtle but fascinating. It implies that we create a kind of geographical simulation of the stories we hear. It's one thing to say, 'Reading stories makes us see pictures in our head.' We'd all find that statement acceptable. It's quite another thing to say that when John left his sweatshirt behind, he left it back at the house in a more remote place in our heads. For that to be true, we cannot simply *visualize* the story on a movie screen in our heads; we must somehow *simulate* it, complete with some analogue (however loose) to the spatial relationships described in the story. These studies suggest that there's no such thing as a passive audience. When we hear a story, our minds move from room to room. When we hear a story, we simulate it. But what good is simulation?

A group of UCLA students were asked to think about a current problem in their lives, one that was 'stressing them out' but was also potentially solvable in the future, such as a problem with schoolwork or with a relationship.

The students were told the goal of the exercise was to help them deal with problem-solving effectively, and they got some brief instructions on problem-solving. After receiving these instructions – think about the problem, look at it from different perspectives – this 'control group' were sent home and asked to report back a week later.

A second group of students, the 'event-simulation' group,

were kept in the lab. They were asked to simulate mentally how the problem had unfolded.

We would like you to visualize how this problem arose. Visualize the beginning of the problem, going over in detail the first incident . . . Go over the incidents as they occurred step by step. Visualize the actions you took. Remember what you said, what you did. Visualize the environment, who was around, where you were.

The event-simulation participants had to retrace, step by step, the events that led to their problem. Presumably, reviewing the chain of events might help the students think about how to fix the problem, like programs engaged in systematic debugging.

A third group, the 'outcome-simulation' group, was asked to simulate mentally a positive outcome emerging from the problem:

Picture this problem beginning to resolve, you are coming out of the stressful situation . . . Picture the relief you feel. Visualize the satisfaction you would feel at having dealt with the problem. Picture the confidence you feel in yourself, knowing that you have dealt successfully with the problem.

The outcome-simulators kept their focus on the desired future outcome: what will it be like once this problem is behind me?

After this initial exercise, both of the simulation groups were sent home. Both groups were asked to spend five minutes every day repeating their simulations, and to report back to the lab a week later.

Make a quick prediction about which group of students you think fared best in coping with their problems. (Tip: it's not the control group.)

Here's the answer: the event-simulation group – the people who simulated how the events unfolded – did better in almost every dimension. Simulating past events is much more helpful than simulating future outcomes. In fact, the gap between the two groups opened up immediately after the first lab session. By the first night, the event-simulation people were already experiencing a positive mood boost compared to the other two groups.

When the groups returned a week later, the event-simulators' advantage had grown wider. They were more likely to have taken specific action to solve their problems. They were more likely to have sought advice and support from others. They were more likely to report that they had learned something new and grown.

You may find these results a bit counter-intuitive, because pop-psychology literature is full of gurus urging you to visualize success. It turns out that a positive mental attitude isn't quite enough to get the job done. Maybe financial gurus shouldn't be telling us to imagine that we're filthy rich; instead, they should be telling us to replay the steps that led to us being poor.

Try the following example.

5.iv   THE DOCTOR AND THE CASTLE

Let's attempt a thought experiment. Or, if you prefer, we can call it a story – one whose ending you will decide for yourself. Imagine that you are one of your country's leading doctors, respected by all patients and revered within the medical community for your practical, common-sense solutions.

A member of the public has been exposed to a disease which causes a cancerous tumour in the stomach. The patient is rushed to the doctor: you.

The patient will die very soon unless the tumour can be removed. However, it is impossible to get to the tumour to remove it, or to inject anything into it. There is a special kind of ray that can kill the tumour from outside the patient's body. The problem is that if the ray is set to a high enough intensity to destroy the tumour, it will also destroy all of the healthy tissues that it passes through along the way, eventually killing the patient.

What is your solution? Take some time to think about how you would answer before reading on.

Solution

This is a very hard problem, and few people are able to come up with the solution. I will give you the answer, but first I would like to replicate Pep Guardiola's methods and tell you a story, a fairy tale.

Once upon a time, there was a wicked king who lived in a huge castle. Everyone who lived in the kingdom hated the wicked king and they got together an army of a hundred brave knights, who agreed to attack the castle and kill him. Although the castle was well defended, the knights knew that, if they all attacked the castle together at exactly the same time, they could break down the defences and get inside. But the knights had a problem. Although there were lots of roads leading up the castle, they were so narrow that only twenty men could pass along each road at any one time. The leader of the knights, however, was very clever. He divided his men up into five groups and told each to approach the castle using a different road. As soon as the leader gave the signal, all one hundred knights charged towards the castle, arriving at exactly the same time. They were easily able to break down the defences and kill the wicked king, and everybody lived happily ever after.

Right, now let's go back to the tumour problem. Actually, wait. You've already figured it out, haven't you?

This pair of stories is used by psychologists to investigate the role of *analogies* in problem-solving. Although the doctor's dilemma and the fairy tale have nothing in common on the surface (a castle does not resemble a tumour, or a knight an anti-cancer ray), the two problems have the same underlying structure. In exactly the same way as the knights can converge on the castle with enough manpower to overcome its defences, so the separate anti-tumour rays converge with enough power to take out the cancer.

It is this underlying structure, rather than the surface similarity, that is useful in an analogy. If, for example, instead of the fairy story I had told you about a patient who had a similar-sized tumour on his abdomen, which doctors easily removed using the same ray turned up to full power, it would have been of no help whatsoever.

5.v   IMAGINATION AND REALITY

Why does mental simulation work?

It works because we can't *imagine* events or sequences without evoking the same modules of the brain that are evoked in real physical activity. Brain scans show that when people *imagine* a flashing light, they activate the visual area of the brain; when they imagine someone tapping on their skin, they activate tactile areas of the brain. The activity of mental simulation is not limited to the insides of our heads. People who imagine words that begin with *B* or *P* can't resist subtle lip movements, and people who imagine looking at the Eiffel Tower can't resist moving their eyes upwards. Mental simulation can even alter visceral physical responses: when people drink water but imagine that it's lemon juice, they salivate more. Even more surprisingly, when people drink lemon juice but imagine it's water, they salivate less.

Mental simulations help us manage emotions. There is a standard treatment for phobias of various kinds – spiders, flying, public speaking, and others. Patients are introduced to a relaxation procedure that inhibits anxiety, and then asked to visualize exposure to the thing they fear. The first visualizations start at the periphery of the fear. For example, someone who is afraid of air travel might start by thinking about the drive to the airport. The therapist leads the patient through a series of visualizations that get closer and closer to the heart of the fear. Each time the visualizations create anxiety; the person pauses for a moment and uses the relaxation technique to restore equilibrium.

Notice that these visualizations focus on the events themselves – the process rather than the outcomes. No one has ever been cured of a phobia by imagining how happy they will be when it is gone.

Mental simulations also help with problem-solving. Even in mundane planning situations, mentally simulating an event helps us to think of things that we might otherwise have neglected. Imagining a trip to the shops reminds us that we could drop off our dry-cleaning at the shop next door. Mental simulations help us anticipate appropriate responses to future situations. Picturing a potential argument with our boss, imagining what they will say, may lead us to have the right words available when the time comes (and to avoid the wrong words as well). Research has suggested that this mental rehearsal can prevent people from relapsing into bad habits such as smoking or excessive drinking. A man trying to kick a drinking problem will be better off if he mentally rehearses how he will handle his Saturday night out. How should he respond when someone offers to buy him a beer?

Perhaps most surprisingly, mental simulation can also build skills. A review of thirty-five studies featuring 3,214 participants showed that mental practice alone – sitting quietly, without moving, and picturing yourself performing a task successfully from start to finish – improves performance significantly. The results were borne out over a large number of tasks: mental simulation helped people throw darts better, figure skaters improve their skating and trombonists improve their playing. Not surprisingly, mental practice is more effective when a task involves more mental activity, such as trombone playing, as opposed to physical activity, but the magnitude of gains is large on average: overall, mental practice alone produced about *two-thirds of the benefits of actual physical practice*.

The takeaway is simple: mental simulation is not as good as actually doing something, but it has significant value. And, to circle back to the world of elite cultures, what I am suggesting is that the right kind of story is, effectively, a simulation. Stories are like flight simulators for the brain. Hearing a story about overcoming adversity to win the league isn't like being there, but it's the next best thing. It was the reason why Brian Clough would target experienced players, whom most observers deemed too old, as he put together his league championship-winning teams at Derby County and Nottingham Forest. When he unveiled the thirty-five-year-old Scottish international Dave Mackay, he explained, 'He knows how to win a league title and that experience is vital.'

In his first season at Derby, Mackay led them to promotion from the second division, and he helped lay the foundations for the club to become First Division champions in 1972.

A story is powerful because it provides the context missing from abstract prose. This is the role stories play – putting knowledge into a framework that is more lifelike, more true to our day-to-day existence. More like a flight simulator. Being the audience for a story isn't so passive, after all. Inside, we're getting ready to act.

This was the method employed in 1998, when University of Tennessee coach Philip Fulmer received a hand-carved walking stick. It arrived just as Fulmer was taking his team out to practice. He took it with him to show the players, who gleefully claimed that it made him 'look like Moses'. Fulmer took it as a jab at his ageing body and greying hair, so he stored the stick away in his office.

Then that night, it hit him. Moses wasn't just some grey-haired old man. He led his people to the Promised Land.

The next day, he took his stick back out to practice and gathered his team in a circle. 'OK,' he said, 'yesterday you said I looked like Moses with this stick.' He then reminded them of the story of Moses and the Israelites and explained how the stick was going to be the focal point of their energy. They wouldn't tell their partners, family or the media about it, but they would take the stick with them wherever they went and it would be a reminder of what they had to do to reach their own Promised Land of winning the league.

The team bought into the story and the stick was passed round to different team members who became responsible for bringing it to practices and meetings. When the team travelled to games, the players would ask whether Fulmer had the stick with him. At every game it stood on the sideline, a constant reminder of the greater story unfolding with every play.

Fulmer said, 'A trip to the Promised Land wasn't just a gimmick; it was my way of inviting the young men into a greater story, an epic bigger than their individual lives. The walking stick wasn't the source of our motivation, it was a visual reminder of the larger story we were writing, in every meeting, at every practice and throughout every game.'[7]

That same year, Tennessee Volunteers won their first National Championship since 1954.

5.vi STORIES AS INSPIRATION

When you describe a compelling story and destination, you're helping to correct one of the front brain's great weaknesses – the tendency to get lost in analysis. Our first instinct, in most situations, is to offer up data: here's why we need to change. Here are the facts and figures to prove it. The front brain – the Rider – loves data. It'll start poring over it, analysing it and poking holes in it, and it'll be inclined to debate the conclusions you've drawn. To the Rider part of your brain, the 'analysing' phase is often more satisfying than the 'doing' phase, and that's dangerous when you're trying to create a winning culture and mindset. 'When all is said and done, there is a lot more said than done,' is how one coach succinctly put it.

Instead, notice what happens when you point to an attractive destination: the brain starts applying its strengths to figuring out how to get there. You have a choice about how to use this energy: by default, allowing it to obsess about which way to move, or by redirecting that energy to help you head towards the destination. For that to happen, you need a story.

Leon Festinger, a leading research psychologist, did a lot of work around the area of cognitive dissonance, the theory that the conscious mind can hold two opposing ideas at the same time. Such conflict (or dissonance) between these ideas creates a psychological tension which throws our system out of order.

When this happens, there is a part of our subconscious, known as the creative subconscious, which springs into action. Among its key functions is maintaining order in our lives. When our system is thrown out of order by an alternative vision of how things could or should be, we get a surge of energy to resolve the tension and put things back in order, the way they should be, or instead, move to the new state. Gestalt psychologists clumsily call this the 'out-of-order-into-order process'.

Let me illustrate this point. Take an elastic band, put your palms together and wrap it around your hands. Keeping one hand still, move the other hand upwards to feel the band tense and stretch. Imagine that your still hand is current reality, where you are now. The tension is the energy created by a move to another goal, the future as you want it to be; as the band stretches, the tension has to be released to prevent the band from snapping. Either the still hand must move upwards or the moving hand must move back down towards it. Which does which will depend on which is the more powerful of the two.

Think about how this works for you in day-to-day life. This morning, when you got out of bed and wandered into the bathroom, switched the light on and had a good look at yourself in the mirror, you would have been in conflict.

You probably have a pretty clear picture in your mind of what you want to look like when you leave your house for work: showered, well groomed, presentable and smart. Did you look like that immediately after getting up and looking in the mirror? If you are like most of us, your internal picture and your external perception didn't match. At this stage, your creative subconscious took over and found the resources to turn that picture into a reality.

Let me give you another example to illustrate this process

and even use it to resolve one of the most frequent areas of disagreement between parents and their kids.

Most children will complain that their parents put them to bed at night when they are wide awake and then drag them out of bed in the morning when they are fast asleep. But I can almost guarantee that there is one morning in the year when parents have no problems getting their children out of bed. Of course, it is Christmas Day, when they tend to get up at a ridiculously early hour.

The children have a really clear picture in their minds of getting up early, staying up late, getting loads of presents, playing with them with their parents and siblings, enjoying a big meal and having lots of visitors. If Father Christmas brings them a new bike, how many times do you think they have played on the bike in their minds before they have ever clapped eyes on it? They have created a positive internal conflict in their minds. The picture is full of so much fun and enjoyment, they can't lie in bed waiting to actually experience their thoughts in reality. This is why a friend of mine regularly gets his kids to identify one thing they are really looking forward to the next day to try and recreate the Christmas Day excitement and get them out of bed.

If there is no disorder then there is no desire or energy produced, to restore the old or create the new. The expression 'comfort zone' is used to describe this state. That is why we need to deliberately create such dissonance and create a destination, describing a better alternative.

The best example of an elite sportsman who has used storytelling is also the best-known sportsman of the twentieth century, a man who once declared, 'I know how to tell and I know what it takes to sell a story.'

5.vii   CREATING FUTURE HISTORY

Cassius Marcellus Clay, Jr, as Muhammad Ali was once known, was born in Louisville, Kentucky on 17 January 1942. Louisville was a city with segregated public facilities, where blacks were the servant class. Growing up in Louisville, the best on the socio-economic ladder that most black people could realistically hope for was to become a clergyman or a teacher at an all-black public school. In a society where it was often felt that might makes right, 'white' was synonymous with both.

When Cassius Clay was twelve years old, his bike was stolen. That led him to take up boxing under the tutelage of a Louisville policeman named Joe Martin. Clay advanced through the amateur ranks, won a gold medal at the 1960 Olympics in Rome, and turned professional under the guidance of Angelo Dundee, a veteran fight trainer in Miami.

'You could spend twenty years studying Ali,' Dave Kindred once wrote, 'and still not know what he is or who he is. He's a wise man and a child. I've never seen anyone who was so giving and, at the same time, so self-centred. He's either the most complex guy I've ever been around or the most simple. And I still can't figure out which it is. We were sure who Ali was only when he danced before us in the dazzle of the ring lights. Then he could hide nothing.'[8]

And so it was that the world came to know Muhammad Ali,

not as a person; not as the social, political or religious figure which he eventually became; but as a fighter. His early professional bouts infuriated and entertained as much as they impressed. Cassius Clay held his hands too low. He backed away from punches, rather than bobbing and weaving out of danger, and he lacked true knockout power.

'Ali fought all wrong,' acknowledges Jerry Izenberg, the esteemed boxing writer. 'Boxing people would say to me, "Any guy who can do this will beat him. Any guy who can do that will beat him." After a while, I started saying back to them, "So you're telling me that any guy who can outjab the fastest jabber in the world can beat him. Any guy who can slip that jab, which is like lightning, not get hit with a hook off the jab, get inside, and pound on his ribs, can beat him. Any guy. Well, you're asking for the greatest fighter who ever lived, so this kid must be pretty good."'[9]

'In the early days,' Ferdie Pacheco, Ali's physician, recalls, 'he fought as though he had a glass jaw and was afraid to get hit. He had the hyper reflexes of a frightened man. He was so fast that you had the feeling, "This guy is scared to death; he can't be that fast normally." Well, he wasn't scared. He was fast beyond belief and smart.'[10]

His smartness, Ali averred, was his greatest strength. Boxing purists cringed when he predicted the round in which he intended to knock out his first nineteen opponents, and grimaced when he did so on seventeen occasions before bragging about each new conquest. He was developing a storytelling technique which he described as 'creating a future history'. And it is this technique which will be of particular use to us in understanding how Ali created a winning mindset for himself.

Then, at the age of twenty-two, Clay challenged Sonny Liston for the world heavyweight crown. Liston was widely regarded as the most intimidating, ferocious, powerful fighter of his era. Clay was such a notable underdog that Robert Lipsyte, who covered the bout for the *New York Times*, said he was instructed to 'find out the directions from the arena to the nearest hospital, so I wouldn't waste deadline time getting there after Clay had been knocked out'. But as the one-time Israeli prime minister David Ben-Gurion once proclaimed, 'Anyone who doesn't believe in miracles is not a realist.' Cassius Clay defeated Sonny Liston in seven rounds to become the heavyweight champion of the world.

Officially, Ali's reign as champion was divided into three segments: before he was exiled from the sport, the years after he returned, and finally, the years after his final defining fight in Manila. And while he fought through the administrations of seven presidents, his greatness as a fighter was most clearly on display in the three years after he first won the crown. During the course of thirty-seven months, Ali fought ten times. No heavyweight in history has defended his crown so frequently against more formidable opposition in more dominant fashion than Ali did in those years.

Boxing, in the first instance, is about not getting hit. 'And I can't be hit,' Ali told the world. 'It's impossible for me to lose, because there's not a man on earth with the speed and ability to beat me.' During this period, he reached a zenith on 14 November 1966 when he did battle against Cleveland Williams. Over the course of three rounds, Ali landed more than one hundred punches, scored four knockdowns, and was hit a total of three times. 'Everything I said would come true, did come true,' he chortled afterwards. 'I said I was The Greatest and they all thought I was acting the fool. Now instead of admitting that I'm the best heavyweight in all of history, they don't know what to do.'

Soon after this, Ali refused induction into the US Army

and was stripped of his title and forced into boxing exile for the next three years, when he was expected to reach his physical peak.

In October 1970, Ali was allowed to return to boxing, but his physical skills were no longer the same. The legs that had allowed him to 'dance' for fifteen rounds without pausing no longer carried him as surely around the ring apron. His reflexes, while still superb, were no longer lightning-fast. In his first challenge to Joe Frazier, the newly minted world champion, Ali was bested over fifteen brutal rounds.

Some fighters can't handle defeat. They fly so high when they're on top that a loss brings them irrevocably crashing down. 'What was interesting to me after the loss to Frazier,' says Ferdie Pacheco, 'was we'd seen this undefeatable guy; now how was he going to handle defeat? Was he going to be a cry-baby? Was he going to be crushed? This was when we learned something else about him. He was one of the toughest guys who ever lived.'[11]

What Ali said was plain and simple: 'I got to whup Joe Frazier, because he beat me. Anybody would like to say, "I retired undefeated." I can't say that no more. But if I could say, "I got beat, but I came back and beat him," I'd feel better.'

Ali won ten fights in a row following his loss to Frazier before he lost to, then avenged himself against, Ken Norton, setting up a rematch against Frazier. From a technical point of view, this rematch was Ali's best performance after his boxing exile, when he showed flashes of what he'd once been as a fighter to record a comprehensive win. Ali next journeyed to Zaire in May 1974 to challenge George Foreman, then the heavyweight champion.

As was the case when he fought Liston, Ali entered the ring a heavy underdog. 'The strategy on Ali's part was to cover up, because he described George as like a tornado,' recalls former boxing great Archie Moore, who helped in Foreman's corner that night. 'And when you see a tornado coming, you run into the house and you cover up. You go into the basement and get out of the way of that strong wind, because you know that otherwise it's going to blow you away. That's what Ali did. He covered up when the storm was raging, knowing that after a while, the storm will blow itself out.'

Ali stopped Foreman in the eighth round to win the championship belt again. Then, over the next thirty months, at the peak of his popularity as champion, he fought nine times. Those fights showed Ali to be a fighter on the decline. Like most ageing combatants, he did his best to put a positive spin on things. But viewed in realistic terms, 'I'm more experienced,' translated to 'I'm getting older.' 'I'm stronger at this weight,' meant 'I need to lose a few pounds.' And 'I'm getting more patient,' was a cover for 'I'm slower.'

Eight of these nine fights during this second reign as champion did little to enhance his legacy, but sandwiched between them, Ali won what may have been the greatest fight of all time, when he and Joe Frazier met in Manila to do battle for the third time.

Ali described the fourteen rounds he shared with his old adversary as the 'closest thing [he'd] ever known to death'. Frazier took the same beating he administered and his corner retired him before the final round could commence.

After Manila, many felt it was a good time for Ali to stop boxing, but too many people had a vested interest in his continuing to fight. Thus he fought on, losing his title again to the novice Leon Spinks, before he regained it. He then finally retired from the sport, bar an ill-advised and futile return two years later. His opponent that night, Larry Holmes, summed it up succinctly. 'Ali's mind is making a date which his body can't keep.'

An era in boxing was over.

His legacy, however, remains, in ways other than the obvious. So how did Ali use stories to create future history? Let's break it down.

It was Aristotle who maintained that there were four primary dramatic plots: Simple Tragic, Simple Fortunate, Complex Tragic, Complex Fortunate. Robert McKee, the screenwriting guru, suggests a more comprehensive twenty-five types of stories in his book *Story*: the modern epic, the disillusionment plot, and so on. When we look at how Ali used stories to create a winning mindset, we find three basic plots: the Challenge plot, the Connection plot and the Creativity plot. It was through these that he would deploy storytelling to propel him throughout his career.

5.viii   THE CHALLENGE PLOT

The story of David and Goliath is the classic Challenge plot. A protagonist overcomes a formidable challenge and succeeds. David felled a giant with his home-made slingshot. There are variations of the challenge plot that we all recognize: the underdog story, the rags-to-riches story, the triumph of sheer willpower over adversity.

The key element of a Challenge plot is that the obstacles seem daunting to the protagonist. We've all got a huge mental inventory of Challenge plot stories. The American hockey team beating the heavily favoured Russians in the 1980 Olympics, the *Star Wars* movies, Rosa Parks.

Challenge plots are inspiring even when they're much less dramatic or historic than these examples. Challenge plots are inspiring in a defined way. They inspire us by appealing to our perseverance and courage. They make us want to work harder, take on new challenges, overcome obstacles. Somehow, after you've heard a story about Matt Busby climbing off his death-bed to win the European Cup ten years later, it's easier to take on the more mundane task of going to the gym. Challenge plots *inspire* us to act.

At the age of twenty-two, when Cassius Clay was facing Sonny Liston in Miami for the world heavyweight champion-ship, an event which most thought would double as his execution, he seized hold of the Challenge plot to establish a narrative that he said would 'shake up the world'.

When he arrived at the weigh-in, his behaviour was extraordinary even measured against the customary antics of a pre-fight event. He seemed out of control. He shrieked at the menacing and intimidating Liston, 'I can beat you any time, chump! You're scared, chump! You ain't no giant! I'm gonna eat you alive,' while being held back by five men. He was apparently bent on slugging Liston right there and then.

Fight officials found that his heart rate registered 120 beats per minute, more than twice its normal rate, and his blood pressure was 200/100. Dr Alexander Robbins, the chief physician of the Miami Boxing Commission, declared that he was 'emotionally unbalanced, scared to death, and liable to crack up before he enters the ring'. He added that if Clay's blood pressure didn't return to normal, the fight would be cancelled. His long-time coach, Angelo Dundee, recalled how during the ensuing chaos, Ali turned and winked at him, to indicate that it was all for pantomime. A second examination conducted an hour later revealed Clay's blood pressure and pulse had returned to normal. It had all been an act.

Angelo Dundee told me that he became a believer when he visited his charge's modest training base in low-rent Miami, where Clay had doodled in light-blue ink on scraps of paper littered around the room. 'Cassius Clay,' they read, in flowery writing, and, 'Cassius Clay is the next champ. Champion of the world. Liston is finished. The next champ: Cassius Clay.' Modern psychologists would call this visualization. Ali said he was merely writing his own future history.

Ali knew that many of Liston's opponents had been beaten before setting foot in the ring, so cowed were they by his granite-like demeanour and terrifying reputation, which had been reaffirmed by his spells in prison and persistent rumours of his Mob connections. 'The one thing that would confuse Liston was to believe that he was stepping into a ring with a madman. If you're crazy, you're unpredictable. Liston's not afraid of me, but he's afraid of a nut,' Ali reasoned.[12]

Yet when he came out for the fight, in his terry-towelling robe with 'The Lip' embroidered on the back, he was coolness and calmness itself. He made a playful, low bow to Sugar Ray Robinson sitting in the crowd. People were astonished at his self-possession and by the start of the seventh round they were even more astonished. Liston remained on his stool in the corner. The new heavyweight champion of the world was Cassius Clay, just as he knew he would be.

5.ix THE CONNECTION PLOT

This is what a Connection plot is all about. It's a story about people who develop a relationship that bridges a gap – racial, class, ethnic, religious, demographic, or otherwise. The Connection plot doesn't have to deal with life-and-death stakes. The connection can be as trivial as you like.

Connection plots are also perfect for romantic stories – think of *Romeo and Juliet* (or one of the highest-grossing movies of all time, *Titanic*). All Connection plots inspire us in social ways. They make us want to help others, be more tolerant of others, work more effectively with others, love others.

Muhammad Ali was invited to address the students of Harvard University. When asked to recite a poem which defined his philosophy of success, he stood up, pointed to himself and said, 'Me.' He then threw his arms wide to the whole audience and said, 'We.'

Ali explained that, 'I truly believe I'm fighting for the betterment of people. I'm not fighting for diamonds or Rolls-Royces or mansions, but to help mankind. Before a fight, I get myself psyched up. It gives me more power, knowing there's so much involved and so many people are gonna be helped by my victory.'

When he was facing George Foreman in Zaire, a fight he was widely expected to lose, he said he was fighting for the disaffected. 'I'm so happy going into this fight,' he said shortly before the bout. 'I'm dedicating this fight to all the people who've been told you can't do it. People who drop out of school because they're told they're dumb. People who go to crime because they don't think they can find jobs. I'm dedicating this fight to all of you people who have a George Foreman in your life. I'm gonna whup my Foreman, and I want you to whup your Foreman.'[13]

Gil Noble, the US television reporter adds, 'When Ali got in the ring, there was a lot more at stake than the title. When that man got in the ring, he took all of us with him.'[14]

Where Challenge plots involve overcoming challenges, Connection plots are about our relationships with others. If you're telling a story at the end-of-season party, it's probably best to use the Connection plot. If you're telling a story at the kick-off party for a new project, go with the Challenge plot.

5.x   THE CREATIVITY PLOT

The third type of inspirational story is the Creativity plot. The prototype might be the story of the apple that falls on Newton's head, inspiring his theory of gravity. The Creativity plot involves someone making a mental breakthrough, solving a long-standing puzzle, or attacking a problem in an innovative way.

The famous explorer Ernest Shackleton faced such enormous odds in his Antarctic exploration (a classic Challenge plot) that maintaining unity amongst his men was critical. A mutiny could leave everyone dead. Shackleton came up with a creative solution for dealing with the whiny, complaining types. He assigned them to sleep in his own tent. When people separated into groups to work on chores, he grouped the complainers with him. Through his constant presence, he minimized their negative influence. Creativity plots make us want to do something different, to be creative, to experiment with new approaches.

Peter Gruber, the successful Hollywood executive, recounts an occasion in the mid 1970s when Muhammad Ali was consumed with the production of a film version of his autobiography *The Greatest*, which Columbia Pictures were to distribute. Although the film wasn't yet in production, he was concerned that the project wasn't getting the support he felt it deserved.

Howard Bigham, Ali's long-time friend, called Columbia and asked if Ali could come and chat with some of the studio's mavens. A handful of them, including John Veitch, head of physical production, and Norman Levy, head of distribution, gathered in CEO David Begelman's office.

After the exchange of pleasantries, it quickly became apparent that Ali's exhortations were losing his audience. It was so early in the development process, and the attendees didn't see the need for his concern. They were looking out of the window, fiddling with their pens, or just watching the champ blankly.

Suddenly Ali went silent. Changing tactics, he got up.

'You want to know how I beat Ken Norton after losing to him in 1973?'

That got their attention. A second later, Ali had the executives standing in a boxing posture. He ordered them to keep their arms up and their bodies moving for thirty minutes, representing ten three-minute rounds. During these thirty minutes of non-stop activity, Ali engaged the execs with the story of the first fight against Norton.

Norton had been a newcomer when the duo first fought at the Inglewood Forum in California. Ali said, 'I was in the worst shape of my career.' He demonstrated how Norton had struck the blow that broke Ali's jaw. As the executives tried the jab, he said, 'You gotta have a plan for every possibility.'

Then he began to demonstrate how he'd trained for the second fight, which took place six months after losing the first. 'He got us all running in place as if our feet were on fire,' recalls Begelman. '"Always be moving." He mimicked jumping rope. He threw punches that we ducked or deflected. "Control, control, control," he repeated. "You got to get fit to win. On the morning of the rematch with Norton, I weighed in at two-twelve – my lightest for any fight during my comeback."'[15]

At the bell for round one, Ali said, he came out fast and was up on his toes circling to the left non-stop. He showed how he wore Norton down by leaning on him or pushing his neck, how he'd taunted him to throw harder punches, sapping his energy further. 'I was ready to dance all night. During the first five rounds, I controlled that fight. Norton couldn't touch me. Then I came down off my toes and Norton started to catch up, scoring to the body. But I fought him off.' He demonstrated the blocks.

'In the twelfth round, I decided I had enough.' Ali mimicked the flurry of punches that had stunned Norton; then paused and delivered the second set, which had finished him off. 'I won seven rounds to five.' As he raised his fists in victory, his story's message was clear: the rematch against Norton had been as much of a triumph of preparation as his movie would be – *if* everyone in that room worked as hard as Ali to make it happen.

Says Begelman: 'At the end of that half hour, we were all banging away, laughing, exhausted, and hugging one another. Ali's story had brought us inside the experience of boxing and made us feel that winning takes more than just punching.'[16] The executives now understood just how much endurance and training and advance work it takes to go the distance in the ring. And that transformed their attitude about the film and the importance of strategizing for ten rounds, from making it to selling the hell out of it.

This interactive approach paid off. With the unconditional commitment of the marketing people as the corner men of his campaign, *The Greatest* would help secure Ali's global appeal.

The purpose of reviewing these plots is not to help us invent stories. Unless you write fiction or advertisements, that won't help much. The goal here is to learn how to spot the stories that have potential to shape your culture. You just need to recognize when life is giving you a gift.

Stories can almost single-handedly defeat the abstraction of the expert. In fact, they naturally embody most of the STEPS framework. Stories are almost always practical. Most of them have emotional and tripwire elements built into them. The hardest part of using stories effectively is making sure they're simple – that they reflect your core message. It's not enough to tell a great story; the story has to reflect your agenda. You don't want a general lining up his troops before battle to tell a Connection plot.

Stories have the amazing dual power to simulate and to inspire. And most of the time we don't have to use much creativity to harness these powers – we just need to be ready to spot the good ones that our environment generates every day.

EXERCISE – PLOT LINES

It is often said that we all have a book in us. True or not, we all have plenty of stories to tell which can point us to where we are heading. The trouble is that we often don't tell them as stories.

I work with teams and individuals to create their own future history by acting as a news reporter: interviewing people involved in the task and then focusing on what they would see, hear, feel, touch, taste and sense when the change actually happens. This is an effective way of preventing the creativity of the task from becoming an intellectual exercise. Instead it becomes something which is practical and relevant to everyone, especially when they can see their own words being quoted back.

I first wrote the following extract after meeting the coaches and playing staff of a Premiership rugby team I worked with. We used it as our season-long story. Here is one version I use, which I have adapted to tell a story about this book:

You have to believe in the Five STEPS to a winning mindset
let me tell you, I believe
that I am indifferent to the impact which books like this
    can have
I don't believe
These messages matter, and implementing the ideas will
    develop my winning mindset
I believe this—
I'm not going to be respected for embracing the need for
    simplicity
so I don't accept
I'll be seen as a leader who gets people to think by using
    innovative approaches to my work
instead
years from now I'll still be plodding along doing the same
    old things
and there's no way that
I'll be able to recognize the moments when our emotions
    have hijacked the ability to be rational and clear-
    headed
that's absurd. I believe
the need to contain, entertain and then explain is good in
    theory but not in practice
as for the idea that
stripping my messages of abstract jargon and replacing it
    with practical terms is the best way to communicate
– that's just bollocks!
A winning mindset can't be developed simply, keeping me
    ahead of the competition
and it's just not true to say that
Storytelling is a key method to helping me achieve success
Winning mindsets are the preserve of the business and
    sporting elite

and it's foolish to keep thinking
There are reasons to believe

(Tripwire: why not choose to reverse it and read it backwards?)

To point you in the right direction, here are four vital elements you need before you can create your own future history.

1. *A protagonist.* This is the lead character, the hero. When writing your future history, the hero must go on a journey. It may be a literal journey – as in *The Wizard of Oz*, when Dorothy travels from Kansas to the Land of Oz. Or it could be a symbolic journey, which takes the hero to a new level of understanding, or teaches them something. (Having started out dissatisfied with her life in Kansas, the journey to Oz teaches Dorothy that 'there's no place like home'.)

2. *A challenge.* To get a story going, our hero needs to be faced with a challenging situation that forces them to take action or make a choice. Something that will get our audience wondering, 'What's going to happen next?' The more unpredictable the outcome, the more engrossed the audience will be. This is where you must decide whether you will choose a Challenge, a Creative or a Connection plot line.

3. *The narrative.* This is where we show what will happen and how. We will look at how to add detail and emotion to enrich the story in the next section of this chapter. The author E. M. Forster put it like this: 'The queen died; the king died. That's a plot. The queen died, the king died of a broken heart – that's narrative.'

4. *Finally, the outcome, the denouement, the resolution.* Here we bring all of the elements together in a way that resolves your hero's predicament and ends the journey.

5.xi HOW TO STRUCTURE A STORY

Once you have the material, how do you shape it?

One answer lies four hundred miles north of Hollywood. In a small city along the eastern edge of San Francisco Bay sits the headquarters of an unlikely entertainment colossus. Pixar Animation Studios, in Emeryville, California, opened in 1979 as the geeky computer-graphics division of Lucasfilm. Thirty-six years later, it's one of the most successful studios in movie history. Starting with *Toy Story* in 1995, Pixar has produced fourteen feature films that together have grossed $7.6 billion worldwide, an astonishing $585 million per film. Six Pixar films – *Finding Nemo*, *The Incredibles*, *Ratatouille*, *WALL-E*, *Up* and *Toy Story 3* – have won the Academy Award for Best Animated Feature, just a few of the twenty-six Oscars the studio has taken home in total.

How does Pixar do it? Success has many parents – the foresight of Steve Jobs, who invested in the company at an early stage of its development; the distribution and marketing muscle of the Walt Disney Company, which struck a development deal with the studio early on and acquired it in 2006; the meticulous attention to detail for which Pixar's army of technical and artistic talent is renowned. But an additional reason might be the stories themselves.

Ed Catmull, the founder of Pixar with John Lasseter, has said, 'Everyone knows how important a well-wrought, emotionally affecting storyline is to any movie. At Pixar, we have a phrase that Story Is King, which differentiated us not just because we said it but also because we believed it and acted accordingly.'[17]

Emma Coats, a former story artist at the studio, has cracked the Pixar code – and, in the process, created a template for an irresistible kind of story. Coats has argued that every Pixar film shares the same narrative DNA, a deep structure of storytelling that involves six sequential sentences:

Once upon a time____. And every day, _____. One day, _____. Because of that, _____. Because of that, _____. Until finally _____.

The six-sentence format is both appealing and supple. It allows the teller to take advantage of the well-documented persuasive force of stories – but within a framework that insists on conciseness and discipline.

Once upon a time . . .

There are many books that explain three-act structure, so I will cover it briefly using the six steps as a template.

Let's look at the first two steps: *Once upon a time* and, *And every day*. They are your Act One. What is the purpose of Act One? It tells the audience everything they need to know to understand the story that is to follow.

Let's look at what legendary film-maker Billy Wilder says about the importance of a good first act. 'If there is something wrong with the third act, it's really in the first act.' Most of us have no problem understanding the importance of the first act of a joke. When someone tells a joke poorly it is more likely than not that they have forgotten to convey an important piece of information in the set-up that makes the punchline funny.

So it seems the joke is in the set-up rather than the punchline. Just as with a joke, a story's set-up must tell the audience everything they need to know to understand the story.

What does an audience need to know? Think of your childhood storybooks. *Once upon a time there were three bears who lived together in the forest: Mummy Bear, Daddy Bear and Baby Bear. They each had a bowl for their porridge – a small bowl for Baby Bear, a middle-sized bowl for Mummy Bear and a big bowl for Daddy Bear.*

We know several things just from those few sentences. Yes, we know there are three bears. We know that there are at least three major characters and we know their relationship to one another. But we also know that these bears behave as people. That is important. You could well have a story where the bears act as animals. Remember, when you create your story, you must let the audience know the reality of your story. It's your world.

'A duck walks into a bar and orders a whisky and Coke.' That joke starts by giving you a major character and letting you know the reality. Notice that when a joke starts with a duck walking into a bar, no one says, 'That's ridiculous.' They accept it because it is the first thing they are told. Whatever your 'talking duck' is, let people know right away.

In the 'Simplicity' chapter, we looked at the idea behind the *Indiana Jones* films. The opening of *Raiders of the Lost Ark* is often talked about because it is exciting. But it is so much more than that. With so many fantastical things happening right at the start of the story, the audience knows a few things about its world. We know that the story's reality is heightened – that it is not to be a film about a soldier coping with his life after Vietnam. It is a fantasy that takes place in the year 1936. We know that in this world, archaeology is much more than just digging for pieces of clay pots. We know, also, that the guy in the battered fedora is good with a whip and good at his job. He appears to be fearless and smart. Things don't always go as planned for him, and he sometimes survives by the skin of his teeth.

We meet Belloq, Indiana Jones's arch-enemy, so we know his is a ruthless business, and that men will kill for the valuable artefacts they seek.

We see that Indiana Jones does have his fears: snakes. He's not a superhuman hero.

And every day . . .

This just supports what has already been set up. It establishes a pattern. A pattern to be broken by . . .

Until one day . . .

An *inciting incident* occurs. The inciting incident is the true beginning of your story. If your story is about an athlete who wants to become a champion, this might be when they meet the coach who will guide them. Or if they have already met, it is when the relationship begins. Alternatively, it may be the moment when your biggest customer expresses dissatisfaction with your product or service and threatens to walk away from the relationship.

Some will tell you that this is when your conflict begins. Comic book writer Jim Shooter has observed that the second act can start with conflict or opportunity. For instance, if you have got a story where the first act is about a young woman who is so poor she can't pay her rent, the first act might end when she finds a million pounds.

This step has been called many things: *act break*, *plot point*, *turning point* and *curtain*. I prefer 'curtain'. The reason I like the term is because it comes from the theatre, where a curtain is literally dropped between the acts. In live theatre, they must get the audience back after a break, so acts end on the highest point, where the stakes are at their most desperate.

In his book *Comedy Writing Step by Step*, writer Gene Perret calls this the 'uh-oh factor'. In a well-constructed sketch, the character and/or the situation is established and then something happens that requires a reaction. He uses an example from an old *Carol Burnett Show* in which Carol plays a woman who has just been released from a hospital psychiatric ward after treatment for addiction to soap operas. She proclaims that she is cured. She says, 'I don't care if Bruce marries Wanda or not.' Her friend's response is, 'Bruce is dead.' As Gene Perret describes it, Carol's eyes widen at this news and the audience thinks, 'Uh-oh, she's hooked on soaps again.'

Drama has its uh-oh moments as well. In Shakespeare's *King Lear*, the king promises his entire kingdom to whichever one of his three daughters can prove she loves him the most. That's an uh-oh moment if ever there was one.

Few people could stop watching a drama after something like this is introduced.

And because of this . . .

This is now your second act. When your first 'curtain' goes down, that is the end of your first act. Now it is time to explore what happens as a result of your first act – everything should be cause and effect. If your character was beaten in an important contest, this is where they deal with it. Does he go into denial? Does he give up and want to quit? In your business story, this is the moment when you decide how you will react to the customer's criticism.

Whatever reaction your character has, it must be in response to the incident at the Act One curtain.

And because of that . . .

Act Two is your longest act and makes up the body of your story. This act is usually split in two. I like to call this split the fulcrum. Because Act Two is so long, it can be difficult to keep an audience engrossed. It helps to cut it in half.

In Billy Wilder's classic film noir *Double Indemnity*, a woman and her lover decide to kill the woman's husband for the insurance money. In the first half of Act Two they plan the murder. At the fulcrum, they carry out their plan and in the second half of Act Two the focus becomes: will they get away with this crime?

Back to our character who has been defeated. Let's say that his initial reaction was to give up on the sport and he begins to alienate the coach who cares for him. But at the fulcrum something happens that makes him want to continue. Now he will stop at nothing to come back and win. In the business scenario, this is where the team decide that they will listen to the feedback and make improvements to win the business back.

Until finally . . .

This is your third act. When the third act curtain 'goes up', it is the beginning of the end of the story. In a cop drama, for instance, it might be the clue that solves the big mystery and puts the detective on the trail of the killer. This event, whatever it is, starts the chain of events that leads to your climax.

Using our example of the player-and-coach relationship, perhaps this is where they make peace and the player accepts the lessons taught to secure victory. In the business story, this is where the customer recognizes the response to their criticism and signs on to continue the working relationship.

In fact, choosing to use storytelling to change behaviour is something which was employed to great effect in order to win a business worth five billion dollars and helped to regenerate one of the world's largest cities as well as inspire a whole generation of children.

5.xii OLYMPIC-STANDARD STORYTELLING

At 7.48 p.m. local time on 6 July 2005, the president of the International Olympic Committee (IOC), Dr Jacques Rogge, stood at a podium in the Singapore Convention Centre with a large white envelope in his hand. Behind him, also standing, according to tradition, were his fellow IOC members. On the floor of the hall, eyes fixed upon the envelope that seemed to be taking him forever to open, were the heads of the National Olympic Committees from around the world and the international federations that represent each Olympic sport, winter and summer alike. This was the 117th session of the IOC, and Jacques Rogge was about to announce which city had been chosen to host the 2012 Summer Olympics.

Also on the floor of the convention centre were delegations from the five cities that had submitted bids to host the Games. Towards the back were those who, earlier in the day, had presented on behalf of Moscow, New York and Madrid. Now depleted in number and understandably subdued, they had learned through three rounds of voting that their bids had been rejected. Moscow had recorded the lowest number of first-round votes. In the second round, New York had come last. In the third round, it was Madrid's turn. As each city was ruled out, another vote was taken among the members of the International Olympic Committee, with those who had voted for the eliminated city now switching their vote elsewhere. Now only two cities remained: London and Paris.

As Rogge looked out from his lectern, he saw the grey-suited delegation from Paris to his right, arms around each other's shoulders. To his left was the London delegation. What the two sets of delegates had in common was that most of them could scarcely breathe. At stake was much more than two weeks of athletic competition. National and civic pride was on the line, with monarchs, presidents, prime ministers and mayors having taken up the cause of the competing cities in the run-up to the vote. In raw business terms, the 2012 Olympic Games was estimated to be worth some eight billion dollars. The legacy of improved infrastructure and sporting facilities that a successful Games leaves behind would benefit future generations. The cost of losing was measured in the opportunity lost, the millions of dollars spent and the weeks, months and years of work that their presentations had represented.

Finally, Rogge succeeded in extricating the card from the envelope. If a 200-metre final had started at the moment he had first tried to break the seal, the winner would by now have been well into his lap of honour.

'The International Olympic Committee,' he read, his face impassive, 'has the honour of announcing that the Games of the Thirtieth Olympiad in 2012 are awarded to the city of . . .' It seemed as if he paused; even if that pause was measured in milliseconds, it was long enough for everyone in the Singapore Convention Centre, and millions of others watching live from all corners of the earth, to imagine him saying the word, *Paris*.

'London,' he said.

One week before the final presentations, London's *Evening Standard* newspaper had run an article about the faint hopes of its city's 'underdog' team. 'According to the latest betting,' it read, 'Paris are 1–6 on to win next week's vote. Given those sort of odds, it would be understandable if Seb Coe [the two-time Olympic champion and London 2012 bid leader] and his London team had decided not to board the plane for Singapore.' Throughout the bidding process Paris had been the favourite, but as Seb Coe had said many times when he sought to inspire his team, the final vote was, 'Paris to lose'. Much depended on the quality of the final presentation and pitch to the International Olympic Committee.

The reason why this final presentation was so important was that the rules surrounding Olympic bidding had changed dramatically since the scandal surrounding Salt Lake City's bid for the 2002 Winter Olympics. To avoid a recurrence of such an embarrassing situation, International Olympic Committee members were banned from visiting any of the bidding cities and so the bids were evaluated by external experts who analysed the technical submissions. The IOC would later visit each of the five cities together and so the playing field was as level as it had ever been, which meant that the delivery of the pitch on 6 July was more important than ever before.

Before Sebastian Coe made his final speech, he had done his homework to understand the audience he was addressing. The 107 members of the IOC represented ninety different nationalities. The average age of a member was sixty-five and more than twenty were in their eighties. Over seventy per cent of the members were former Olympians, some of whom had competed when the Games were last hosted in London, in 1948.

A final video was shown. It began with a small African boy, wearing a distinctive wristband, throwing stones on a dusty street and having his attention drawn to the commentary of the London 2012 100-metre final. The film now cut to a Chinese girl, sitting on the floor of a small apartment, watching gymnastics. Somewhere in South America, a young boy watched cycling. And in Russia a little girl was transfixed by swimming. All from the London 2012 Games. Shots of running shoes, gymnastic slippers, a bicycle, and a pair of blue swimming goggles followed.

Now the young Russian girl was at the side of the swimming pool, adjusting the same blue goggles before belly-flopping unceremoniously into the water. Swimming breaststroke, she went below the surface. But with each stroke, each time she surfaced, she was older, stronger, until she was a young woman in an Olympic competition. So too the Chinese gymnast ran onto the mat and with each flip left her childhood behind and brought her dreams closer to reality. The South American boy rode his bicycle through the marketplace in his village and into an Olympic velodrome. And finally, back in Africa, the young boy with the wristband grew up and into athletics, national championships, and finally the Olympics. The film ended with him on the line of the Olympic 100-metre final. The starting gun sounded, and the film faded to black with the words, 'Choose London. And inspire young people everywhere to choose sport.'

When Sebastian Coe came to deliver his emotive speech, the IOC members applauded. Some of those in the audience might have pondered about the power of the emotion employed at the end of his presentation compared to that of the last speaker from the Paris bid team.

'On behalf of the youth of today, the athletes of tomorrow, and the Olympians of the future,' said Coe, 'we humbly submit the bid of London 2012.'

The Paris presentation had ended with a similar structure. But it had an entirely different orientation.

'Paris needs the Games. Paris wants the Games. Paris loves the Games.'

Paris's presentation was not about appealing to the positive emotions of the Olympic Committee. It was simply about Paris.

And therein lies a lesson for us all about storytelling.

EXERCISE – PIXAR

You can even summarize this book with a Pixar pitch:

Once upon a time, it was generally assumed that the leaders working within the world of elite sport were using techniques completely removed from the real world of non-sporting competition. Every day, we assumed that the challenges they faced were somehow different to ours and so whilst we enjoyed watching them operate, we knew there was nothing to learn. One day, you picked up this book and began to read about the STEPS to create a winning mindset. Because of that, you understood the parallels between their world and yours, and because of this understanding, you were able to incorporate some simple practices into your own role. Finally, you and your team are now seeing the benefits of a winning mindset and are enjoying the spoils of your success.

CONCLUSION

Being raised by a boxing coach has its ups and downs. On the one hand, you learn valuable lessons like how to skip rope, anticipate danger, learn to control your emotions and cope under pressure. The downsides are you learn to exercise extreme caution when answering back, and you get experimented on. A lot.

Here's an example, similar to one my dad made me do when I expressed an interest in learning how to become a coach. He listened to my reasons for wanting to find out more about the demands of his world and then promised to show me the first – and most important – lesson of all elite coaches.

He instructed me to find a sheet a paper and draw a rough picture of a coffee mug.

Sounds easy, right? You'd be surprised. When I now do this experiment with the coaches I work with, the drawings tend to be of a nursery-school standard. It is clear that elite coaching is not based on artistic skills.

However, when I do the experiment again, I echo my dad's next instruction, asking the coaches to 'be creative'.

This time, the drawings are a bit better. Now, rather than the plain mug, I receive pictures of mugs that look like the Holy Grail in *Indiana Jones* or elaborate goblets with ornate handles. I get small mugs, big mugs and many people add a slogan, like

'World's Greatest Coach'. From each coach, I receive a unique shape, size and pattern.

Yet for all their individuality, the drawings all have one thing in common. They are all drawn from the side view, rather than from above. Every single one.

Studies have found that when most people draw a coffee mug, they do it from the side and not the top. But why? We've all seen a coffee mug when we were standing above it. So why do people never think of drawing the mug from above?

It comes back to the point which my dad sought to make about elite coaching. When we try and create a winning mindset using only one type of approach, we may see different solutions (or styles of mugs), but we still see it from only one perspective. Great coaches strive to see things from a full range of perspectives. They have the willingness to look as widely as possible for ideas that can help them deliver their message.

'If you are an apple picker and you keep coming back to the same trees every day, eventually you're going to run out of fruit,' my dad advised. Learning to see your world from different angles and perspectives allows you to see the details, connections and solutions that no one else can see.

Whilst the thinking that inspired this book is taken from the practices of those coaches operating within their chosen sport at an elite level, that doesn't mean you have to work in sport to apply it – far from it. The approach is both broader and simpler than that. It relies on an understanding of human beings and their ways of thinking and learning.

In the introduction, I challenged the common assumption that you need to be a coaching genius to use the STEPS process to create a winning mindset within your own field of endeavour. You don't. There is nothing magical about this way of thinking. It usually traffics in the obvious and places a huge premium on common sense. We all have the ability to apply the STEPS checklist, and you can use it as an ideal tool to make a difference and start creating a winning mindset within your own world.

You might just surprise yourself.

Acknowledgements

There's an old proverb that it takes a village to raise a child and it is the same when it comes to writing a book. This book you are holding in your hands would not exist without the help of the following team of superstars.

Geraldine, thank you for being my best friend, for freely giving me your constant encouragement, patience, love, support and wonderful company, and allowing me to follow my dreams all the way from that first bus stop.

George and Rose, you are the two greatest things ever to happen for me. Thank you for blessing me with your love, laughter and continued sense of fun and curiosity. I love you both.

Thank you Anthony, Chris and Rachael. Your encouragement, interest and unfailing friendship mean so much to me.

Blaise Tapp, thank you for sharing your thoughts and ideas, and then offering your considerable talents at every turn.

Rob Smyth and Bernard Niven, please accept my immense gratitude for generously sharing your insights, talent and support.

Thank you to Susan Czerski for being part of the team and making my life so much easier.

Thank you also to my brilliant editor, Robin Harvie. Your faith, trust and support are greatly appreciated. Equally, thank you to all at Pan Macmillan for your support of the initial idea and subsequent book.

Deep gratitude is also due to David Luxton, my incredibly talented literary agent.

To all the great players, coaches and leaders with whom I have had the immense good fortune to work – and learn from. Experience is a great teacher and you have all given so freely. I hope that you continue to apply the STEPS to achieve your own dreams.

Finally, to my Mum, Rosemarie. Thank you for your quiet but unstinting encouragement and courage to have a go at chasing my dreams. I hope you see your own influence within these pages.

This book is dedicated to my father, Brian Hughes. It has been my incredible good fortune to have had the best father, coach, teacher and person I could have wished for. I hope that the messages contained within reflect the alchemy that has defined your life and all those who have been blessed by your influence. Thank you.

Notes

Introducing the Five Steps

1 Damian Hughes, *How to Think Like Sir Alex Ferguson: The Business of Winning and Managing Success* (Aurum Press, 2014).

2 James Kerr, *Legacy* (Constable, 2013).

3 *Daily Telegraph*, 29 October 2015.

4 Dominic Carman, *No Ordinary Man: A Life of George Carman* (Hodder and Stoughton, 2002).

5 Barry J. Gibbons, *If You Want to Make God Really Laugh, Show Him Your Business Plan: 101 Universal Laws of Business* (Capstone, 1999).

6 *Daily Telegraph*, 27 March 2005.

7 Dr Kevin Dutton, *The Wisdom of Psychopaths* (Arrow, 2013).

8 Ibid.

9 Colin Powell, *My American Journey* (Ballantine Books, 2003); *It Worked For Me: In Life and Leadership* (Harper, 2012).

10 Sebastian Coe, *Running My Life: The Autobiography* (Hodder & Stoughton, 2012); *The Winning Mind: What it Takes to Become a True Champion* (Business Plus, 2010).

11 Dave Bowler, *Shanks: The Authorised Biography of Bill Shankly* (Orion, 1996).

Trapdoors

1 Paul Kimmage, *Full Time: The Secret Life of Tony Cascarino* (Simon & Schuster UK, 2013).

The First Step: Simplicity

1 Andrea Pirlo with Alessandro Alciato, *I think therefore I play* (BackPage Press, 2014).

2 TV documentary, 'What makes the perfect World Cup penalty?' See http://www.bbc.co.uk/guides/zgg334j#z22qq6f.

3 Pirlo with Alciato, *I think therefore I play*.

4 Sir Alex Ferguson, *Managing My Life* (Hodder Paperbacks, 2000).

5 Marcello Lippi, *A Game of Ideas: Thoughts and Passions from the Sidelines* (Editrice San Raffaele, 2008).

6 John P. Kotter, *Heart of Change: Real-Life Stories of How People Change Their Organizations* (Harvard Business Review Press, 2012).

7 Edward Halliwell, 'Death by Information Overload', *Harvard Business Review* 87, 9, pp. 83–9.

8 Barry Schwartz, *The Paradox of Choice: Why More is Less* (Harper Perennial, 2005).

9 Roland G. Tharp and Ronald Gallimore, *Rousing Minds to Life: Teaching, Learning and Schooling in Social Context* (Cambridge University Press, 2010).

10 Swen Nater and Ronald Gallimore, *You Haven't Taught Until They Have Learned: John Wooden's Teaching Principles & Practices* (Fitness Information Technology Inc., US, 2010).

11 John Wooden and Steve Jamison, *The Wisdom of Wooden: My Century On and Off the Court* (McGraw-Hill Contemporary, 2010).

12 Nater and Gallimore, *You Haven't Taught Until They Have Learned.*

13 Tharp and Gallimore, *Rousing Minds to Life.*

14 Sam Delaney, *Mad Men & Bad Men: What Happened When British Politics Met Advertising* (Faber & Faber, 2015).

15 Kelvin MacKenzie and John Essery, *Gotcha! Classic Headlines from The Sun* (Signet Books, 1993).

16 Michael Buerk, *The Road Taken* (Arrow, 2005).

17 Ibid.

18 Seth Godin, *Purple Cow: Transform Your Business by Being Remarkable* (Penguin, 2005).

19 Gary Neville, *Red: My Autobiography* (Corgi, 2012).

20 Damian Hughes, *How to Think Like Sir Alex Ferguson: The Business of Winning and Managing Success* (Aurum Press, 2014).

21 Roy Keane with Roddy Doyle, *The Second Half* (Weidenfeld & Nicolson, 2015).

22 Alastair Campbell, *Winners: And How They Succeed* (Pegasus, 2015).

23 Rio Ferdinand, *#2sides: My Autobiography* (Blink Publishing, 2014).

24 *Sunday Times*, September 2014.

25 Rory Ross with Tim Foster, *Four Men in a Boat: The Inside Story of the Sydney 2000 Coxless Four* (Weidenfeld & Nicolson, 2015).

26 Matthew Pinsent, *A Lifetime in a Race* (Ebury Press, 2005).

27 Ross with Foster, *Four Men in a Boat.*

28 Pinsent, *A Lifetime in a Race.*

29 Ross with Foster, *Four Men in a Boat.*

The Second Step: Thinking

1 Noreena Hertz, *Eyes Wide Open: How to Make Smart Decisions in a Confusing World* (William Collins, 2014).

2 Ferdinand, *#2sides: My Autobiography*.

3 *Daily Telegraph*, 20 March 2015.

4 Rinus Michels, *Teambuilding: The Road to Success* (Reedswain Incorporated, 2013).

5 Denis Bergkamp, *Stillness and Speed* (Simon & Schuster UK, 2014).

6 Richard Moore, *Heroes, Villains and Velodromes: Chris Hoy and Britain's Track Cycling Revolution* (HarperSport, 2012).

7 Richard Moore, *Sky's the Limit: British Cycling's Quest to Conquer the Tour de France* (HarperSport, 2011).

8 Ibid.

9 Moore, *Heroes, Villains and Velodromes*.

10 Ibid.

11 Rod Ellingworth, *Project Rainbow: How British Cycling Reached the Top of the World* (Faber & Faber, 2014).

12 Ibid.

13 Moore, *Heroes, Villains and Velodromes*.

14 *Cycling Weekly* interview, 18 February 2013.

15 Paul Ekman and Wallace V. Friesen, *Unmasking the Face* (Malor Books, 2003).

16 Brian and Damian Hughes, *Marvelous: The Marvin Hagler Story* (Pitch Publishing Ltd, 2013).

17 Sir Alex Ferguson, *Managing My Life* (Hodder Paperbacks, 2000).

18 BBC News Website interview, 9 April 2015.

19 Luis Lourenço and José Mourinho, *José Mourinho: Made in Portugal* (Dewi Lewis Media Ltd, 2004).

20 Ibid.

21 Ibid.

22 BBC Radio 4 interview, December 2011.

23 Lourenço and Mourinho, *José Mourinho*.

24 BT Sport interview, December 2014.

25 Lourenço and Mourinho, *José Mourinho*.

26 Luis Lourenço, *José Mourinho – Special Leadership: Creating and Managing Successful Teams* (Prime Books, 2014).

27 Lourenço and Mourinho, *José Mourinho*.

28 Ibid.

29 Daniel Coyle, *The Talent Code: Greatness isn't Born. It's Grown* (Arrow, 2010).

The Third Step: Emotions

1 Scott Weiss and Paige Stover, *Confusing the Enemy: The Cus D'Amato Story* (Acanthus, 2014).

2 Teddy Atlas, *Atlas: From the Streets to the Ring: A Son's Struggle to Become a Man* (Harper Paperbacks, 2007).

3 Mike Tyson, *Undisputed Truth: My Autobiography* (HarperSport, 2014).

4 Atlas, *Atlas: From the Streets to the Ring.*

5 Tyson, *Undisputed Truth.*

6 Atlas, *Atlas: From the Streets to the Ring.*

7 Ibid.

8 Tyson, *Undisputed Truth.*

9 David Adam, *The Man Who Couldn't Stop: The Truth About OCD* (Picador, 2015).

10 James Watson, *Avoid Boring People and Other Lessons from a Life in Science* (OUP, 2007).

11 Atlas, *Atlas: From the Streets to the Ring.*

12 James Kerr, *Legacy* (Constable, 2013); Kevin Roberts, *Lovemarks: The Future Beyond Brands* (PowerHouse Books, US, 2006).

13 Ian Gilbert, *Essential Motivation in the Classroom* (Routledge, 2012).

14 Clive Woodward, *Winning!* (Hodder Paperbacks, 2005).

15 Kerr, *Legacy.*

16 Ibid.

17 Ibid.

18 Ibid.

19 *Daily Telegraph*, 29 October 2015.

20 Steve Peters, *The Chimp Paradox: The Mind Management Programme to Help You Achieve Success, Confidence and Happiness* (Vermilion, 2012).

21 Richard Moore, *Heroes, Villains and Velodromes: Chris Hoy and Britain's Track Cycling Revolution* (HarperSport, 2012).

22 Ibid.

23 Brian Hughes and Damian Hughes, *Hit Man: The Thomas Hearns Story* (Milo Books, 2009).

24 Chris Evans, *It's Not What You Think* (HarperCollins, 2010).

25 Phil Jackson, *Eleven Rings* (Virgin Books, 2015).

26 Brad Gilbert and Steve Jamison, *Winning Ugly* (Simon & Schuster UK, 2007).

27 David Woods and Tim Brighouse, *The A–Z of School Improvement: Principles and Practice* (Bloomsbury Education, 2013).

28 Didier Drogba, *The Autobiography* (Aurum Press, 2008).

29 Zlatan Ibrahimovic, David Lagercrantz and Ruth Urbom, *I Am Zlatan Ibrahimovic* (Penguin, 2013).

30 *Daily Telegraph*, 27 December 2008.

31 *Daily Mail*, 27 April 2010.

The Fourth Step: Practical

1 *Daily Telegraph*, 3 July 2013. See also: http://www.shortlist.com/entertainment/sport/the-curious-mind-of-gary-neville.

2 David Epstein, *The Sports Gene: Talent, Practice and the Truth About Success* (Yellow Jersey, 2014).

3 Mark Hodgkinson, *Ivan Lendl: The Man Who Made Murray* (Aurum Press, 2014).

4 Ibid.

5 Bruce Abernethy, Vaughan Kippers, Stephanie J. Hanrahan, Marcus G. Pandy, Alison M. McManus and Laurel Mackinnon, *The Biophysical Foundations of Human Movement* (Human Kinestics, 2013).

6 Tom English, *The Grudge: Two Nations, One Match, No Holds Barred* (Yellow Jersey, 2011).

7 Louis van Gaal and Robert Heukels et al, *Louis van Gaal Biographie & Vision* (Visiesport Gmbh, 2010).

8 *The Correspondent*, 8 August 2014. See also: https://www.youtube.com/watch?v=_CCTLCW6l-c.

The Fifth Step: Stories

1 *Sunday Times*, 18 January 2013.

2 Guillem Balague, *Pep Guardiola: Another Way of Winning: The Biography* (Orion, 2013).

3 Martí Perarnau, *Pep Confidential: Inside Guardiola's First Season at Bayern Munich* (Arena Sport, 2014).

4 Balague, *Pep Guardiola: Another Way of Winning*.

5 Ibid.

6 Perarnau, *Pep Confidential*.

7 Ray Glier and Phillip Fulmer, *What It Means to Be a Volunteer: Phillip Fulmer and Tennessee's Greatest Players* (Triumph Books, 2008).

8 Thomas Hauser, *Muhammad Ali: His Life and Times* (Portico, 2012).

9 Ibid.

10 Ferdie Pacheco, *Blood in My Coffee: The Life of the Fight Doctor* (Sports Publishing, 2013).

11 Ibid.

12 Hauser, *Muhammad Ali*.

13 Ibid.

14 Ibid.

15 Peter Gruber, *Tell to Win: Connect, Persuade and Triumph with the Hidden Power of Story* (Profile Books, 2012).

16 Ibid.

17 Ed Catmull, *Creativity, Inc.: Overcoming the Unseen Forces That Stand in the Way of True Inspiration* (Bantam Press, 2014).

Bibliography

Abernethy, Bruce, Vaughan Kippers, Stephanie J. Hanrahan, Marcus G. Pandy, Alison M. McManus, Laurel Mackinnon, *The Biophysical Foundations of Human Movement* (Human Kinestics, 2013)

Achor, Shawn, *Before Happiness: Five Actionable Strategies to Create a Positive Path to Success* (Virgin Books, 2013)

Adam, David, *The Man Who Couldn't Stop: The Truth About OCD* (Picador, 2015)

Agassi, Andre, *Open: An Autobiography* (HarperCollins, 2010)

Ambridge, Ben, *Psy-Q: A Mind-Bending Miscellany of Everyday Psychology* (Profile Books, 2015)

Andersson, Patric, Peter Ayton and Carsten Schmidt, *Myths and Facts about Football: The Economics and Psychology of the World's Greatest Sport* (Cambridge Scholars Publishing, 2008)

Angel, Violan Miguel, *Pep Guardiola: The Philosophy That Changed the Game* (Meyer & Meyer Sport (UK), 2014)

Atlas, Teddy, *Atlas: From the Streets to the Ring: A Son's Struggle to Become a Man* (Harper Paperbacks, 2007)

Balague, Guillem, *Pep Guardiola: Another Way of Winning: The Biography* (Orion, 2013)

Barclay, Patrick, *Mourinho: Further Anatomy of a Winner* (Orion, 2015)

Beilock, Sian, *Choke* (Constable, 2011)

Benjamin, Aaron S., ed., *Successful Remembering and Successful*

Forgetting: A Festschrift in Honor of Robert A. Bjork (Psychology Press, 2011)

Bergkamp, Denis, *Stillness and Speed* (Simon & Schuster UK, 2014)

Beveridge, Harriet and Ben Hunt-Davis, *Will it Make the Boat Go Faster?: Olympic-winning Strategies for Everyday Success* (Matador, 2011)

Birla, Madan, *FedEx Delivers: How the World's Leading Shipping Company Keeps Innovating and Outperforming the Competition* (John Wiley & Sons, 2005)

Black, Campbell, *Raiders of the Lost Ark* (Ballantine Books, 2008)

Boardman, Chris, *Triumphs and Turbulence: My Autobiography* (Ebury Publishing, 2016)

Borst, Hugo, David Doherty (translator), *O, Louis: In Search of Louis van Gaal* (Yellow Jersey, 2014)

Bowlby, John, *A Secure Base* (Routledge, 2005)

Bowler, Dave, *Shanks: The Authorised Biography of Bill Shankly* (Orion, 1996)

Brown, Derren, *Tricks Of The Mind* (Channel 4, 2007)

Buerk, Michael, *The Road Taken* (Arrow, 2005)

Butcher, Pat, *The Perfect Distance: Ovett and Coe: The Record Breaking Rivalry* (Phoenix, 2005)

Calne, Donald, *Within Reason: Rationality and Human Behaviour* (Vintage, 2000)

Campbell, Alastair, *Winners: And How They Succeed* (Pegasus, 2015)

Carman, Dominic, *No Ordinary Man: A Life of George Carman* (Hodder & Stoughton, 2002)

Carter, Rita, *Mapping the Mind* (University of California Press, 2010)

Catmull, Ed, *Creativity, Inc.: Overcoming the Unseen Forces That Stand in the Way of True Inspiration* (Bantam Press, 2014)

Cialdini, Robert B., *Influence: The Psychology of Persuasion* (HarperBusiness, 2007)

Clough, Brian, *Clough The Autobiography* (Corgi, 1995)

Coe, Sebastian, *Running My Life: The Autobiography* (Hodder & Stoughton, 2012)

Coe, Sebastian, *The Winning Mind: What It Takes to Become a True Champion* (Business Plus, 2010)

Collins, Tim, *Rules of Engagement: A Life in Conflict* (Headline Review, 2006)

Copeland, Eugene, *Earl Scruggs 131 Success Facts – Everything You Need to Know about Earl Scruggs* (Emereo Publishing, 2014)

Coyle, Daniel, *The Talent Code: Greatness isn't born. It's grown* (Arrow, 2010)

Curran, Andrew, *The Little Book of Big Stuff about the Brain: The True Story of Your Amazing Brain* (Crown House Publishing, 2008)

de Shazer, Steve, *Keys to Solution in Brief Therapy* (W. W. Norton, 1985)

Delaney, Sam, *Mad Men & Bad Men: What Happened When British Politics Met Advertising* (Faber & Faber, 2015)

DiBernardo, Marcus, *Train Like Bayern Munich. Play Like Bayern Munich: 15+ Training Exercises Used By Pep Guardiola* (CreateSpace Independent Publishing Platform, 2015)

Drogba, Didier, *The Autobiography* (Aurum Press, 2008)

Dubner, Stephen. J. and Steven D. Levitt, *Think Like a Freak: Secrets of the Rogue Economist* (Penguin, 2015)

Dundee, Angelo and Bert Randolph Sugar, *My View from the Corner: A Life in Boxing* (McGraw-Hill Contemporary, 2009)

Dundee, Angelo with Mike Winters, *I Only Talk Winning* (Robson Books, 1988)

Dunker, Karl, *On problem-solving. Psychological Monographs* (American Psychological Association, 1945), 58(5), 1–113

Dutton, Kevin, *The Wisdom of Psychopaths* (Arrow, 2013)

Dweck, Carol, *Mindset: How You Can Fulfil Your Potential* (Robinson, 2012)

Ekman, Paul and Wallace V. Friesen, *Unmasking the Face* (Malor Books, 2003)

Ellingworth, Rod, *Project Rainbow: How British Cycling Reached the Top of the World* (Faber & Faber, 2014)

English, Tom, *The Grudge: Two Nations, One Match, No Holds Barred* (Yellow Jersey, 2011)

Epstein, David, *The Sports Gene: Talent, Practice and the Truth About Success* (Yellow Jersey, 2014)

Evans, Chris, *It's Not What You Think* (HarperCollins, 2010)

Ferdinand, Rio, *#2sides: My Autobiography* (Blink Publishing, 2014)

Ferguson, Alex, *Managing My Life* (Hodder Paperbacks, 2000)

Festinger, Leon, *A Theory of Cognitive Dissonance* (Stanford University Press, 1957)

Frazier, Joe with Phil Berger, *Smokin' Joe: The Autobiography* (Robson Books, 1998)

Fredrickson, Barbara, *Positivity: Groundbreaking Research to Release Your Inner Optimist and Thrive* (Oneworld Publications, 2011)

Gardner, Howard, *Frames of Mind: The Theory of Multiple Intelligences* (Basic Books, 2011)

Gibbons, Barry J., *If You Want to Make God Really Laugh, Show Him Your Business Plan: 101 Universal Laws of Business* (Capstone, 1999)

Gibbons, Barry, *This Indecision is Final: 32 Management Secrets of Albert Einstein, Billie Holliday and a Bunch of Other People Who Never Worked 9–5* (Irwin Professional Publishing, 1996)

Gilbert, Brad and James Kaplan, *I've Got Your Back: Coaching Top Performers from Center Court to the Corner Office* (Portfolio, 2005)

Gilbert, Brad and Steve Jamison, *Winning Ugly* (Simon & Schuster UK, 2007)

Gilbert, Ian, *Essential Motivation in the Classroom* (Routledge, 2012)

Glier, Ray and Phillip Fulmer, *What It Means to Be a Volunteer: Phillip Fulmer and Tennessee's Greatest Players* (Triumph Books (IL), 2008)

Godin, Seth, *Purple Cow: Transform Your Business by Being Remarkable* (Penguin, 2005)

Goldstein, Noah J., Steve J. Martin and Robert B. Cialdini, *Yes! 50 Secrets from the Science of Persuasion* (Profile Books, 2007)

Gottman, John M. and Nan Silver, *The Seven Principles for Making Marriage Work: A Practical Guide from the Country's Foremost Relationship Expert* (Harmony, 2015)

Granato, Len, *Newspaper Feature Writing* (NewSouth Publishing, 2002)

Gruber, Peter, *Tell to Win: Connect, Persuade and Triumph with the Hidden Power of Story* (Profile Books, 2012)

Haidt, Jonathan, *The Happiness Hypothesis: Putting Ancient Wisdom to the Test of Modern Science* (Arrow, 2007)

Haidt, Jonathan, *The Righteous Mind: Why Good People are Divided by Politics and Religion* (Penguin, 2013)

Hartley, Simon, *Two Lengths of the Pool: Sometimes the Simplest Ideas Have the Greatest Impact* (CreateSpace Independent Publishing Platform, 2013)

Hauser, Thomas and Muhammad Ali, *Muhammad, Ali: In Perspective* (HarperSanFrancisco, 1996)

Hauser, Thomas, *A Beautiful Sickness: Reflections on the Sweet Science* (University of Arkansas Press, 2001)

Hauser, Thomas, *Muhammad Ali: His Life and Times* (Portico, 2012)

Hawk, Tony and Sean Mortimer, *Tony Hawk: Professional Skateboarder* (ReganBooks, 2002)

Heath, Chip and Dan, *Made to Stick: Why Some Ideas Take Hold and Others Come Unstuck* (Arrow, 2008)

Heath, Dan and Chip Heath, *Switch: How to Change Things When Change is Hard* (Random House Business, 2011)

Henderson, Michael, *50 People Who Fouled Up Football* (Constable, 2009)

Hertz, Noreena, *Eyes Wide Open: How to Make Smart Decisions in a Confusing World* (William Collins, 2014)

Hiddema, B., *Cruijff! Van Jopie tot Johan* (Luitingh-Sijthoff, 1996)

Hodgkinson, Mark, *Ivan Lendl: The Man Who Made Murray* (Aurum Press, 2014)

Hoffer, Richard, *Bouts of Mania: Ali, Frazier and Foreman and an America on the Ropes* (Aurum Press, 2015)

Hughes, Brian and Damian Hughes, *Hit Man: The Thomas Hearns Story* (Milo Books, 2009)

Hughes, Brian and Damian Hughes, *Marvelous: The Marvin Hagler Story* (Pitch Publishing Ltd, 2013)

Hughes, Brian and Damian Hughes, *Peerless: The Sugar Ray Robinson Story* (Damian Hughes, 2007)

Hughes, Damian, *How to Change Absolutely Anything* (Pearson Life, 2012)

Hughes, Damian, *How to Think Like Sir Alex Ferguson: The Business of Winning and Managing Success* (Aurum Press, 2014)

Hughes, Damian, *Liquid Leadership: Inspirational Lessons from the World's Great Leaders* (Capstone, 2009)

Hughes, Simon, *Men in White Suits: Liverpool FC in the 1990s: The Players' Stories* (Bantam Press, 2015)

Humphrys, John, *Lost For Words: The Mangling and Manipulating of the English Language* (Hodder & Stoughton, 2005)

Ibrahimovic, Zlatan, David Lagercrantz and Ruth Urbom, *I Am Zlatan Ibrahimovic* (Penguin, 2013)

Isaacson, Walter, *Steve Jobs: The Exclusive Biography* (Abacus, 2015)

Jackson, Phil, *Eleven Rings* (Virgin Books, 2015)

Jones, John, *The Magic-Weaving Business: Finding the Heart of Learning and Teaching* (Leannta Publishing, 2011)

Kahneman, Daniel, *Thinking, Fast and Slow* (Penguin, 2012)

Keane, Roy with Roddy Doyle, *The Second Half* (Weidenfeld & Nicolson, 2015)

Keith, John, *Shanks for the Memory: Wit and Wisdom of Bill Shankly* (Robson Books, 1998)

Kelly, Stephen F., *It's Much More Important Than That: Bill Shankly, The Biography* (Virgin Books, 1997)

Kerr, James, *Legacy* (Constable, 2013)

Kimball, George, *Four Kings: Leonard, Hagler, Hearns, Duran and the Last Great Era of Boxing* (Mainstream Publishing, 2008)

Kimmage, Paul, *Full Time: The Secret Life of Tony Cascarino* (Simon & Schuster UK, 2013)

Klein, Gary, *Seeing What Others Don't: The Remarkable Ways We Gain Insights* (Nicholas Brealey Publishing, 2014)

Klein, Gary, *Sources of Power: How People Make Decisions* (MIT Press, 1999)

Klein, Gary, *The Power of Intuition: How to Use Your Gut Feelings to Make Better Decisions at Work* (Crown Business, 2004)

Kormelink, Henny and Tjeu Seeverens, *The Coaching Philosophies of Louis van Gaal and the Ajax Coaches* (Reedswain Inc., 2003)

Kotter, John P., *Heart of Change: Real-Life Stories of How People Change Their Organizations* (Harvard Business Review Press, 2012)

Kuper, Simon and Stefan Szymanski, *Soccernomics: Why England Loses, Why Spain, Germany, and Brazil Win, and Why the U.S., Japan, Australia . . .* (Nation Books, 2014)

Kuper, Simon, *The Football Men: Up Close with the Giants of the Modern Game* (Simon & Schuster UK, 2012)

Lampard, Frank, *Totally Frank* (HarperSport, 2006)

Lehman, Scott, *More than a Game: Finding Life's Answers Through Golf* (In His Grip Golf Association, 2015)

Lemov, Doug, *Teach Like a Champion* (Jossey-Bass, 2010)

Lewis, David, *Impulse: Why We Do What We Do Without Knowing Why We Do It* (Random House Books, 2014)

Lewis, Jack and Adrian Webster, *Sort Your Brain Out: Boost Your Performance, Manage Stress and Achieve More* (Capstone, 2014)

Lippi, Marcello, *A Game of Ideas: Thoughts and Passions from the Sidelines* (Editrice San Raffaele, 2008)

Lourenço, Luis and José Mourinho, *José Mourinho: Made in Portugal* (Dewi Lewis Media Ltd, 2004)

Lourenço, Luis, *José Mourinho – Special Leadership: Creating and Managing Successful Teams* (Prime Books, 2014)

Lumet, Sidney, *Making Movies* (Vintage Books, 1996)

Lyttleton, Ben, *Twelve Yards: The Art and Psychology of the Perfect Penalty Kick* (Penguin Books, 2015)

MacKenzie, Kelvin and John Essery, *Gotcha! Classic Headlines from The Sun* (Signet Books, 1993)

MacLean, Paul D., *The Triune Brain in Evolution: Role in Paleocerebral Functions* (Plenum Publishing Co., 1990)

McGeechan, Ian, *Lion Man: The Autobiography* (Simon & Schuster UK, 2010)

McGuinness, Jim and Keith Duggan, *Until Victory Always* (Gill & Macmillan, 2015)

McKee, Robert, *Story: Substance, Structure, Style and the Principles of Screenwriting* (Methuen Publishing, 1999)

McKinstry, Leo, *Sir Alf: A Major Reappraisal of the Life and Times of England's Greatest Football Manager* (HarperSport, 2010)

McLean, Ray, *Any Given Team: Improving Leadership and Team Performance* (Leading Teams Australia, 2015)

McNab, Andy and Kevin Dutton, *The Good Psychopath's Guide to Success* (Corgi, 2015)

McRae, Donald, *Dark Trade: Lost in Boxing* (Simon & Schuster UK, 2014)

Meijer, Maarten, *Louis van Gaal: The Biography* (Ebury Press, 2015)

Michel, Rinus, *Teambuilding: The Road to Success* (Reedswain Incorporated, 2013)

Moore, Richard, *Heroes, Villains and Velodromes: Chris Hoy and Britain's Track Cycling Revolution* (HarperSport, 2012)

Moore, Richard, *Sky's the Limit: British Cycling's Quest to Conquer the Tour de France* (HarperSport, 2011)

Morrell, Margot and Stephanie Capparell, *Shackleton's Way:*

Leadership Lessons from the Great Antarctic Explorer (Nicholas Brealey Publishing, 2003)

Nater, Swen and Ronald Gallimore, *You Haven't Taught Until They Have Learned: John Wooden's Teaching Principles & Practices* (Fitness Information Technology, Inc, US, 2010)

Neto, Joel, *Mourinho, the True Story: The Book José Mourinho Tried to Ban* (First Stone Publishing, 2005)

Neville, Gary, *Red: My Autobiography* (Corgi, 2012)

O'Neil, William J., *Sports Leaders & Success: 55 Top Sports Leaders & How They Achieved Greatness* (McGraw-Hill Professional, 2004)

Pace, Michael, *Dark Psychology 101: Learn The Secrets Of Covert Emotional Manipulation, Dark Persuasion, Undetected Mind Control, Mind Games, Deception, Hypnotism, Brainwashing and Other Tricks of the Trade* (CreateSpace Independent Publishing Platform, 2015)

Pacheco, Ferdie, *Blood in My Coffee: The Life of the Fight Doctor* (Sports Publishing, 2013)

Pagano, Chuck with Bruce A. Tollner, *Sidelined: Overcoming Odds through Unity, Passion, and Perseverance* (Zondervan, 2014)

Palmer, S. E., E. Rosch and P. Chase, 'Canonical Perspective and the Perception of Objects', in *Attention and Performance IX*, ed. John B. Long and Alan D. Baddeley (Lawrence Erlbaum, 1981), 135–51

Peacock, Jamie with Phil Caplan, *Jamie Peacock: No White Flag* (The History Press, 2014)

Perarnau, Martí, *Pep Confidential: Inside Guardiola's First Season at Bayern Munich* (Arena Sport, 2014)

Perret, Gene, *New Comedy Writing Step by Step* (Quill Driver Books, US, 2007)

Peters, Steve, *The Chimp Paradox: The Mind Management Programme to Help You Achieve Success, Confidence and Happiness* (Vermilion, 2012)

Phelps, Michael with Alan Abrahamson, *No Limits: The Will to Succeed* (Simon & Schuster UK, 2009)

Pink, Daniel H., *A Whole New Mind: Why Right-brainers Will Rule the Future* (Riverhead Books, US, 2006)

Pinsent, Matthew, *A Lifetime in a Race* (Ebury Press, 2005)

Pirlo, Andrea with Alessandro Alciato, *I think therefore I play* (BackPage Press, 2014)

Powell, Colin, *It Worked For Me: In Life and Leadership* (Harper, 2012)

Powell, Colin, *My American Journey* (Ballantine Books, 2003)

Remnick, David, *King of the World: Muhammad Ali and the Rise of an American Hero* (Picador, 2015)

Roberts, Kevin, *Lovemarks: The Future Beyond Brands* (PowerHouse Books, US, 2006)

Ross, Rory with Tim Foster, *Four Men in a Boat: The Inside Story of the Sydney 2000 Coxless Four* (Weidenfeld & Nicolson, 2015)

Roth, Dave Lee, *Crazy from the Heat* (Ebury Press, 2000)

Rubin, David C., *Memory in Oral Traditions: The Cognitive Psychology of Epic, Ballads, and Counting-out Rhymes* (Oxford University Press, 1998)

Schultz, Howard, *Pour Your Heart into It: How Starbucks Built a Company One Cup at a Time* (Hyperion, 1998)

Schwartz, Barry, *The Paradox of Choice: Why More is Less* (Harper Perennial, 2005)

Shinar, Yehuda, *Think Like a Winner* (Vermilion, 2008)

Simmons, John, *We, Me, Them and It: The Power of Words in Business* (Texere Publishing, 2000)

Slide, Anthony, *It's the Pictures That Got Small: Charles Brackett on Billy Wilder and Hollywood's Golden Age* (Columbia University Press, 2014)

St John, Ian, *The Saint, My Autobiography* (Hodder Paperbacks, 2006)

Steele, Jon, *Perfect Pitch: The Art of Selling Ideas and Winning New Business* (John Wiley & Sons, 2006)

Stratton, W. K., *Floyd Patterson: The Fighting Life of Boxing's Invisible Champion* (Mainstream Publishing, 2014)

Sunstein, Cass R. and Reid Hastie, *Wiser: Getting Beyond Groupthink to Make Groups Smarter* (Harvard Business School Press, 2015)

Sunstein, Cass R. and Richard H. Thaler, *Nudge: Improving Decisions About Health, Wealth and Happiness* (Penguin, 2009)

Tharp, Roland G. and Ronald Gallimore, *Rousing Minds to Life: Teaching, Learning and Schooling in Social Context* (Cambridge University Press, 2010)

Torres, Diego, *The Special One* (HarperSport, 2014)

Tosches, Nick, *Night Train: The Sonny Liston Story* (Hamish Hamilton, 2000)

Trott, Dave, *One Plus One Equals Three: A Masterclass in Creative Thinking* (Macmillan, 2015)

Trott, Dave, *Predatory Thinking* (Pan, 2014)

Tufte, Edward R., *The Cognitive Style of PowerPoint: Pitching Out Corrupts Within* (Graphics Press, 2006)

Tyson, Mike, *Undisputed Truth: My Autobiography* (HarperSport, 2014)

van Gaal, Louis and Robert Heukels et al, *Louis van Gaal Biographie & Vision* (Visiesport Gmbh, 2010)

Vialli, Gianluca and Gabriele Marcotti, *The Italian Job* (Bantam, 2007)

Vogt, Manfred, Heinrich Dreesen and Peter Sundman, *Encounters with Steve de Shazer and Insoo Kim Berg: Inside Stories of Solution-Focused Brief Therapy* (Solutions Books, 2015)

Walsh, Bill with Steve Jamison and Craig Walsh, *The Score Takes Care of Itself: My Philosophy of Leadership* (Portfolio, 2010)

Walsh, David, *Inside Team Sky* (Simon & Schuster UK, 2014)

Watson, James, *Avoid Boring People and Other Lessons from a Life in Science* (OUP, 2007)

Watson, James, *DNA: The Secret of Life* (Arrow, 2004)

Weiss, Scott and Paige Stover, *Confusing the Enemy: The Cus D'Amato Story* (Acanthus, 2014)

Wilson, Jonathan, *Brian Clough: Nobody Ever Says Thank You: The Biography* (Orion, 2012)

Winner, David, *Brilliant Orange: The Neurotic Genius of Dutch Football* (Bloomsbury, 2001)

Wiseman, Richard, *59 Seconds: Think a Little, Change a Lot* (Pan, 2015)

Wiseman, Richard, *Quirkology: The Curious Science of Everyday Lives* (Pan, 2015)

Witt, Christopher, *Real Leaders Don't Do PowerPoint: How to Speak So People Listen: How to Sell Yourself and Your Ideas* (Piatkus, 2009)

Wooden, John and Steve Jamison, *The Wisdom of Wooden: My Century On and Off the Court* (McGraw-Hill Contemporary, 2010)

Woods, David and Tim Brighouse, *Inspirations: A Collection of Commentaries and Quotations to Promote School Improvement* (Network Continuum Education, 2006)

Woods, David and Tim Brighouse, *The A–Z of School Improvement: Principles and Practice* (Bloomsbury Education, 2013)

Woodward, Clive, *Winning!* (Hodder Paperbacks, 2005)

Zander, Rosamund Stone and Benjamin Zander, *The Art of Possibility: Transforming Professional and Personal Life* (Penguin Books, 2002)

Academic papers

Banbury, S. and D. C. Berry (1998). 'Disruption of office-related tasks by speech and office noise', *British Journal of Psychology*, 89, 500

Bar-Eli, M., O. H. Azar, I. Ritov, Y. Keidar-Levin and G. Schein, 'Action bias among elite soccer goalkeepers: the case of penalty kicks', *Journal of Economic Psychology*, 28, 606–21

Baumeister, R. F., E. Bratslavsky, C. Finkenauer and K. D. Vohs (2001). 'Bad is stronger than good', *Review of General Psychology*, 5, 323–70

Blackwell, Lisa, Kali H. Trzesniewski and Carol S. Dweck (2007). 'Implicit Theories of Intelligence Predict Achievement Across an Adolescent Transition: A Longitudinal Study and an Intervention', *Child Development*, 78, 246–63

Elsbach, Kimberley D. (2003). 'How to Pitch a Brilliant Idea', *Harvard Business Review* 81, 9, 117–23

Elsbach, Kimberley D. and Roderick M. Kramer (2003). 'Assessing Creativity in Hollywood Pitch Meetings: Evidence for a Dual Model of Creativity Judgements', *Academy of Management Journal*, 46, 3, 283–301

Flegal, K. E. and M. C. Anderson (2008). 'Overthinking skilled motor performance: Or why those who teach can't do', *Psychonomic Bulletin & Review*, 15, 927–32

Frank, M. G. and T. Gilovich (1988). 'The dark side of self- and social perception: Black uniforms and aggression in professional sports', *Journal of Personality and Social Psychology*, 54, 1, 74–85

Hemp, Paul (2009). 'Death by Information Overload', *Harvard Business Review* 87, 9, 83–9

Iqbal, S. T. and E. Horvitz, (2007). 'Disruption and recovery of computing tasks: field study, analysis and directions', *Proceedings of the SIGCHI Conference on Human Factors in Computing Systems*, 677–86

Iyengar, Sheena S. and Mark R. Lepper (2000). 'When Choice is Demotivating: Can One Desire Too Much of a Good Thing?', *Journal of Personality and Social Psychology*, 79, 995–1006

Jordet, G. (2009). 'When superstars flop: public status and "choking under pressure" in international soccer penalty shootouts', *Journal of Applied Sports Psychology*, 21, 2, 125–30

Mack, A., 'Inattentional Blindness: Looking Without Seeing', *Current Directions in Psychological Science*, 12, 5, 180–84

McCafferty, J. (1998). 'Coping with Infoglut', *CFO Magazine*, September 1998

Miner, H. (1956). 'Body Ritual Among the Nacirema', *American Anthropologist*, New Series, 58, 3, 305–7

Perez, Sarah (2008). 'Twitpitch: The Elevator Pitch Hits Twitter', *ReadWriteWeb*

'Pixar Story Rules', *Pixar Touch Blog*, 15 May 2011

Sunstein, C. R. (2006). 'When Crowds Aren't Wise', *Harvard Business Review*, 84, 9, 20–21

The Economist (1995). 'Garbage in, garbage out', 3 June 1995

Wansiki, B. (2005). 'How Descriptive Food Names Bias Sensory Perception in Restaurants. Food Quality and Preference', *Science Direct*, 16, 5, 393–400

Weste, D., P. S. Blagov, K. Harenski, C. Kilts and S. Hamann (2006). 'Neural Biases of Motivated Reasoning: an fMRI Study of Emotional Constraints on Partisan Political Judgement in the 2004 U.S Presidential Election', *Journal of Cognitive Neuroscience*, 18, 11, 1947–58

extracts reading groups
competitions books new
discounts extracts
extracts
competitions discounts
books new events
events books
extracts
new reading groups
interviews
events extracts
discounts
new books events
events new

www.panmacmillan.com

extracts events reading groups
competitions books extracts new